T0319907

How to Get Published in the Best Entrepreneurship Journals

How to Get Published in the Best Entrepreneurship Journals

A Guide to Steer Your Academic Career

Edited by

Alain Fayolle

Professor of Entrepreneurship and Director, Entrepreneurship Research Centre, EMLYON Business School, France

Mike Wright

Professor of Entrepreneurship and Director, Centre for Management Buy-out Research, Imperial College Business School, Imperial College London, UK and University of Ghent, Belgium

Edward Elgar

Cheltenham, UK • Northampton, MA, USA

Published by
Edward Elgar Publishing Limited
The Lypiatts
15 Lansdown Road
Cheltenham
Glos GL50 2JA
UK

Edward Elgar Publishing, Inc.
William Pratt House
9 Dewey Court
Northampton
Massachusetts 01060
USA

A catalogue record for this book
is available from the British Library

Library of Congress Control Number: 2013943232

This book is available electronically in the ElgarOnline.com
Business Subject Collection, E-ISBN 978 1 78254 062 5

ISBN 978 1 78254 061 8 (cased)
ISBN 978 1 78347 147 8 (paperback)

Typeset by Columns DesignXMLLtd, Reading
Printed on FSC approved paper
Printed and bound in Great Britain by Marston Book Services Ltd, Oxfordshire

Contents

Contributors

David Ahlstrom is Professor of Management at The Chinese University of Hong Kong. He is a former chief editor of *Asia Pacific Journal of Management* and is currently international editor for the *Journal of World Business*.

David B. Audretsch is Distinguished Professor and Ameritech Chair of Economic Development at Indiana University and Director, Research Department on Entrepreneurship, Growth and Public Policy, Max Planck Institute of Economics. He is an editor of *Small Business Economics* and Chair of the Academy of Management Entrepreneurship Division.

Melissa Baucus is Professor of Entrepreneurship at University of Otago in New Zealand. Most recently, she served on the entrepreneurship faculty at the University of Louisville. She has published in academic journals including *Academy of Management Journal*, *Entrepreneurship Theory and Practice*, *Journal of Business Venturing* and *Journal of Management*. She has also published cases focusing on venture capital funding and business ethics in *Entrepreneurship Theory and Practice* and *Journal of Business Ethics*, respectively, and has presented at the U.S. Association for Small Business and Entrepreneurship (USASBE) conference on successful case writing for classroom use and publication.

Robert Blackburn is Professor of Small Business and Entrepreneurship and Director of the Small Business Research Centre at Kingston University. He is editor in chief of *International Small Business Journal*.

Garry Bruton is Professor of Management and Fehmi Zeko Family Fellowship at Neeley School of Business, Texas Christian University, Co-director of the Institute for Global Innovation and Chinese Entrepreneurship at Tongji University, and Honorary Professor at Sun Yat-sen Business School, China. He is a former editor of *Academy of Management Perspectives* and former action editor at the *Asia Pacific Journal of Management*.

Charles Carson is Associate Dean of Brock School of Business, Samford University. He has published in academic journals including *Educational and Psychological Measurement*, *Management Decision* and

Human Performance. He has also published case-based research and pedagogical cases in journals such as *The Case Journal* and the *Journal of Applied Case Research*. He currently serves on the Editorial Review Board for *The Case Journal* and previously served on the Executive Board of the North American Case Research Association (NACRA). In 2011, he was selected as the Outstanding Educator by the Federation of Business Disciplines/Southwest Case Research Association.

Andrew Corbett is Professor of Entrepreneurship at Babson College. He is an editor of *Journal of Management Studies*.

Nicole Coviello is Betty and Peter Sims Professor of Entrepreneurship and Professor of Marketing in the School of Business and Economics, Wilfrid Laurier University, Canada. She is a field editor of the *Journal of Business Venturing*.

Per Davidsson is Professor, Director and Talbot Family Foundation Chair in Entrepreneurship, Australian Centre for Entrepreneurship Research (ACE), Queensland University of Technology (QUT) Business School. He is also Professor at the Jönköping International Business School. He is a field editor of the *Journal of Business Venturing* and a former associate editor of *Entrepreneurship Theory and Practice* and *Small Business Economics*, as well as Past Chair of the Academy of Management Entrepreneurship Division.

Dimo Dimov is Professor of Innovation and Entrepreneurship at the University of Bath. He is a field editor of the *Journal of Business Venturing*.

Alain Fayolle is Professor of Entrepreneurship and Director of the Entrepreneurship Research Centre at EMLYON Business School. He is an associate editor of *Journal of Small Business Management*.

Hermann Frank is Associate Professor of Small Business Management and Entrepreneurship and Director of the Research Institute for Family Business at WU Vienna University of Economics and Business. He is an associate editor of *Journal of Small Business Management*.

Isabella Hatak is Assistant Professor at the Institute for Small Business Management and Entrepreneurship at WU Vienna University of Economics and Business. She has published contributions on trust, relational competence, and knowledge transfer to peer-reviewed journals and international conferences. She is a reviewer of *Journal of Small Business Management* and *International Small Business Journal*.

Benson Honig is Teresa Cascioli Chair in Entrepreneurial Leadership at DeGroote School of Business, McMaster University, Canada. He is also a decision editor of *Entrepreneurship Theory and Practice*.

Sally Jones is Teaching Fellow in Enterprise at the Leeds Enterprise Centre.

Franz Lohrke holds the Brock Family Endowed Chair in Entrepreneurship and is Chair of the Entrepreneurship, Management, and Marketing Department in the Brock School of Business, Samford University. He has published in academic journals including *Entrepreneurship Theory and Practice*, *International Small Business Journal*, *Journal of Business Research* and *Organizational Research Methods*, and he has co-edited two books on entrepreneurship theory. He has also published theory-development and pedagogical cases, and in 2011, he was chosen as the Outstanding Case Reviewer for *Entrepreneurship Theory and Practice*.

Helle Neergaard is Professor of Entrepreneurship, iCARE, at Aarhus University. She is President Elect of European Council of Small Business.

Friederike Welter is Managing Director at the Institut für Mittelstandsforschung in Bonn and Professor of SME Management and Entrepreneurship at University Siegen. She is associate editor of *Entrepreneurship Theory and Practice*.

Mike Wright is Director of the Centre for Management Buy-out Research, Head of the Innovation and Entrepreneurship Group and Professor of Entrepreneurship at Imperial College Business School and Visiting Professor at the University of Ghent, Belgium. He is a co-editor of *Strategic Entrepreneurship Journal*, a former editor of *Journal of Management Studies* and *Entrepreneurship Theory and Practice*, and a Past Chair of the Academy of Management Entrepreneurship Division.

Foreword

The value of this book surfaces in sharp relief when I reflect on my beginnings as a scholar. I enrolled in an 'ad hoc' PhD programme – one of three students – two adults with business and teaching experience, and my young self. Our only formal instruction was a course in statistics and a seminar on pedagogy. Most productive interaction came in the form of papers written for faculty in different departments. Then came the dissertation, mine an agglomeration of inductive, semi-qualitative and semi-quantitative analyses. By working with some superb scholars I had caught the research bug and certainly graduated with many more conceptual resources than I began with. However, I was in no way prepared for the rigours of academic publication. My first submission was greeted with a desk reject beginning with the words, 'Quite simply, I don't know where to begin'.

Life would have been so much easier had I had the benefit of this terrific book. It provides concrete and actionable advice on all aspects of publishing in the field of entrepreneurship, and indeed other domains of management. It counsels young researchers on how to develop and formulate research questions, how to integrate them into the existing literature and to highlight their contribution, and how to build and argue sound hypotheses. It provides insight and guidance for conducting both quantitative and qualitative research. It even shows which journals might be most useful for scholars aiming to 'up their game'. There is no question that the sound advice given here by Audretsch, Corbett, Fayolle, Honig, Wright and other stars in the field will focus readers on the essentials so vital in today's highly competitive and ever more exacting publishing environment.

What I also like about this collection are its more unconventional and liberating offerings by scholars more removed from the North American orthodoxy. I identified personally with Per Davidsson's reflections on how his early start, with little pressure to publish, allowed him to focus on the topics he cared most about – and enabled him to exploit the enthusiasm and relevance that brought him countless citations. Valuable lessons too are to be found in Jones and Neergaard's insights on turning a dissertation monograph into publishable articles, Coviello's guidelines for working with qualitative methods, and Ahlstrom and Bruton's and Dimov's analyses of the challenges of researching other cultures. A constructive subtext that runs through this collection is that although conceptual and methodological rigour is critical to crafting a publishable contribution, it is not always necessary to 'contribute to theory' (Miller, 2007). Although that is a useful option for many scholars, there is also room for relevant contributions that bring to bear solid data to garner new insights into practical problems confronting entrepreneurs.

What is especially edifying about this collection is that it demonstrates that there is no one best way to do research and that a wide variety of points of view may be brought to bear. It reflects an openness to different approaches, topics, methods and cultures, and that very scope for selection allows people with very different interests and skills to pursue their research passion and remain motivated and persistent in the face of a potential avalanche of rejections.

I wish you all fruitful reading and best of luck in your careers. *Bon courage*!

Danny Miller
Montreal, April 2013

REFERENCE

Miller, D. (2007), 'Paradigm prison', *Strategic Organization*, **5** (2), 177–84.

Preface

Entrepreneurship is becoming a well-established field of research. Entrepreneurship research now appears in the best journals in management, and some entrepreneurship scholars have a worldwide reputation in social and human sciences. However, the field still needs to improve its scientific legitimacy and most researchers need to improve their ability and skills in top-level research and writing. In particular, in a 'publish or perish' era, entrepreneurship researchers need to get published in the best entrepreneurship journals and also in the best journals in management, finance, economics, and so on. These thoughts led one of the editors of this book (Alain Fayolle) to design and set up for French-speaking researchers a four-day academic seminar entitled 'Meet the Editors' (of entrepreneurship journals).

The objective of this workshop organized in Paris with the help of the French Foundation for Management Education (FNEGE) was to support young entrepreneurship faculty members mainly from France in their effort to publish their research in the most prestigious outlets within the entrepreneurship discipline. Over a period of four days (23–26 January 2012), the editors of leading entrepreneurship journals[1] worked together with the 21 participants in an interactive way to provide hands-on advice on the research publication process. Topics of discussion included: how to submit a paper to a top journal, manage the review process and respond to reviewers; how to build up a successful research team; how to position a manuscript and clearly define its contribution to theory; how to get publication from a doctoral monograph; how to do a critical review of the literature and write a state of the art review; and how to get publication in leading American journals.

Mike Wright (the other editor of this volume), a speaker at the workshop, had for some time been involved in a number of meet the editor and paper development workshops, as well as writing articles on getting published, in his role as a journal editor and at the time Chair of the Academy of Management Entrepreneurship Division. He had observed the marked raising of the threshold needed to publish in leading journals and the demands this placed on entrepreneurship scholars to 'tool up' if they were successfully to meet this challenge.

At breakfast on the first day of the Paris workshop, there was a discussion between the two of us from which emerged the idea of the book. We believe together that the field of entrepreneurship is on the road to institutionalization. In such context young researchers need to be supported in their quest for socialization into the community of entrepreneurship scholars. Membership of the entrepreneurship division of the Academy of Management is a means towards this end. More specifically, keeping in mind the need to get published to fully belong to a community, we think that this book will add some value to the existing set of means.

We believe that this book will bring useful answers and insights to young entrepreneurship researchers' issues when taking the decision to commit to long and complex research processes in an emergent field. We advise them to keep in mind that research is not only a matter of the competences and talent they believe they have, but is above all a collective process. Getting published in entrepreneurship journals can thus be seen through the lenses of learning from the experiences and knowledge of experienced and successful scholars. We warmly thank all of our colleagues, editors and associate editors of entrepreneurship journals, who have accepted to contribute to this book in order to offer their expertise and share their experience.

Alain Fayolle
EMLyon

Mike Wright
CMBOR

NOTE

1. *Journal of Business Venturing, Entrepreneurship Theory and Practice, Small Business Economics, Strategic Entrepreneurship Journal, Journal of Small Business Management, Entrepreneurship & Regional Development, International Small Business Journal* and *International Journal of Entrepreneurship and Innovation.*

1. Thinking and writing for scholarly publication in entrepreneurship

Alain Fayolle

INTRODUCTION

As any researcher, entrepreneurship scholars are aiming at getting published in good academic journals. They have a wide range of choices both in the fields of management and entrepreneurship. Entrepreneurship scholars may also target journals in other disciplines such as psychology, sociology, philosophy, finance or economics. Obviously, a key question is in which journal(s) could we submit our research? But, probably much more important issues are in relation to why should we publish our work and on what topics and research objects/domains?

In this introductory chapter, we bring insights and answers to these questions based on the literature and our knowledge in entrepreneurship. The chapter is organized as follows. Our first part is an attempt to answer the above questions. In a first section, we analyze the main reasons leading entrepreneurship scholars to get published in academic journals. Of course, the 'publish or perish' logic plays a role, but there are also other arguments in relation to our social role and mission. The second section is around the choice of research topics in our field. What kind of topics could be usefully studied and why? Finally, our third section is around the choice of academic journals. We notably present here the best entrepreneurship journals, the big seven: *Journal of Business Venturing* (JBV), *Entrepreneurship Theory and Practice* (ETP), *Strategic Entrepreneurship Journal* (SEJ), *Journal of Small Business Management* (JSBM), *Small Business Economics* (SBE), *Entrepreneurship & Regional Development* (ERD) and *International Small Business Journal* (ISBJ).

Our second part allows us to present the different contributions of this book, including 13 chapters, each of them addressing a key topic in relation to getting published with entrepreneurship manuscripts. Topics of discussion in the book include: how to submit a paper to a top journal, manage the review process and respond to reviewers; how to build up a successful research team; how to position a manuscript and clearly define its contribution to theory; how to publish from a doctoral monograph; how to do a critical review of the literature and write a state of the art review; how to publish entrepreneurship research in general management journals; how to publish policy-oriented research and, for scholars outside North America, how to get published in leading American journals.

The objective of this book is to provide entrepreneurship researchers with relevant material and insights in order to support them in their efforts to publish their research in the most prestigious outlets within the entrepreneurship discipline, but also in management journals that are open to entrepreneurship research. The contributors of this book are the editors of leading entrepreneurship and management journals. Based on their experience as researchers and editors they bring useful hands-on advice on the research publication process.

GETTING PUBLISHED IN ENTREPRENEURSHIP: THE WHY AND THE WHAT

As the second part of this chapter is mainly centered on the how (to get published in entrepreneurship journals), this first part offers insights around the why and what issues.

Why Should We Publish?

We know that scholarly interest in entrepreneurship is becoming more and more important. As underlined by Sorenson and Stuart (2008, p. 518), 'the number of articles published with the term "entrepreneur/ship" in the title, abstract, or keywords tripled each year from roughly 50 in 1990 to more than 150 in 2000 … the annual count of articles doubled again between 2000 and 2005, and authors published more than 370 academic papers on entrepreneurship in 2006 alone'.

This growing interest for entrepreneurship as a field of research reflects a number of factors. First, entrepreneurship is increasingly recognized at social and economic levels, in its capacity to generate new jobs, innovation and economic growth. There is consequently a growing social demand due to policy concerns. Zahra and Wright (2011) notably claim that there is a strong need to strengthen the link between entrepreneurship research and public policy. How we should evaluate public policies in entrepreneurship to get useful knowledge about their impact on entrepreneurial attitudes, behaviors and results is a key question. Student demand for content and the practice-oriented needs expressed by entrepreneurs and would-be entrepreneurs are also important parts of the social demand towards entrepreneurship research.

Taking into consideration the strength of this social demand, many entrepreneurship scholars are focusing their research on deepening understanding of the antecedents, processes and consequences of entrepreneurship (Sorenson and Stuart, 2008). However, as for any research community, there is a risk of deviance and losing our way in the field. The pressure of 'publish or perish' and the risk of being isolated in our academic 'ivory tower' are real threats for the future of entrepreneurship research. Willing to avoid such deviance, influential scholars have reflected on ideas and ways towards a better future (see, for example, Welter, 2011; Wiklund et al., 2011; Zahra and Wright, 2011), highlighting the importance of contexts or the necessity to shift the focus, content and methods of entrepreneurship research.

As a conclusion, our dream for the future of entrepreneurship research would be:

- Having more impact on the actual practices of entrepreneurship at the different levels: individual, organization and country.
- Helping would-be entrepreneurs, novice and experienced entrepreneurs to be more intelligent in complex situations and more successful in founding and growing their new companies.
- Helping policymakers in rethinking, designing and implementing public policies for entrepreneurship at different stages of the entrepreneurial processes and for different groups of people.
- Contributing to the constitution of a strong research community aimed at reducing the level of fragmentation in entrepreneurship research and bridging the worlds of academia and practice.

What Topics to be Studied?

Different perspectives may be useful to make relevant choices to answer the question: what topics to be studied? If we take the point of view of scientific journals, they are looking for influential research and articles that bring into a field new ideas, new theories and new contributions (Gambardella and Zollo, 2009). Bruce Kogut, the editor of the *European Management Review* from 2005 until 2008, wrote in one editorial introduction: 'The *European Management Review* has the ambition of being the journal of first choice for scholars interested in the theory and empirical study of management' (Gambardella and Zollo, 2009, p. 1). A scientific paper must be original and/or interesting, bringing added value to the existing knowledge. Originality and newness can come from:

- studying a topic that has not been studied before in relation to academic and/or managerial issues;
- using or creating a new methodology to treat a research problem;
- importing a theory from a given field and applying it in one other field;
- elaborating a new theory;
- using a new database to study a research question;
- doing a meta-analysis or a literature review, and so on.

Another perspective could be to actively participate in a scientific conversation based on personal interests and preferences in research. Anne Huff considers that scholarship is conversation: 'To share your ideas and fully participate in the scholarship of your field, you therefore must write' (1999, p. 5). For her, good thinking and good writing are intrinsically linked within a virtuous circle (1999, p. 7). An example of scientific conversation can be found in the literature on the concept of opportunity. The conversation started with Shane and Venkataraman's article (2000) and 12 years later, Shane (2012) offered a review showing the impact on the research community and the scientific outcomes of this initial article.

As a conclusion, choosing a good topic is equivalent to having something interesting to say to someone (a researcher and/or a scientific journal), keeping in mind that getting published strongly relates to good thinking and good writing.

What Journals to be Considered?

We present first an overview of the journals which could be of interest for entrepreneurship scholars before focusing on the best entrepreneurship journals, the big seven.

An overview

There are many lists and rankings of journals both in entrepreneurship and management fields. In his 2012 revised list,[1] Jerry Katz indicates that a lot has changed since the previous list published in 2003. At that time there were four entrepreneurship journals listed in the Social Science Citation Index (SSCI). Today there are ten (JBV, ETP, JSBM, ERD, SBE, SEJ, *Family Business Review*, ISBJ, *Technovation* and *Journal of Technology Transfer*). There are also ten mainstream management journals

(*Administrative Science Quarterly*, *Academy of Management Review*, *Academy of Management Journal*, *Academy of Management Learning & Education*, *Academy of Management Perspective*, *Journal of Management*, *Journal of Management Studies*, *Management Science*, *Simulation & Gaming*, *Strategic Management Journal*) which publish entrepreneurship articles. Of course, we could discuss the *sensu stricto* inclusion in the list of entrepreneurship journals of *Technovation*, *Journal of Technology Transfer* and *Family Business Review*.

In a study defining a forum for entrepreneurship scholars, Fried (2003) identified six entrepreneurship journals, JBV, ETP, SBE, ERD, JSBM and ISBJ, and 14 journals in management. Most of them belong to the Katz list. The highest rated journals at that time (outstanding) were *Academy of Management Journal*, *Academy of Management Review*, *Journal of Business Venturing*, *Strategic Management Journal*, *Administrative Science Quarterly*, *Organization Science* and *Management Science*. The second group of journals (significant) includes *Entrepreneurship Theory and Practice*, *Small Business Economics*, *American Journal of Sociology*, *Journal of Management*, *Harvard Business Review*, *Research Policy*, *California Management Review*, *Sloan Management Review*, *Journal of Management Studies* and *Academy of Management Executive* (now *Academy of Management Perspectives*). The third and last group of journals (acceptable), those having the lowest group highlights, were *Entrepreneurship & Regional Development*, *Journal of Small Business Management*, *Journal of Private Equity*, *Venture Capital*, *Journal of Small Business Finance*, *Regional Studies*, *Journal of High Technology Management Research* and *International Small Business Journal*.

The British Association of Business Schools (ABS) offers in its 2010 Academic Journal Quality Guide a ranking (see Appendix 1.1) of entrepreneurship and small business management journals including four categories (grades). This list ranks the best entrepreneurship journals, the big seven, into grades four and three.

In its 2011 'Categorization of Journals in Economics and Management', the French National Committee of the Scientific Research (*Comité National de la Recherche Scientifique*) has identified 32 journals in its list of innovation and entrepreneurship journals. Both ETP and JBV appear with the highest rating, ISBJ, JSBM, SBE and SEJ are in the second group, while ERD is in the third (out of four).

Finally, to complete this initial overview of some lists and rankings of entrepreneurship journals, the list of the 45 journals used in the FT (*Financial Times*) research ranking only proposes two journals in entrepreneurship: JBV and ETP.

The big seven

At the beginning of 2013, we sent the following message to the editors of the big seven:[2] 'We are preparing a book on "How to get published in the best entrepreneurship journals"… and we would like to get data about your journal on trends in submissions, acceptance rates and journal quality measures.' We received a response and data from the seven journals. In the rest of this section, we present the key data for each journal introduced in our development from the higher Institute for Scientific Information (ISI) two-year impact factor in 2011 to the lower.

Journal of Business Venturing   The journal receives 500–575 manuscripts per year. The acceptance rate was 10 percent in 2011 and about 12 percent in previous years.

The impact factor increased from 2.149 in 2010 to 3.062 in 2011. Depending on the rankings, JBV ranked 25th in the ISI 2010 Business list and 13th in the 2011 list. A current key concern relates to possible retractions of articles due to non-ethical behavior.

Entrepreneurship Theory and Practice   The acceptance rate of the journal has ranged from 6 percent to 9.9 percent for 2005–10 (an average of 8.5 percent). The desk rejection rate has remained near 40 percent, and 60–70 percent of the manuscripts are rejected after the first round of review.

The impact factor increased from 2.272 in 2010 to 2.542 in 2011. Based on the rankings, ETP was at 23rd in the ISI 2010 Business list and at 19th in the 2011 list. ETP expresses the same kind of concerns as JBV. The journal is dealing with possible retractions, notably due to self-plagiarism issues, simultaneous submissions and related matters. As for trends, other than ethical issues, there are an increasing number of manuscripts from outside the US. Many of these are not appropriate for the journal, primarily because of the lack of significant theoretical contribution.

In relation to the ethical issues highlighted by both JBV and ETP, we would like to underline the contribution brought by our book through Chapter 7 by Benson Honig.

Strategic Entrepreneurship Journal   SEJ is younger than the two previous journals and its youth probably explains that the number of submissions has been lower than those of JBV and ETP. In the last five years, the number of submitted papers was

- 2008: 129;
- 2009: 151;

- 2010: 176;
- 2011: 220;
- 2012: 193.

The impact factor has increased from 2.026 in 2010 to 2.053 in 2011. Based on the rankings, SEJ was at 28th rank in the ISI 2010 Business list and at 29th in the 2011 list.

Small Business Economics   The journal received 279 manuscripts in 2009, 337 in 2010 and 338 in 2011. The acceptance rate for each year of this period was 18 percent in 2009, 12 percent in 2010 and 21 percent in 2011. Acceptance rates, especially in this case, are difficult to interpret as the number of papers accepted in a year relates to prior year submissions.

The impact factor has decreased slightly from 1.555 in 2010 to 1.549 in 2011. Based on the rankings, SBE was at 42nd in the ISI 2010 Business list and roughly at the same rank (41st) in the 2011 list.

International Small Business Journal   The journal is experiencing an interesting progression among the best entrepreneurship journals. The number of submissions grew from 269 in 2010, to 341 in 2011 and to 444 in 2012. The acceptance rates within this period were: 8.1 percent (2010), 9.8 percent (2011) and 10.8 percent (2012).

The impact factor has increased strongly from 0.927 in 2010 to 1.492 in 2011. Based on the rankings, ISBJ was at 63rd in the ISI 2010 Business list and at 47th in the 2011 list.

Journal of Small Business Management   The journal received 513 manu-scripts in 2010, 598 in 2011 and 635 in 2012. The acceptance rates are 8.2 percent (2010), 9 percent (2011) and 8 percent (2012). The desk rejection rate has ranged from 20 percent to 25 percent.

The impact factor experienced a modest increase from 1.189 in 2010 to 1.392 in 2011. JSBM does not appear in the ISI Business list but in the 2010 ISI Management list, the journal is ranked 72nd, compared to SEJ (45th), SBE (59th) and ISBJ (85th).

Entrepreneurship & Regional Development   The journal receives over 300 direct submissions a year on average and the 2012 acceptance rate was 5.4 percent. The Editor of ERD, Alistair Anderson, has been the only one to send us a two-page Editor's reflections on his journal (see Appendix 1.2). In these reflections, he develops interesting thoughts about the way we should read and interpret metrics such as the number of submissions or the acceptance rate, particularly when it comes to taking into consideration, or not, special issues. In broad terms, ERD is regularly rejecting more than half of all submitted papers at the first editorial review.

The ERD impact factor fell sharply from 1.353 in 2010 to 0.943 in 2011. Based on the rankings, ERD was at 52nd in the ISI 2010 Business list and at 73rd in the 2011 list.

GETTING PUBLISHED IN ENTREPRENEURSHIP: THE HOW

We introduce here the 13 other chapters which constitute the main contribution of this book.

In Chapters 2 and 3, 'Getting published in entrepreneurship journals' and 'The review process', Mike Wright focuses on processes involved in getting published, outlining the stages from submission through review to final acceptance. In addition, he gives insightful advice to entrepreneurship scholars in order to help them in elaborating a publication strategy.

Per Davidsson in Chapter 4, 'Getting published – and cited – in entrepreneurship: reflections on ten papers', based on his personal background and experience, gives us a set of reasons for publication success and to get cited. The chapter is mainly a discussion of the key success factors he has identified – importance of the research question and the contribution, hard work and tenacity to publish, fit with the journal, high quality of (or unique) data, and having good co-authors and timing – in relation to a selection of ten articles published in the last couple of decades.

In Chapter 5, 'From idea to publication: managing the research process', Robert Blackburn and Friederike Welter describe the complex and challenging process leading to publication. The main objective of the chapter is to map out the journey from idea to publication. The authors show what lessons can be learned from previous experiences and how important it is to accumulate and share experiences in this domain. Despite the abundant documentation on research process, methods and writing in management and entrepreneurship, 'the actual process of converting a research idea into publication remains complex and subject to a variety of challenges, but it is ultimately rewarding'.

Hermann Frank and Isabella Hatak in Chapter 6, 'Doing a research literature review', address a very important topic in research. Reviewing the literature allows researchers aiming at publishing high-quality academic research to increase their awareness and understanding of existing work in the research field, so they can better position their own research on the map of knowledge creation. The chapter offers an overview of types of literature reviews (narrative, meta-analysis) and of the processes of doing a (successful) literature review.

In Chapter 7, 'Ethics and publishing in entrepreneurship research', Benson Honig states that ethics in entrepreneurship research is an increasingly important component of the field, echoing actual issues and concerns raised in our field, as we have seen above, at least by the two leading entrepreneurship journals, JBV and ETP. This chapter examines the ethical implications of the role and impact entrepreneurship research and education play in developing more and/or better entrepreneurs. Moreover, it focuses on non-ethical behaviors from scholars and researchers in our field, and their consequences at different levels.

Sally Jones and Helle Neergaard in Chapter 8, 'Moving from the periphery to the inner circle: getting published from your thesis', propose, as a starting point, an auto-ethnographic narrative of the doctoral process. Based on this narrative, the authors address the specificities of getting published from a doctoral thesis and present the pros and cons of two strategies: monograph and article-based thesis. They also give general advice on how to publish from a PhD, highlighting the importance of academic identity and emotions involved in the process of development.

In Chapter 9, 'Do European scholars have specific problems getting published in Anglo-Saxon journals?', Dimo Dimov makes an attempt to answer a cultural question in the field of entrepreneurship. In the conclusion, he says: 'not all European scholars face difficulties in publishing in top international journals, but some of them do'. Based on his own experience and those of other European scholars among the most cited authors in the field, being editors or associate editors or editorial board members of leading entrepreneurship journals, strongly involved in the entrepreneurship division of the Academy of Management, Dimo Dimov examines and discusses the key factors which throw some light on why some European scholars have no specific problems while others may have. These factors relate to socialization for publishing, training (mainly at the doctoral level), focus and communication.

Nicole Coviello starts, in Chapter 10, 'How to publish qualitative entrepreneurship research in top journals', by reminding us that 'six of the last ten winners of the *Academy of Management Journal*'s Best Article award (to 2011) are qualitative'. It is a strong sign that qualitative studies are important and impactful, but we know how difficult and challenging it is to get published with such qualitative works. In this chapter, based on her experience as an author, reviewer and editor, Nicole

Coviello offers powerful guidance to improve our chances, as entrepreneurship scholars, to succeed in publishing qualitative research in a top journal.

In Chapter 11, 'Laying the foundations for Asia-focused research through qualitative research', David Ahlstrom and Garry Bruton clearly explain the way research should be conducted in the context of Asia. For the authors, too often scholars examining issues in Asia are repeating research questions from mature Western economies. However, the institutional setting in Asia clearly is different than mature Western economies and so these questions may not be the best to drive research in Asia. Qualitative studies have the potential to lay the foundation to identify those questions that should be driving Asia-focused research. This chapter discusses how scholars should conduct such qualitative research about Asia so that it not only generates valid results but also is publishable in leading business journals.

Franz Lohrke, Melissa Baucus and Charles Carson in Chapter 12, 'Publishing cases in entrepreneurship journals', show the importance of the case study method to build and teach theory. In entrepreneurship research, case studies have provided key theories in the areas of motivation, clusters, corporate entrepreneurship and new international ventures. In this chapter, the authors explain and discuss important issues in relation to publishing theory-building and pedagogical cases in top journals. As a consequence, they offer insightful suggestions to improve the quality of research processes and scholarly writing based on cases.

In Chapter 13, 'Getting published in entrepreneurship policy', David Audretsch shows that the increasing demand for understanding and learning more about entrepreneurship policy relates to the emergence of entrepreneurship as a driving force leading to economic growth and job creation, and improving performance and competitiveness. He then describes the domain of entrepreneurship policy research, identifying five distinctive levels or types and arguing that it is much more than taking into consideration research aiming at providing policymakers with instrumental recommendations. Finally, in this chapter, David Audretsch illustrates each type of entrepreneurship policy research, analyzing their link with actual publication modes or outlets.

Finally, Andrew Corbett in Chapter 14, 'Positioning entrepreneurship research for general management journals', addresses the difficulties entrepreneurship scholars may have to get published in broader management journals. In this chapter, he examines how entrepreneurship scholars need to build their manuscripts to fit well within general management journals. The main differences relate to the review process and the way the contribution needs to be presented, by taking into account related research from scholars outside the field of entrepreneurship. Andrew Corbett gives useful suggestions for dealing with the particularities of general management journals.

NOTES

1. The message has been sent to Dean Shepherd (JBV), Ray Bagby (ETP), Mike Wright (SEJ), George Solomon (JSBM), Robert Blackburn (ISBJ), David Audretsch (SBE) and Alistair Anderson (ERD).
2. www.slu.edu/x17970.xml.

REFERENCES

Fried, V.H. (2003), 'Defining a forum for entrepreneurship scholars', *Journal of Business Venturing*, **18** (1), 1–11.

Gambardella, A. and M. Zollo (2009), 'Editor's introduction', *European Management Journal*, **6** (1), 1–4.

Huff, A.S. (1999), *Writing for Scholarly Publication*, Thousand Oaks, CA: Sage Publications.

Shane, S. (2012), 'Reflections on the 2010 AMR decade award: delivering on the promise of entrepreneurship as a field of research', *Academy of Management Review*, **37** (1), 10–20.

Shane, S. and S. Venkataraman (2000), 'The promise of entrepreneurship as a field of research', *Academy of Management Review*, **25** (1), 217–26.

Sorenson, O. and T.E. Stuart (2008), '12 Entrepreneurship: a field of dreams?', *The Academy of Management Annals*, **2** (1), 517–43.

Welter, F. (2011), 'Contextualizing entrepreneurship – conceptual challenges and way forward', *Entrepreneurship Theory and Practice*, **35** (1), 165–84.

Wiklund, J., P. Davidsson, D.B. Audretsch and C. Karlsson (2011), 'The future of entrepreneurship research', *Entrepreneurship Theory and Practice*, **35** (1), 1–9.

Zahra, S.A. and M. Wright (2011), 'Entrepreneurship's next act', *Academy of Management Perspectives*, **25** (4), 67–83.

APPENDIX 1.1

Table 1A.1   Rankings of entrepreneurship and small business journals

Journal and ABS grade	ISI two-year impact factor 2011
Grade Four	
Journal of Business Venturing	3.062
Entrepreneurship, Theory and Practice	2.542
Grade Three	
International Small Business Journal	1.492
Entrepreneurship & Regional Development	0.943
Small Business Economics	1.549
Journal of Small Business Management	1.392
Strategic Entrepreneurship Journal	2.053
Grade Two	
Journal of Small Business and Enterprise Development	n.a.
International Journal of Entrepreneurial Behavior and Research	n.a.
Venture Capital: An International Journal of Entrepreneurial Finance	n.a.
International Journal of Entrepreneurship and Innovation	n.a.
Family Business Review	2.600
Grade One	
Journal of International Entrepreneurship	n.a.
World Review of Entrepreneurship, Management and Sustainable Development	n.a.
Journal of Enterprising Culture	n.a.
International Entrepreneurship and Management Journal	n.a.
Journal of Entrepreneurship	n.a.
Social Enterprise	n.a.

APPENDIX 1.2   EDITOR'S REFLECTIONS ON *ENTREPRENEURSHIP & REGIONAL DEVELOPMENT*

The scope of the journal is, as the title implies, entrepreneurship and how it contributes to development. But we are particularly interested in papers that contribute to our understanding of the topics, papers that make a useful conceptual contribution. This means that work which is primarily descriptive is unlikely to be published. This is true even if the paper uses sophisticated analysis methods. Papers should add to, or challenge, our understanding of these fascinating phenomena. In broad terms, we appreciate papers that build from, or engage with, topics that have previously been published in the journal, or in related journals.

But conceptual contributions may cover a variety of topics and do so in a number of different ways. A simple test of a paper's suitability is 'is this interesting?' This test can be seen as a threshold in the sense that if the paper is not 'interesting' it will not be considered further. A second test is 'after reading this paper do I know something now that I didn't know before?' We encourage a variety of methodological approaches. Hence good quantitative papers that address interesting questions are very welcome. But papers that take too sweeping an approach, and hence lack depth and the fine grain that is interesting, may be rejected, especially if the hypotheses seem trivial. Papers which merely confirm established views are unlikely to be accepted. Good qualitative papers are often well received because they tend to address interesting questions of 'why' and 'how'. For many such papers the problem is not the nature of the research question or proposition, but the quality and rigor of the study. We insist that this is demonstrated in the paper and again of course, that the contribution is well founded and interesting. Entirely theoretical papers are also welcome. But here the standard required is different and demanding. Such papers must fit the themes already established in the journal and must build soundly from the existing literature and offer insights or novelty. Armchair musings and ungrounded assertions are not very appealing.

We receive over 300 direct submissions a year and have a final acceptance rate (2012) of 5.4%. But these bold figures mask much of the process and don't give a very accurate picture. First these figures largely exclude special issues. We usually have at least a couple of special issues each year focusing in depth on a very specific topic. Typically, these produce high quality specialist material. The editors of the special issues judge what they deem to be interesting and sufficiently robust for the special issues. In some cases the numbers of submissions to a special issue are high, but in others a lower number of good papers are submitted. However, it has never been the case that not enough good quality papers are submitted to cancel a special issue. Most special issues publish around five papers from the call. We now have ten issues a year, delivered as five double issues. The number of issues was increased to cope with the increasing number of good papers submitted.

Nonetheless, in broad terms, we decline more than half of all submitted paper at the first editorial review. Some of these are simply not well suited to the journal; many are not very interesting; others are underdeveloped, whilst others are simply not robust enough to consider sending to reviewers. As editor I always try to explain why I have declined the paper and take great satisfaction when I receive a note thanking me for rejecting the paper because the author now knows how to improve it! For me this is a ringing endorsement of the benefits of our peer review system. As an author it can be hard to judge what is good, or what is weak in our own papers. I have the dubious merit of having had one of my own papers rejected by my own journal!

This stage typically takes about ten days from submission. But there are peaks in submissions, usually around the ends of academic terms, when editorial decisions can be delayed. We have two associate editors, Ed Malecki and Sarah Jack; they tend to deal only with promising papers, those most likely to be sent for review. Papers that pass the 'interesting' – *the so what* – test and appear to be well framed in the literature and rigorously researched are sent to two anonymous reviewers. In addition to our experienced editorial board, we have a number of excellent reviewers. Their wisdom, insights and empathy are absolutely vital in maintaining the quality of the journal. In effect they are the gatekeepers of our academic standards. But if a paper has promise, but falls a little short of our publication standards, mostly our reviewers will try to show authors how they could reach the standards. Our high-quality reviewers spend considerable time effort and their expertise in reviewing papers. They don't just advise editors about the acceptability or not of the paper. Instead they may offer suggestions, advice and help to improve the paper. Reviewing times vary greatly, but we hope to be able to provide a decision on the paper in about three months. Often the best or specialist reviewers are busy, so sometimes it can take much longer. I don't have precise data for the number of papers that progress from this first round of peer review, but my estimate is that about 35% are asked to revise and resubmit. I can only recall one paper that was accepted at this stage.

If a paper has progressed, there may be several iterations of revisions required. One annoying problem is that some authors don't seem to try very hard to address the reviewers' concerns. If they only pay lip service, not genuinely and carefully engaging with the spirit of the constructive critiques and simply making changes that superficially address points, these papers rarely progress. (This, of course, is not the same as the author explaining why they did not follow the guidance.) I am often surprised at this attitude and not only because it seems to ignore the usefulness and the considerable efforts made by the reviewers. But especially because if an author has taken the time and made the effort investments required getting a paper to this stage, it seems strange to me that they don't care enough to make sufficient changes to satisfy the reviewers. The final rounds of reviews are usually quite fast, taking a month or so.

When a paper is finally accepted it moves immediately into the publication process, with stages of proofing and so on. The period from acceptance to publication varies according to how many accepted papers are in the pipeline. But after proofing, we place the paper on our early cite section of our website. Papers are allocated a unique DOI number which serves as a unique reference for citations. Interestingly, a substantial number of papers are cited at this early publication stage.

In sum then, we endeavor to publish papers that our readers will find interesting and useful, but we welcome a broad church of approaches allow papers to satisfy these criteria.

We expect high standards of scholarship, but are open to how this is achieved. Our editors and reviews, in a genuine spirit of peer review, strive to maintain our standards by constructive critique.

Alistair Anderson

2. Getting published in entrepreneurship journals

Mike Wright

INTRODUCTION

Getting published in entrepreneurship journals is an increasingly highly competitive process. As entrepreneurship as a discipline grows in popularity among students, more and more schools in a growing number of countries are recruiting faculty who are expected to publish quality academic research. The result has been a sharp rise in submissions to journals as was observed in Chapter 1. In parallel with this development, there has also been a sharp increase in submissions to general management journals in which entrepreneurship scholars may be aiming to publish. Unfortunately, the space available in journals has remained relatively constant so that acceptance rates have fallen commensurately.

By no means all the increase in the volume of submissions is accompanied by an increase in the quality of articles. Much of the influx of papers is coming from less developed regions or from schools without a research tradition where faculty lack rigorous research training (Clark et al., 2013). Yet, the situation is changing rapidly and there is no room for complacency. In this environment it becomes important for entrepreneurship scholars to 'up their game' by developing their expertise if they are to be successful in publishing in leading journals.

This chapter and the next contribute to developing entrepreneurship scholars' publishing expertise by focusing on the processes involved in getting published. In this chapter, I begin by discussing the development of a publication strategy and targeting journals. Details are then provided on the specific elements to take into account in writing and preparing a paper for submission.

DEVELOPING A PUBLICATION STRATEGY AND JOURNAL TARGETING

You need to be realistic about publishing in the very top journals. As we have seen, acceptance rates are low and timescales are long. The distribution of academics system-wide who publish even one article in the very top-tier journals in their career is highly skewed, even more so from outside the US. Nevertheless, the returns to publishing in a top journal are high.

In contrast, there is a serious danger of an adverse career effect from publishing a stream of low-level CV-fillers. This generally sends a negative signal to potential employers that a candidate's work is not of sufficient quality. A preferable strategy is to develop a portfolio approach that focuses on papers that count. Not all papers will have the potential to be published in a top journal. There is therefore a need to balance the desire to get your research published with the quality of journal and the 'perceived' quality of the paper. One might consider publishing initial work in a lower-level journal to build confidence and become familiar with the review process. However, it is important to be mindful of aiming for journals with a quality threshold that will count. Moreover, the learning benefits from getting an 'easy hit' may be quite limited.

Frustrating though it may be, we just have to accept that having work rejected is part and parcel of being an academic. As Don Siegel, editor of *Academy of Management Perspectives* and formerly a field editor at *Journal of Business Venturing* (JBV), commented to the author: 'If you're not being rejected, you're not aiming high enough.' The key is to develop strategies to minimize the chances of being rejected and to maximize the chances of receiving a 'revise and resubmit' decision, the most realistic initial best outcome that one might expect.

You need to be aware of the journals in the entrepreneurship field, the scope of the kind of papers they accept, their quality and their ranking relative to other journals. Authors also need to make sure that they are aware of the journal lists used for tenure and promotion purposes held by their departments, schools or institutions. These lists may be specific to particular institutions in terms of the approved journals they include and how journals are rated. It is also important to note whether specific entrepreneurship field journals are rated compared to more general management and other relevant journals. This may influence the extent to which a publication strategy for an entrepreneurship scholar needs to include mainly field or mainly general management journals.

Schools' publication lists may be based on recognized published rankings of journals, of which there are many. The website www.harzing.com contains many examples of these lists. Two of the most well known are the UK's Association of Business Schools' (ABS's) list and the ISI impact factors list. As the 'Harzing' website shows, there is a great deal of consistency between lists but there are some differences especially in relation to how entrepreneurship field and general management journals are included and rated, especially among the lower level journals. The Institute for Scientific Information (ISI) impact factor lists only those journals that have satisfied criteria for inclusion and mainly covers the more established stronger journals. The impact factor of a journal is a measure of the extent to which the articles published in a journal during two-year and five-year periods have been cited in other articles.

The principal entrepreneurship journals as ranked by the UK ABS are shown in Appendix 1.1 to Chapter 1. The appendix also indicates the impact factor for those journals in the list included in the ISI.

PREPARING AN ARTICLE FOR SUBMISSION

In this section I develop an outline of the things to consider in writing an article in preparation for its submission to a leading academic journal. The intention is not to be too formulaic but to highlight key areas that reviewers will likely focus upon in their reports. As noted earlier, it is advisable to look carefully at how articles are constructed in the particular journal to which a submission is planned. For ease of exposition, this section is structured in terms of the sequence of parts of an article.

Introduction and Framing

This section is perhaps the most important part of an article. Framing and positioning the paper in the relevant literature is crucial to establishing its contribution. For good entrepreneurship journals, it is not sufficient that an article has 'perfectly formed empirics' that address a methodological gap – such articles may be better targeted towards a journal focused on methods.

Articles need to establish both that there is a gap in the existing literature and to be convincing as to why it is important to fill that gap. A gap may exist but this may be because the topic is trivial or uninteresting.

Articles may make a novel contribution either because they disconfirm existing assumptions or they address observed puzzles. To make a contribution, papers need to do more than fill in the potholes in a well-trodden path (Barley, 2006). Rather, they need to challenge the consensus. This can be achieved by seeking to bring a new theoretical lens to an established area. To be interesting, however, the new lens will need to lead to different relationships and findings from what is already known from existing studies. There is a need to demonstrate the shortcomings of existing approaches and how the new lens helps us to see a topic differently.

An alternative approach is to open up a new topic or phenomenon that has not been addressed before. Such work may be published in more prestigious journals only once its validity has been established. Connecting a new phenomenon to existing debates by showing how it leads us to reconsider how we have previously thought about an area is a good way to break into a top journal. For example, when work first began to appear on repeat entrepreneurs it challenged insights into how entrepreneurs behave, which had previously tended to assume that entrepreneurs starting a business were doing so for the first time. As a result, work on the role of entrepreneurial experience and learning began to develop.

Successful entrepreneurs need to be adept at opportunity recognition and exploitation. Similarly, to identify an interesting research gap, researchers also need to be entrepreneurial. Interaction with practitioners and the real problems and challenges they face can help in identifying new topics and perspectives not covered in the existing literature (McGrath, 2007).

The data and methods adopted in an article have to be rigorous and to 'industry standard', even when examining a new phenomenon. Sometimes there is a temptation to want to move quickly to stake a claim over a new area. Authors may attempt to deflect criticism by claiming that a study is exploratory, but doing so can suggest that a paper is flawed because it is relying on convenience samples and variables that do not measure the constructs claimed.

Whatever approach is adopted, it is crucial to be explicit about the research question that the article is seeking to address. The research question needs to follow directly from the material in the introduction that establishes the gap in the literature and the need to address that gap.

The introduction should then contain a brief paragraph in which the contributions of the paper to the literature are stated. One approach is to state a general contribution to theory and a specific contribution to the particular topic being considered. Writing this paragraph can be challenging but presents a good test. If you struggle to convey your contribution in this paragraph after having conducted the research and analysis, then an editor and reviewer coming to the paper for the first time may also wonder what the paper is adding and form a negative view even at this early stage in their reading. The introduction can conclude with a brief recognition of the data being used, and its novelty and appropriateness for the particular research questions.

Positioning an entrepreneurship paper for submission to a general management journal requires a different approach. Rather than leading with an emphasis on filling a gap in the entrepreneurship literature, it is important to identify the shortcomings in existing management debates and research, on which recourse to an entrepreneurship context helps shed new light. For more on this aspect see Andrew Corbett's chapter.

Finally, a common lament is that US journals are not interested in non-US or that top-tier journals are not interested in qualitative papers. The problems here probably relate more to non-US papers not keying into current debates and conversations in the US literature. With respect to qualitative papers, a common problem is the failure of authors to be clear about the purpose of the study and to convey that leading-edge or even 'industry standard' methods have been used (Davidsson, 2012). In other words, papers tend to be judged by editors and reviewers on their merits within the particular conceptual and methodological paradigm they adopt. Recent editorials, for example in the *Academy of Management Journal* (AMJ), have set out what is looked for in qualitative articles that are to be publishable in that journal (Bansal and Corley, 2011).

Literature and Theoretical Framework

The literature review needs to be focused on the issues to be covered in the article rather than a longer more general review. There is a need to provide clear justification for why a particular theory or set of theories is appropriate. The integration of theories can be an advantage and open the way to new conceptual insights. The danger comes from having too many theories that are incompatible and which make the empirics impossible.

Hypothesis Development

It is useful to introduce up front the overarching framework to be adopted. This helps the reader to appreciate that the hypotheses fit together in a coherent manner rather than being just an ad hoc list of items. Drawing a diagram of your model further helps convey how the elements connect. Having introduced your conceptual framework it is important to use the theory to develop your hypotheses rather than previous empirical studies. The danger with relying on prior empirical studies is that it can lead to the questioning of what is new in the study if previous research has already presented findings. In developing a novel contribution, it is important to avoid replicative and uninteresting hypotheses. For example, if direct effects have already been examined and the article is focusing on moderating relationships, the direct effects will need to be included as control variables even though they may not appear as a formal hypothesis. Similarly, since all hypotheses need to connect to the theoretical framework being adopted, other relationships that may have been tested in prior literature will need to be included in the control variables in order to avoid problems relating to omitted variable bias.

Data and Method

All empirical papers, whether qualitative or quantitative, need to include a data and method section. This section needs to convey a great deal of information that provides a convincing explanation that the data and measures used are the most appropriate for the study. Rather than involving a lengthy chapter as in a doctoral dissertation, this material needs to be presented in only a few pages. Bear in mind that this section is being written for an expert audience who will have a clear idea of 'industry standard' measures and techniques. This is not the place to provide a detailed exposition of research methods. However, in what follows I outline some of the key issues to be addressed in a data and methods section.

The section should provide a clear explanation and justification of the sample being used. The data need to be up to date, especially if the study is based on publicly available databases that are known to be updated regularly. For questionnaires, there is a need to state when the study was undertaken. Studies that were carried out a considerable time ago may both appear to be no longer relevant and suggest that the work has been around for a long time and has been unsuccessful at being published elsewhere.

Studies published in leading journals are increasingly being based on longitudinal data, whether they are quantitative performance studies or qualitative studies of entrepreneurial processes. Cross-sectional studies especially need to be careful in ascribing causality to relationships, and standard techniques to deal with endogeneity are expected to be used.

Traditional mail surveys increasingly face the problem of low response rates. This makes it imperative to have both a large sample and to provide detailed diagnostics on representation and lack of non-response bias. Comparisons should also be made with response rates in other recently published articles on related topics.

Online questionnaires are being used as an alternative to traditional mail surveys as they can enable higher response rates. However, they can pose major challenges in establishing representativeness, and the tendency to use shorter questionnaires can mean that scales are not sufficiently rigorous.

Developing a novel data-set that, through diligent collection of hard-to-access data from multiple sources, contains a rich set of variables not available from 'off the shelf' data-sets can give a paper an extra edge. Editors seem increasingly to be in receipt of papers where the authors claim that the data is 'hand collected' but this is becoming something of a cliché and a little unconvincing when it refers to data-sets containing tens of thousands of variables.

Authors can also demonstrate conceptual and methodological novelty by developing papers with multi-level analyses. It is increasingly being recognized that authors need to use multi-level methods if they have multi-level constructs. Journals are also increasingly interested in articles that adopt mixed-method approaches. However, it is important that authors justify why such an approach is necessary. Qualitative analysis, for example, should not just replicate the quantitative findings but help explain puzzling results that have emerged from the hypothesis testing.

The method section also needs to convey that the appropriate tests to establish the validity and reliability of measures have been undertaken. Archival data-sets may overcome the problem of low response rates faced by questionnaire surveys, but the shortcomings in the coverage of such data-sets are sometimes overlooked. For example, archival data-sets may only include entrepreneurial ventures above a certain size, so biases may be introduced if the study is focusing upon early-stage small ventures. A further problem is that archival data-sets may be more limited in the measures they use to capture entrepreneurial behaviour. Besides providing a careful justification as to why a particular measure is a good proxy for a conceptual construct, there may be a need to undertake robustness analyses using different measures.

A standard problem to be addressed in quantitative studies concerns common method bias. Here authors need to recognize that for the better journals there is a need to go beyond traditional standard tests such as the Harman one-factor test. Practice in these journals involves the need for at least part of a sample to undertake and report inter-reliability tests and to obtain data from other independent sources (for example, financial performance data).

The article will need to include a section providing explicit definitions of variables, along with citations to papers that have previously used these measures where relevant. It is of key importance to show a convincing connection between the constructs used in the theory section and the measures operationalized.

Quantitative articles will need to include control variables that, although not part of the article's theoretical framework, may influence the relationships being tested. Inclusion of these variables should be accompanied by reference to studies that have previously used them. Failure to include obvious control variables that have appeared in other studies can signal lack of knowledge or competence and lead to recommendations to reject. Inclusion of the main control variables but omission of specifically relevant measures can result in a not uncommon demand to collect further data. Collecting further data is not only time-consuming but may be near impossible with some research designs. For example, with an anonymous questionnaire survey it is likely impossible to go back to respondents. This potentially serious problem emphasizes the need for careful and thorough thought in research design.

Before the presentation of the main findings, articles need to include tables and text presenting brief descriptive results (typically means and standard deviations), as well as a correlation matrix accompanied by variance inflation factor scores (where appropriate) to demonstrate that the potential problem of multicollinearity has been recognized.

Analytical Methods

Articles need to outline and provide a brief justification for the analytical approach adopted. In some areas, there may be debate about whether alternative approaches should/could also be used, in which case there needs to be an indication that tests have been undertaken using different methods and, hopefully, similar results obtained.

Where appropriate the potential problems relating to selection bias issues need to be addressed. For example, in the international entrepreneurship literature many earlier studies might simply use exporting propensity and exporting intensity as alternative dependent variables in analyses of the determinants of exporting. However, a potential selection bias may be introduced because the reasons to select into exporting may differ from the factors driving the percentage of sales that are exported once the decision to export is made. Standard techniques, such as Heckman two-step analysis, are available to address these issues.

Results and Analysis

Presentation of results needs to be concise and structured in the order of the hypotheses. Studies also need to report not only the statistical significance of analyses but also their economic significance. Presentation should be restricted to reporting the results with discussion saved for the next section. It is important to avoid surprising the reader by introducing tests that have not been theorized in the hypothesis section. For example, if moderating effects are thought to be important, there should be argumentation leading to hypotheses early on rather than them only appearing in the results section.

Practice in reporting results tends to vary a little between disciplines. In entrepreneurship and management journals, standard practice is to build up from models involving only control variables to final models that include all variables. Results tables need to show whether the significance of the incremental R-squared is moving from one model to the next.

Lastly in reporting the significance of findings, authors need to be aware that the better journals tend to frown on 10 percent significance levels as not being sufficiently strong to claim support for a hypothesis.

With the increasing use of archival data-sets, it is becoming more common for entrepreneurship journals to expect to see robustness analyses using different proxies or techniques. There needs to be a justification and explanation of why particular robustness checks are being undertaken.

Discussion

The discussion section needs to begin with a brief summary of the research questions and how the findings addressed these questions. The discussion should then go on to show how the findings link to and extend prior literature, highlighting what is surprising or unexpected. Where possible and appropriate some *post hoc* analysis may be carried out to explore further unexpected results. This may be a role for qualitative analysis or preliminary quantitative analysis on a reduced sample.

The discussion section should also consider the implications of findings for management, other practitioners and policy. It is important while discussing the implications of a study's findings, however, not to go beyond them to make unsubstantiated claims either in these areas or for academic research. Recent wider policy debates about the role of academic research in business have drawn attention to the relevance and impact of research findings. As such, comments on practical implications are assuming greater importance.

A final part of the discussion section needs to consider limitations of the study and implications for further research. Care needs to be taken in writing this section not to undermine completely what has gone before.

All papers have some shortcomings, but it is important to convey that the principal potential problems have been considered and attempts made to address them rather than ignoring them and hoping that a reviewer and editor will not notice either. The chances are that they will notice and take a negative view because if the author was immersed in the field to the level expected he or she should have been aware of these issues. Demonstrating that you are aware of the problems and have attempted to deal with them is a preferable strategy since either the reviewer will accept what has been done as a reasonable solution or may take a constructive approach to suggesting alternative remedies that can be tried.

Conclusions

Rather than ending on a negative note by highlighting limitations, an article needs to conclude with a short paragraph that emphasizes the novel contribution to the literature.

The main body of the text of an article needs to be followed by a reference list in the journal style. The reference list needs to match the citations in the text. References should be complete. Major discrepancies in these aspects convey a sloppiness that can raise questions in the editor's and reviewers' minds about the degree of care that has been taken with the research itself. Journal practice varies regarding usage of footnotes. As a general rule these should be minimized. Tables and figures should follow, each on a separate page. They should have a title that clearly conveys the contents. Where figures convey the model used in the analysis they should refer to the hypotheses being tested. Tables should be self-explanatory – some journals require the inclusion of a paragraph explaining what the table is about and definitions of the variables being used. Significance levels of variables need to be indicated and explained.

CONCLUSIONS

To summarize what I would see as the main message to take away from this chapter: to get published in a good entrepreneurship journal, or any good academic journal for that matter, requires you to be willing and able to FITE:

- **F** – be focused (on research, on journals); be able to frame (the paper in the literature).

- **I** – have ideas, inspiration and insight (you need to go beyond replicating what others have done).
- **T** – be tenacious (take rejection and deal with adversity); develop techniques (conceptual and empirical); develop working in complementary teams (to be able to cover the various aspects of a paper) to the required 'industry standard'.
- **E** – have energy (to deal with sheer amount of input needed), enjoyment and be enamoured (have passion) about your topic.

REFERENCES

Bansal, P. and K. Corley (2011), 'From the editors: the coming of age for qualitative research: embracing the diversity of qualitative methods', *Academy of Management Journal*, **54** (2), 233–7.

Barley, S. (2006), 'When I write my masterpiece: thoughts on what makes a paper interesting', *Academy of Management Journal*, **49** (1), 16–20.

Clark, T., S. Floyd and M. Wright (2013), 'JMS at 50: editors reflections: in search of the interesting and impactful', *Journal of Management Studies*, forthcoming.

Davidsson, P. (2012), 'Some reflection on research "schools" and geographies', *Entrepreneurship & Regional Development*, forthcoming.

McGrath, R. (2007), 'No longer a stepchild: how the management field can come into its own', *Academy of Management Journal*, **50** (6), 1365–78.

3.   The review process

Mike Wright

INTRODUCTION

While most authors probably have an outline understanding of the journal review process, some of the details, such as how editors make decisions about whether to accept or reject a paper and how they select reviewers, may be less clear. Similarly, appropriate ways to respond to reviewers may be less well understood. In this chapter I discuss the stages in the review process from submission through review to final acceptance. It is also important for authors to understand the perspective of the editors and the reviewers both in preparing an article for submission and in revising a paper. Accordingly, the last section of the chapter spends some time discussing these aspects.

THE REVIEW PROCESS

The general decision-making process for articles submitted to a journal is as shown in Figure 3.1. The figure indicates the various stages that an article can go through as well as the range of decisions available. Essentially, there are four stages in the decision process. First, editors take an initial decision whether to send an article out to review or not. Second, having sent an article out for review and received reviewers' reports, the editor decides whether to progress the paper further or not. Third, where a decision is taken to ask for an article to be revised, the editor, having asked for a further round of reviews on the revised paper, decides whether to progress the article further or not. This stage may involve several iterations. Finally, after various stages of revision, the editor will make a final decision whether to accept the paper for publication.

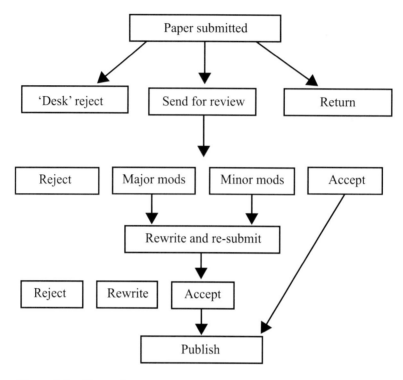

Figure 3.1   The review process

The Initial Decision

Most entrepreneurship journals have now adopted an online submission process (for example, Manuscriptcentral). Prospective authors and reviewers will need to register their affiliations and other details before being guided through the stages in the process of uploading a submission. Typically, authors will receive an email acknowledgement that the article has been successfully submitted. Some journals (for example, *Journal of Management Studies*) maintain an electronic submission process involving the submission of an article as an email attachment to an editorial office. This latter system can have advantages to authors in providing a more personalized service than an online submission process where it can be difficult to gain access to an administrator or and editor. Some journals using an online system are especially unresponsive to queries by authors.

Typically, when an article is received by a journal, the managing editor (either an administrator or a senior editor) will allocate it to one of the editors by matching the topic with their areas of expertise. If the journal has associate editors (or equivalent) the editors will then decide whether to handle the paper themselves or to allocate it to an associate editor whose expertise is a better fit. It will be appreciated that, given the wide scope of topics, even within entrepreneurship, that submissions may cover, it is not feasible for all articles to have a precise fit with the expertise of an editor. Partly to help improve the degree of fit, and hence provide a better service to authors, some entrepreneurship journals have increased the size and scope of expertise of their editorial teams.

It is useful to be aware of the background of the editors and associate editors at journals. *Strategic Entrepreneurship Journal*, for example, has four co-editors and nine associate editors (http://sej.strategicmanagement. net/editorial.php). The underlying rationale for this approach was to appoint individuals who have experience in publishing in top-tier management journals who bring differing perspectives on themes within entre-preneurship, such as family firms, entrepreneurial finance and micro-aspects of entrepreneurship. In something of a contrast, *Journal of Business Venturing* has an editor-in-chief, a senior editor and 14 field editors who are all publishing in entrepreneurship but come from different disciplines, such as economics, marketing, psychology, sociology and accounting (http://www.journals.elsevier.com/journal-of-business-venturing/editorial-board/). As the topics being submitted to a journal are quite random, and in order to maintain equity in editors' workloads, editors need to be able to handle papers outside their narrow area of expertise.

Once a paper has been allocated to an editor or associate editor, they are responsible for deciding whether to send the paper out for review and, if so, to whom. In a small number of cases, articles may be returned to authors with a request to address minor issues, such as: removing author-identifying information from the article, reducing the word count so that it falls within the journal's word limit, correcting grammatical and typographical mistakes, inserting missing references, clarifying certain concepts and areas, and further develop the contribution of the paper. In these cases the editor is essentially saying that the paper appears to be interesting but these issues may adversely deflect from the reviewers' perceptions of its underlying worth.

Journals vary in the percentage of papers that they send out for review. However, the percentage of papers rejected at this initial stage (desk rejects) has increased considerably in recent years.

Even at this desk reject stage, good editorial practice is to provide specific constructive feedback outlining the reasons for the decision and suggesting ways in which the author might develop the paper. Such feedback, coupled with a timely decision (sometimes within a week, and possibly much less) can leave an author with a positive feeling about the process.

Editors may decide not to send an article out for review for various reasons. Although a journal clearly states itself to be an entrepreneurship journal, some submissions fall outside its scope. Typically, these articles are not relevant because either they do not cover entrepreneurship in any recognized form and/or are written for another discipline. For example, while an important aspect of the development of an entrepreneurial venture may be its entry onto a stock market through an initial public offering, an article in this area may include little if any connection to the now extensive entrepreneurial literature on this topic. Rather, the article may be concerned purely with the more general finance literature and contain no citations to the entrepreneurship literature. As such, the article may be more appropriately targeted towards a specialist finance journal. Indeed, an editor may suspect that the article has already been rejected by a leading finance journal and that the author has submitted it to the entrepreneurship journal because that journal happens to be on the list of tenure-approved journals at the author's institution. Some articles may be desk rejected as they deal with practical aspects relating to entrepreneurship that are more appropriately dealt with in a practitioner journal.

Articles may be desk rejected by leading entrepreneurship journals because they simply replicate previous studies in a different context without developing a conceptual argumentation as to why that context offers new insights beyond what we already know from, say, a US or UK context. In other words, the authors of such articles are missing an important opportunity to extend theory or delineate the boundary conditions of existing theory in a particular area. Examples of articles that illustrate the kind of approach to consider are contained in the special issue of *Strategic Entrepreneurship Journal* on 'Entrepreneurship in emerging economies' (Bruton et al., 2013).

Underdeveloped articles are also likely to receive an initial editorial rejection. While an article may contain a potential interesting idea, it may be seriously lacking in terms of the articulation of its contribution, its positioning within the literature, the development of its conceptual arguments, its research design and analysis, and the discussion of its insights. In such cases, it is beyond the scope of the review process effectively to set out to the author how to write a paper, and the very underdeveloped nature of the article may give the editor little confidence that the author would be able to rework the paper. Authors may be under some pressure to publish in order to be able to gain their first post or to pass through probation or tenure, but a rush to premature submission is highly unlikely to achieve this goal. It is strongly advised that authors take the time to obtain and incorporate feedback from colleagues prior to submitting to a journal. Colleagues can involve supervisors, other PhD students and other authors in a particular area. Presenting a paper at a faculty/student 'brown bag' seminar which are typically designed specifically for colleagues to air work in progress is a good way to start the writing and review process.

Finally, it is important to take care that a submitted article is checked carefully for typographical and other presentational glitches, including deletions and 'track changes' left over from earlier iterations. It is also important to follow journal style guidelines regarding the inclusion of an abstract, hierarchies of section headings (with or without numbering), referencing style, placement of reference to where tables and figures should be inserted, and exclusion of author-identifying information in the text. Apparent lack of attention to such detail may be indicative of more substantive problems. It may distract an editor or reviewer from the underlying quality of a paper if the flow of their reading is constantly disrupted by such easily avoided errors. Lack of page numbers is a particular important omission that can be an irritation to editors and reviewers wishing to refer to particular points in their report.

These problems may be exacerbated by the typical tendency to read through papers on screen. It can be useful to read a hard-copy version of a paper as it nears completion in order to pick up presentational shortcomings that might otherwise be missed. Reading a paper through carefully in this way can help pick up inappropriate structure and section headings, as well as poor flow in argumentation.

Journals do vary in their style and it is important for authors to look closely at how articles in different journals are presented. Authors for whom English is not their first language may find it useful to have a native English speaker edit their manuscript. Indeed, even for native English speakers from outside the US submitting to US journals it is useful to be aware of not just US spellings but also different phrasings. After all, the US and the UK are two countries separated by a common language! An example of a desk rejection letter is shown in Box 3.1.

BOX 3.1   EXAMPLE OF A DESK REJECTION LETTER

Dear xxxx

Thank you for submitting your paper. I have now read your manuscript carefully and have decided not to send it out for review. Accordingly, I am sorry to tell you that I am unable to progress your paper further with this journal.

Essentially, the main reasons for this decision are as follows:

1. The positioning of your paper needs to be strengthened in order to do a much more convincing job in justifying why this remains an interesting topic rather than one that has been neglected for some years. There is a very well-established literature in this area that you need to recognize in order to establish why and where there is still a gap to fill. One aspect that you may want to consider is whether new environmental conditions might lead us to reconsider existing conceptual frameworks.

2. As there is existing literature containing conceptual arguments you may want to take a closer look to help frame your study (you may also want to take a look at Suddaby's 2006 paper in AMJ on what grounded theory is not).

3. Your propositions are quite limited and not well derived. Further, they relate to firms in general rather than to your particular focus. More generally, I am concerned about the way you approach the paper. You develop propositions but then state that as the aim is theory-building you are going to use an inductive approach to test them. This creates a methodological confusion that needs to be resolved by reframing your approach.

4. As it is, it is unclear that what you are adding is theory-building. Rather, in your results section and in your discussion you make empirical generalizations rather than advancing novel propositions that can be developed into testable hypotheses.

5. There is also a disconnect between the parts of the paper, as in the empirical and discussion section you do not refer back to the propositions developed in the literature section.

6. You should also reflect on the selection of your sample. If you are engaged in theoretical sampling as a basis for theory development about the differences between small and large firms, you need to have some large firms in your sample.
7. Your findings section was quite descriptive and did not seem to lead anywhere. How can you use this material to generate richer insights for theory-building? For example, you may want to consider theorizing about the process of strategy development in these types of firms.
8. The final section of the study is quite disappointing. This needs to be developed to elaborate on your contribution to the field and to consider the implications of your findings. As this is a qualitative study, you could also outline insights into how one might go about undertaking more general quantitative studies to test your insights.
9. You should aim to finish the paper with a short paragraph stressing the positive contribution of your study, rather than finishing on a negative.

I am sorry that I am unable to progress your paper further. I hope that the above comments are helpful to you as you continue your work in this area. Thank you for considering our journal as a potential outlet for your work.

As shown in Chapter 1, journals have received substantial increases in submissions in recent years while the space available has typically remained fairly constant. This has been a particular problem for more highly regarded journals. Quality thresholds in entrepreneurship especially have increased as doctoral programmes do a better job of training students in both theoretical and empirical aspects of research. At the same, time reviewing capacity remains limited. Good reviewers are likely in demand from many journals. As a result, editors have to manage both their reviewers as well as their authors, and do not want to send them articles that are clear rejections. Not surprisingly, therefore, the better journals have desk reject rates of around 50 per cent or more. Removing articles at this early stage means that editors can focus scarce reviewing resources on articles with the greatest potential to make a substantial contribution to the literature. Nevertheless, the risk of a type II error, that is, of rejecting a paper that should have been accepted, remains.

Selecting Reviewers

Journals vary in the number of reviewers they seek to comment on a paper. With a range generally between one and four, the norm in entrepreneurship journals is likely two or three. Journals typically seek to match reviewers in their reviewer database with expertise in the topic area of a submitted article as well as the method being used. Some journals may also select someone from their editorial board to comment as a general reader on the likely appeal of an article to the journal's wider readership. Journals with online submission systems, for example, can enable the action editor handling a manuscript to select reviewers based on the match of the topic area of an article and reviewer with an expertise in that area. But the reviewer selection process is not quite so straight-forward.

Qualitative researchers in an area may be able to comment on aspects of an article relating to the concepts but be uncomfortable reviewing a paper that adopts a quantitative approach. Similarly, reviewers with a quantitative background may not be appropriate to comment on the method in a qualitative paper.

Reviewers who have previously published on the topic of a submitted paper may recently have been sent other articles to review by the journal. As the journal will not want to overload a reviewer and risk losing their goodwill in the future, editors will not want to send a new paper to them. Other potential reviewers will be excluded because, although well-known authors on a particular topic, they are known either not to be willing to review for the journal or to be not particularly effective or timely reviewers. Some may be editors or associate editors of journals with little capacity to take on further ad hoc reviews. It must be acknowledged that some individuals make a remarkable contribution despite the other demands on their time.

For these reasons, editors need to rely on the tacit knowledge they have built up about the individuals who are likely to be actually available and willing to review a paper.

It is important for authors to ensure that they cite key recent works on their topic, especially if they have been published in the journal to which they are submitting. This shows awareness of the field and also helps fit an article into the conversations taking place in that journal. It also helps the editor in selecting reviewers. Not to be underestimated, if a particular individual who has published in an area is selected as a reviewer, they are less likely to be antagonized if their work is cited. Authors who have published in an area some time ago may have moved on to other areas and no longer be willing or able to undertake a review.

Comments Following Review

If it is decided to seek reviewer reports on an article, experts in that particular area will be asked to comment on the topic, the theoretical appropriateness and conceptual development, the research design and the method of analysis, and the extent and nature of contribution.

Thoroughness and timeliness of reviews are important in the competition between journals to attract the best authors and papers. Electronic submission processes have helped enhance the timeliness aspect of the review process, although not all journals engage in systematic follow-up of tardy reviewers. As a result of the increased competition between journals, the time given to reviewers to prepare their reports has reduced dramatically in recent years, from months to weeks. Journals will grade reviewers based on the timeliness and quality of their reviews. Quality may be judged in terms of the insightfulness of the comments and their developmental nature. Reviewers who provide slow, incomplete and non-developmental reviews are unlikely to be asked again to perform a review since this behaviour is detrimental to the journal's reputation. Reviewers are expected to be critical, but it is possible to do this without being abusive.

When you submit an article to a journal, you need to be patient. The overall time from initial submission to publication, if the paper is accepted, can be well over a year and probably nearer two years in most cases. This may seem excessive but consider the practicalities:

- initial response – time for the editor to read the paper in the context of a flow of other manuscripts that need to be dealt with, identify potential reviewers and get their agreement to write a review: up to one month;
- receipt of reviews and make a decision – time for the reviewers to schedule the review among their other work commitments and for the editor to read the reviews, reread the paper and write a reasoned decision letter: three to four months;
- time for the author to rework the paper and resubmit – time to digest lengthy reviewer reports, consult papers suggested by reviewers, brainstorm and rework the positioning of the paper, possibly collect and analyse new data, and write a detailed response to the reviewers' comments: six to eight months;
- processing of the revised paper – sending out to the original reviewers, time for them to re-engage with what may be a substantially changed paper and write their reviews, and similarly for the editor in writing their decision letter: three to four months;

- second round of revisions: as above, four to eight months;
- third (and subsequent) round(s) of revisions: these stages may or may not involve the reviewers, but even if they do not, action editors may still seek significant changes to bring out the full contribution of the paper: three to six months;
- acceptance to online publication: one month;
- acceptance to hard copy publication – six to 18 months.

The time to take a decision on an article following a first round of reviews does vary, and can be significantly increased if tardy reviewers are not chased. *Family Business Review*, for example, reports an average time to first decision of 34 days. General practice in the management and entrepreneurship areas has generally improved greatly and now appears to be between two and three months. Some decision letters can arrive much sooner but if you receive a very quick decision from a journal after it has been sent out for review, this often means a rejection. Some journals are still woeful. At the time of writing, this author has had a paper under first review at a journal for over 15 months, and counting. The online system simply shows that the paper is under review (well we knew that) and the editor does not respond to either emails or phone calls.

Following an initial round of comments from reviewers, approximately a further 30 per cent of papers are likely to be rejected. After further rounds of review, the average acceptance rate for good journals is likely below 10 per cent of papers submitted. For some journals in the general management area that publish entrepreneurship papers, the acceptance rate may be around 5 per cent. The editor's decision letter accompanied by copies of the reviews will be sent to the author and also to the reviewers. This process provides developmental feedback for both authors and reviewers. The reviewers can both see how the points they have made have fed into the decision being made as well as appreciating the comments and approach adopted by the other reviewer(s).

The editorial letter synthesizes the main themes arising from the reviewers' reports and gives additional comments based on the editor's own reading of the paper. In this way, whether the decision is reject or revise, guidance is provided on the way(s) forward. If the decision is made to invite a revision and re-submission, the editor will have reflected on their view of the likely feasibility of making the changes required. There is little point in inviting a re-submission if it is clear that the changes requested essentially involve a new research design and effect- ively a new paper. In some cases, it may not be clear at the point of first review decision whether or not it will be feasible to make the changes sufficiently to satisfy the reviewers. However, if the reviewers are signalling that the paper is potentially of novel interest and the editor agrees, then the decision may be to invite a revision but to signal that this is risky or even high risk. An example of a revise and resubmit decision letter following review is presented in Box 3.2.

BOX 3.2   AN EXAMPLE REVISE AND RE-SUBMIT LETTER

Dear xxxx

I have now read your paper in conjunction with the reviewers' comments. The reviewers find the topic of interest, but in their insightful reports both have a number of major concerns. Having read the paper myself, I agree with their points. I am of the view that very major changes will need to be made in order to address our concerns. I am willing to offer you the opportunity to revise and resubmit the paper but must stress that this is a high risk revise and re-submit.

Essentially, the main concerns are as follows:

1. I agree with reviewer 1 that the research gap and the focus of your study needs better justification. At present the Introduction and positioning are not particularly convincing. For this journal we would need to see a strong conceptual contribution and at present this is missing. Your key contribution seems to me to be about why firms that originate from one source subsequently generate the creation of further firms. You may want to consider positioning the paper more firmly in this theme.

2. The reviewers are concerned about the size of your sample. You need to do a better job of justifying why this is a significant phenomenon that requires specific study. For example, it may be appropriate to extend the sample beyond the small subset of parent organizations that you currently look at.

3. I agree with reviewer 2's concerns about how you frame the learning argument since you include reference to material that does not appear to be especially relevant.

4. Reviewer 3 comments that your introduction of the role of two particular sets of actors seems to come from

nowhere. This is not necessarily to say that they are not important, but at present it is not evident why you believe this to be the case. So, you need to provide explanation and justification for incorporating these actors.

5. The reviewers have problems with your unit of analysis. There seems to be a mismatch here between the individual level of learning and the organizational level of your study. This does need to be reconciled.

6. Reviewer 3 raises concerns about hypothesis 4. It may be preferable to just include this as a control variable since it is not part of the central framework of your study. In developing several of your hypotheses you draw heavily upon existing empirical studies. Given the conceptual framework you adopt, you need to use this framework to develop your arguments.

7. As the data relate to a long period, you need to provide the reader with an outline of the evolution of the context you are studying over this time. This issue also suggests that you need to gather more data to enable you to include more specific measures of context than the general contextual control variables that you have at present. The reviewers also comment on the absence of other important controls, such as individual level controls.

8. You comment that the study is part of a larger project. However, your explanation of the data collection and method does need to be free-standing. This helps to emphasize the significance and novelty of your study as well as helping readers who may not be familiar with this data-set.

9. You refer to entrepreneurs with particular experience but you exclude some recent important work in this area. This omission needs to be rectified and may help you to strengthen some of your arguments about learning from entrepreneurial experience.

10. More generally, as I read the paper it seemed that at times the citations seem rather dated. There has been more recent work comparing firms from different contexts that you need to include.

11. Your discussion section needs to be reworked so that you stress your conceptual contribution without going beyond your findings.

12. The reviewers make a number of other points that also need to be addressed.

I do hope that the comments of the reviewers will assist you in developing your work. Good luck as you continue your research in this area.

An indication of the relative importance of the kind of issues that can lead to a paper being rejected after being sent out for review is provided by Table 3.1. The information in the table is based on a survey of 270 papers rejected by the *Journal of Management Studies* (JMS) between 2003 and 2004 when the author was one of the editors (Clark et al., 2006). Articles rejected after receiving reviewers' reports generally had more than one fundamental or fatal flaw. The most important features of these deficiencies were as follows.

Table 3.1   Reasons for rejection after review

Reason	No.	%
Lack of contribution	248	92
Failure to develop theoretical contribution	205	76
Fatal flaws in methods	189	70
Deficiencies in analysis	156	58

Note: Based on 270 decision letters relating to papers submitted to *Journal of Management Studies* in 2003–04.

Source: Clark et al. (2006).

First, the overwhelmingly prevalent problem was that the contribution to the existing literature was either not evident or at best marginal. Typically, authors failed to position the article so that it identified a specific gap in the existing literature that it was important to address. Relatedly, an article claims several potential contributions that are either disconnected or convey a lack of clarity about the focus of the paper. Importantly for leading journals such as JMS, articles need to distinguish between conceptual and empirical contributions related to data-sets and methods of analysis. Of central importance is the contribution to extending conceptual understanding.

Authors need to anticipate that reviewers will likely pose the 'so what' question, that is, how does the article take us beyond what is already known? Reviewers who are experts in a particular field may take the view that the contribution is not novel. Finally, reviewers may comment that even though a contribution is clearly stated, it is not of sufficient significance for publication in a leading journal.

Secondly, an article may be rejected because it fails to make a theoretical contribution. Such a contribution could be derived from developing and testing new hypotheses or by developing or extending conceptual understanding of a newly observed phenomenon. The reason that articles like this are rejected by leading journals is their tendency to be overly descriptive. They lack convincing explanations for the relationships they identify between variables or for the patterns in the phenomena being analysed.

Third, the research design is either fundamentally flawed or inappropriate for the research question. For example, the sample frame may be inappropriate. In quantitative studies the sample may not be representative or large enough for the analysis being conducted. In qualitative studies, there may be a lack of a justification for the selection of the case study firms in relation to the particular methodological approach being adopted. For example, if the purpose of the qualitative study is theory-building, cases may need to be selected on the basis of theoretical sampling yet this may not be evident in the paper. For leading entrepreneurship journals, qualitative papers typically need to develop new conceptual insights rather than to illustrate the application of an established theory. Some recent editorial articles provide indications of how to approach the development of qualitative papers for leading journals (for example, Suddaby, 2006).

Additional methodological issues relate to the constructs and measures not being adequately operationalized, interrelationships between constructs not being specified, and there being a disconnect between the measures employed and the hypotheses or model. A danger in quantitative studies is that data-sets are used that were designed for other purposes than those of the submission, so that the variables do not capture the constructs being analysed. A further concern is that data is cut too finely ('salami slicing') so that the article overlaps too closely with other articles from the same data-set.

Finally, relatively least common in the reasons for rejection is the presence of fundamental problems in how the data are analysed. Articles may adopt inappropriate or inadequate methods in relation to the research question posed. In some cases, if the conceptual argumentation is robust and the data-set being used is appropriate to test the hypotheses that have been set out, then it may be relatively straightforward to apply another analytical technique. The problem comes if the data-set is not configured in the appropriate manner to address the research question.

By no means all papers invited to be revised and resubmitted eventually survive the review process. Authors may take the view that they cannot meet reviewers' requests and withdraw the paper. However, although inexperienced authors especially may recoil in horror at being presented with a vast list of seemingly insurmountable demands, it is worth taking time to reflect on how changes can be addressed before giving up and submitting the paper elsewhere. If a paper is submitted elsewhere the clock starts again when several months have already gone by. Further, in a specialist topic area, there is a risk that at least some of the reviewers at another journal may be the same as at the first journal. These reviewers likely will come up with the same points as before but if they have not been addressed may take a less benign view.

Journals typically set a time limit for article re-submission, although many will extend that limit if the editor is approached in advance with a reasonable justification (for example, significant time was needed to collect further data). But it is important to be timely in revising a paper, without rushing and doing an inadequate or perfunctory job. Topic areas can move on quite quickly, and the longer a revision is delayed the more likely it is that further work will appear that either takes away the novelty of a contribution completely or requires further major reworking of the paper.

In re-submitting an article it is critically important to try to address fully all the reviewers' comments. Reviewers tend to notice if authors have tried to sidestep what they see as particularly tricky points. It is good practice to provide a detailed and not just a perfunctory response to each point raised by the editor and the reviewers. Given the effort that reviewers have put into commenting on a paper, they are unlikely to appreciate a grudging response that fails adequately to show and explain what changes have been made. A good response document can speed up the second-round review process by providing reviewers with a clear guide as to what has been done. Remember that it may be several months since the reviewer last saw the paper and, while the author remains intimately familiar with it, this is unlikely to be the case for the reviewer. Further, a detailed and courteous response letter is a good way to avoid antagonizing the reviewer.

Approaches to responding to reviewers vary, but one useful way is to copy the editor's and reviewers' comments into a file. Then go through the comments in detail, identifying initial responses to each point. This helps ensure that all points get addressed and that you as an author immerse yourself in the detail of the points being raised. In this way it is possible to identify the most important points, those that are difficult to address, those that are straightforward and those that need some further consideration. Then you can iterate between revising parts of the paper and building up the response document.

An example reviewer comment and author response is as follows. The reviewer is quite critical but appreciates that there is an underlying interesting aspect to the article and makes constructive suggestions that help the authors identify a more novel contribution while at the same time dropping some earlier features:

> *Reviewer comment* 8. As for your results, it is frankly not too surprising that more experienced entrepreneurs would identify and pursue more business opportunities (models b and c). The more interesting differences relate to characteristics such as serial vs. portfolio entrepreneurs and the nature of their prior experience. It is not until the Discussion that we read why those aspects of ownership/experience might be important. As a reader, I am not sure I would have ever gotten to your Discussion because your front-end seems rather uninteresting. I recommend you make a much stronger effort to spell out those differences in the beginning of the manuscript.
>
> In fact, consider the following: shorten your subsections on identification (3.1), pursuit (3.2) and 'nature of' (3.3), and add subsections on habitual, total, serial vs. portfolio, failure, and portfolio of failure. Then, organize your hypotheses under the later set of subsections: habitual-identify, habitual-pursuit, habitual-nature of, then total-identify, total-pursuit, and so forth. This approach would shift the attention to the role of human capital/ownership experience (rather than identification vs. pursuit) which is what your Introduction says you are most interested in.

> Author response: Thank you for these invaluable suggestions. We have revised the paper in line with these. We have also sought to remove some of the more obvious hypotheses. We now focus on three aspects of experience (extent of experience, experience of failure and mode of experience acquisition) and two aspects of opportunity identification (intensity (i.e., number of opportunities identified) and innovativeness of the latest opportunity). For example, rather than focusing on whether the entrepreneur is experienced or not, we now focus on the extent of experience and develop arguments suggesting a non-linear relationship. Because we were concerned that we would end up with too many hypotheses that would distract from the core message, we decided to remove discussion of opportunity pursuit.

(After further revisions covering a number of other points, the paper was eventually published.)

Editors' decision letters should provide guidance on both the main points that need to be addressed and suggestions as to how disagreements between reviewers might be addressed. Even so, there may be points of legitimate disagreement with reviewers. A convincing explanation needs to be provided as to why a reviewer's suggestion has not been followed. Judgement may be needed in terms of deciding how critical a particularly contentious point is for the reviewer. It is important to maintain a courteous and polite tone in responses, without being obsequious, and to leave the door open in case a reviewer comes back to revisit the point next time around because they really do feel that the point is a critical one.

Acceptance for Publication

As an article nears acceptance, the reviewers may effectively sign off, leaving the editor to address remaining comments without recourse to the reviewers. There may still be significant work to be done to finally get the article fit to publish. This part of the process may take several iterations. It will typically involve sharpening and polishing the introduction and conclusion to bring out the article's contribution. It may also require some sharpening of the argumentation surrounding hypotheses and explanation of the analysis and its implications for practice and policy.

Through the review process an article can become significantly longer and lose some of its sharpness as the authors seek to meet the reviewers' comments. The complaint from authors that 'you've asked me to put this material in, now you're asking me to take it out' is not uncommon. Editors may ask authors to reduce the length of a conditionally accepted article by anything up to, say, a third and guide them as to where cuts are needed. From my experience as both an editor and an author this can usually be accomplished without loss of content and the final version will read better and convey the essential message in a much punchier way.

Once a paper is accepted, the lead time to hard-copy publication can vary significantly. If a journal does not have much of a time pipeline, the article may appear in the next issue. In contrast, authors can wait well in excess of a year. Reflecting the delay in the publication process, many journals now publish at the start of the article the dates of submission, when an article was revised and when it was accepted. The emergence of online access to accepted articles does help to alleviate the problem in the delay in publication. These papers can typically be accessed at the journal's website and/or through a university library's electronic journals. As such, readers can access information faster and a journal's citation impact can also be enhanced. To further aid the dissemination of articles, many journals make final proof pages of articles to authors prior to publication in pdf format for circulation to key contacts.

THE EDITOR'S AND REVIEWERS' PERSPECTIVES

It is helpful for authors to appreciate the editor's and reviewers' perspectives in submitting papers to journals. Editors are stewards of a journal's reputation. Their role is to ensure that papers published in the journal do not detract from the audience's perception of the quality of the journal. Publishing weak papers sends an adverse signal about the journal and the quality of the review process.

Editors operate in the context both of increasing competition among journals for a restricted number of good papers that will be highly cited and contributing to a higher score or position in the various rankings of journal quality.

As noted earlier, editors have to manage their reviewers as well as their authors. Good reviewers are a scarce resource as they are likely to be in demand from other journals. Asking them to write reports on weak papers that should have been desk rejected is likely to lead to complaints and to them being unwilling to review further for the journal.

Some editors may be especially active and push the authors to undertake significantly more analysis once the reviewers have signed off. This may be because they have a particular expertise in an area or are more attuned to what is needed to make a contribution in a journal that regards itself as in the top tier. Occasionally, the editor may be identifying points that reviewers have not picked up or have not fully pursued but which need to be.

Reviewers generally provide their service voluntarily and for free, although some journals mainly in finance and economics do pay a modest fee. To undertake a serious review to a level of quality expected by leading journals, a reviewer can easily devote the best part of a day. There is therefore an important opportunity cost to reviewers in terms of time foregone when they could have been working on their own research.

CONCLUSIONS

Publishing in good entrepreneurship journals is increasingly challenging. But it is a challenge that, armed with some insights into the process as outlined in this chapter, can be overcome. It may not seem like it during the process when as an author your goal is to get your paper accepted, but the positive side of the review process is that the paper that does eventually emerge is the better for it and is more likely to get cited. However, there is continuing debate about the benefits of an onerous review process for traditional journals. There have been suggestions from some that papers should be accepted or rejected on an 'as is' basis (Tsang and Frey, 2007). The whole format of traditional academic journals is also being challenged by the revolution in publishing online and open access outlets, policy developments relating to the relevance and impact of academic research and what is required to obtain tenure in universities (Clark et al., 2013). Yet universities continue to seek ways to outsource the assessment of the quality of the research produced by their faculty. At present, these developments are unresolved.

REFERENCES

Bruton, G., I. Filatotchev, S. Si and M. Wright (2013), 'Strategy and entrepreneurship in emerging economies', *Strategic Entrepreneurship Journal*, forthcoming.

Clark, T., S.W. Floyd and M. Wright (2006), 'On the review process and journal development', *Journal of Management Studies*, **43** (3), 655–64.

Clark, T., S. Floyd and M. Wright (2013), 'JMS at 50: editors reflections: in search of the interesting and impactful', *Journal of Management Studies*, forthcoming.

Suddaby, R. (2006), 'What grounded theory is not', *Academy of Management Journal*, **49** (4), 633–42.

Tsang, E. and B. Frey (2007), 'The as-is journal review process: let authors own their ideas', *Academy of Management Learning and Education*, **6** (1), 128–36.

4. Getting published – and cited – in entrepreneurship: reflections on ten papers

Per Davidsson

BACKGROUND

I grew up in academic heaven. At least for me it was. Not only was Sweden in the late 1980s paradise for any kind of empirical research, with rich and high-quality business statistics being made available to researchers without them having to sign away their lives, over 70 percent response rates achieved in mail surveys to almost any group (if you knew how to do them), and boards of directors opening their doors to more qualitatively orientated researchers to sit in during their meetings. In addition, I perceived an environment with a very high degree of academic freedom, letting me do whatever I found interesting and important. I am sure for others it was sheer hell, with very unclear career paths and rules of the game. Career progression (something which rarely entered my mind) meant that you tried as best you could and then you put all your work – reports, books, book chapters, conference papers, maybe even published articles – in a box and had some external committee of professors look at it. If you were lucky they liked what they saw for whatever reasons their professorial wisdom dictated, and you got hired or promoted. If you were not so lucky you would not get the job or the promotion, without quite knowing why. So people could easily imagine an old boys' club – whose members were themselves largely unproven in international, peer review publishing – picking whoever they wanted by whatever criteria they chose to apply. Neither the fact that assessors were external nor the presence of an appeals system might have completely appeased your suspicious and skeptical mind, considering the balance of power.

I did not bother much about these things and naively believed that if I did good things – with high integrity – good things would happen to me.

Rather than trying to understand the prevailing incentive system and maximizing my performance by its criteria, I did what interested me; what felt right, and what made sense to me. It is a philosophy I have basically applied throughout my career. That is, I have not bothered much about politics, tactics, sheer rhetoric, bean counting or the 'Kremlin-ology' of putting in the right references and other cues to please potential editors and reviewers (or trying to tease out who they are). By my criteria this has worked wonderfully – which is not to say I could not have achieved more had I sometimes been more thoughtful and careful about how I positioned and disseminated my research.

The academic culture I was brought up in, more precisely, was the Stockholm School of Economics – the elite business school in Sweden – and its Department of Economic Psychology. I then spent four years at the still relatively young Umeå University, before moving to the entrepreneurship-focused academic start-up venture called the Jönköping International Business School (JIBS) in 1994. The system I saw was one with great academic freedom (and integrity). I was allowed to ask almost any research questions I came up with, using any methods I saw fit (and which were approved of somewhere in existing academic literature). It certainly helped that I was in an emerging field – entrepreneurship – where there was lots of virgin ground. But note that I was allowed to choose to enter this field; no one tried to stop me from making this 'risky' choice. The *perception* of existence of virgin ground was further helped by ignorance. The absence of the Internet, electronic repositories and an agreed upon set of outlets to which 'everybody that mattered' had access and paid attention meant that if you could not get it directly or indirectly through institution's library, it did not exist. It was a very different world.

Publishing in peer-reviewed, international journals was optional, and we had little sense of a hierarchy of journal prestige, and we had not heard of impact factors, the H-index (it was not yet invented!) or anything like that. In economic psychology, with its closer links to the underlying disciplines, journal publication was more encouraged than it was for other young management scholars, but there was no strong pressure. So I did not have to worry about maximizing the number of publications I got my name on; splitting up my work into 'minimum publishable units' or spending much time 'kneading the dough' in rounds of revisions – perhaps on papers I did not believe had that much of importance to say anyway. Instead, I moved on to the next thing that had triggered my curiosity. I enjoyed the luxury of leaving things be after writing a conference paper or research report – the point where *I* thought *I* had learnt what *I* could learn from that particular piece of research –

only sending manuscripts to journals when I felt like it or thought I had something important to say. Besides, I was not very interested in having to listen to how others thought I should streak the brush when I composed my pieces of art.

I had my first real encounter with the US academic system and culture during an extended trip to three universities in 1991. I found them absolutely absurd. This goes especially for the obsession with numbers of works; I have later found reason to contemplate the strong emphasis on competition and relative disregard for true collegiality and having some intellectual fun, and the strong reliance on indicators like journal ratings rather than direct evaluation of contents. I remember on this first trip asking a dean what to me was a most obvious question: 'Why don't you limit the number of works on which an applicant can base their application (so they can focus on doing deeper, better studies and you get less material to assess – I naively assumed they would actually read the works of applicants rather than just scoring them based on proxy indicators)? The suggestion was so alien that he laughed out loud. After more than 50 academic visits to the US I still think aspects of the US-type research publication and evaluation system – to which I have never been fully subjected employment-wise as I have pursued my career in Sweden and Australia – are extreme, absurd or, at least, unsound. I also fear that other parts of the world may currently be importing too much of it, and that we are, and will be, paying dearly for this in some respects. But there are two sides to everything. There is no perfect system, and the ideal system of academic publishing and promotion would probably be something in between the US of today and the academic Sweden I grew up in. Upon moving to Australia, I was baffled by a national evaluation system which assigned one point equally to every peer-reviewed output, whether it was an award-winning paper in the *Administrative Science Quarterly* or some dodgy little conference the participants had colluded to arrange for the specific purpose of scoring points in this system.

An important drawback of the Swedish system I was part of during my early career was the incredible waste of not (regularly) taking research to such dissemination that international colleagues could realistically learn from and build on it. As a case in point, one important reason that it took a while for Gregor Mendel's important findings on inheritance to catch on was that he published them in the local dust collector *Verhandlungen des naturforschenden Vereins Brünn*, where it was lucky to get cited three times over the first 35 years after its publication. We owe it to research funders and our colleagues to disseminate our research better; it is not just about satisfying one's own curiosity in the incredibly self-centered way the younger version of me did.[1] Further, if we want our colleagues to learn from and build on our research, it is certainly fair enough that we be asked to subject them to tough scrutiny of our peers before they are accepted and published. I have come around completely as concerns appreciation for the peer review process. It is not perfect, but arguably it is our most important tool for continuous competence development. It is by subjecting our work to the scrutiny of competent colleagues that we force ourselves to learn more theory, the latest developments in methods, and important findings that we may have missed in our own review, as well as helping us improve our writing skills. The biggest regret I have about the early years of my career is that had I been pushed more to (expand) my limits by sending more work to more competitive journals, I would have learned more and achieved more. It was nice to get all the positive feedback I received back then in my immediate environment, but some 'tough love' would probably have helped taking my scholarship to higher levels, or – if I have reached my maximum – to do so earlier. The lost opportunities to learn and develop are the other big waste of the system from which I came. And most Scandinavian colleagues of my cohort did much less than I did in terms of trying to get published in international journals.

This said, it is also worth emphasizing that I did certainly not need to be forced to put in over 60-hour weeks back then. That came from pure love of the work I was doing. This raises concerns about the extreme pressure and unrealistic expectations that are imposed on some junior colleagues of today by deans who have not done the math and expect their particular crew to take an unreachable percentage of the space in a small number of elite journals. Under such conditions, the perhaps arrogant young man I then was may not have chosen to stay in this game at all. In more general terms, by increasing the demands universities may end up not with better and more highly motivated young scholars; selection effects may lead to just the opposite.

This background hopefully helps explain what I look like as an entrepreneurship researcher if you examine my CV or the results of a search on Google Scholar (GS) or Publish or Perish (PoP). The combination of entering an emerging field and the allowing culture I came from has permitted me to publish works using different disciplinary perspectives and levels of analysis, ranging from empirical fact-finding to suggestions for methods improvements to conceptual developments, and being published in journals with orientations towards sociology, psychology, economics, geography, ethics and management, in addition to entrepreneurship and small business management. This is unlikely to be achievable – and trying is not recommended – for new entrants into entrepreneurship research today. The early entry into the field, and the culture I came from, have probably also helped me get – and take – some voice in this field, through publications and otherwise. I have not, however, excelled in numbers of published articles, or been one of the primary leaders in elevating entrepreneurship to top-tier disciplinary or mainstream management journals. In these regards, I am miles behind good friends and valued colleagues, such as Dean Shepherd, Mike Wright and Shaker Zahra, and about to be overtaken by some of my best 'disciples', such as Johan Wiklund. Although I have some articles in broader journals in the top tier, what I can claim is rather a good track record in leading entrepreneurship journals. In particular, I have reached comparatively high citation rates for most of my articles in this primary playing field of mine – which can also be interpreted as sometimes not having aimed as high as I should in the journal hierarchy.

OVERALL REASONS FOR PUBLICATION SUCCESS, IF I CAN SAY I HAD ANY

When I reflect on any possible common denominator as regards why some of my work has been well received, what comes to mind most strongly is the importance of the research question, and hence the contribution. I know this may sound pretentious, but it is my honest analysis. This is subtly different from being able to claim addressing a gap in the literature – a notion that triggers ambiguous feelings in me when I encounter it as editor or reviewer. The literature is full of gaps, and mostly for good reason: the perceived gap may not be important or interesting enough. Instead of claiming that something I did fills a gap in some research stream, I think some of my best appreciated work started from my own understanding of what is it that the field of entre-preneurship really needs at this point? Thus, it is something along the lines of the criterion Don Hambrick suggests should replace the ever-present requirement of a 'contribution to theory', namely 'Does the paper have a high likelihood of stimulating future research that will substan-tially alter managerial theory and/or practice?' (Hambrick, 2007, p. 1350). Over time, I have grown very sympathetic to Anne Huff's (1999) notion of conversations, and the importance of positioning one's work in relation to an ongoing conversation. However, sometimes some of us also need to do something about ongoing silence – those conversa-tions that ought to be going on in our field, but are not – or help take a conversation to a new level rather than adding an aspect to it. This is not something all of us can or should aspire to do all of the time – 'normal science' should not be frowned upon – but when we see an opportunity to make a contribution of a more fundamental type, I think we should take it. As discussed below, I think that although none of them revolutionized anything, my best appreciated articles have in common at least an element of this nature.

Apart from the importance of the research question, I see a number of other recurring themes that my better published or better cited articles have in common. One, which arguably comes with taking on important research questions in not yet established conversations, is to take on the hard work that goes with, for example, getting relevant data to address these less well-trodden paths, and to have the tenacity to see it through to publication in a good place. The fit with the journal is another aspect, which I perhaps did not emphasize or master at the time, but which I can see in retrospect is important. Having good co-authors that take on different roles in the process is also of essence – it is almost impossible today to have all the theory, methods and writing skills – and 'review process stamina' – needed for top-tier publication residing in one person. Further, timing sometimes seems to be a really crucial factor. Below I discuss these factors in relation to a selection of ten articles published since 1990. It is my hope that although the playing field has changed over time, young scholars of today will find some useful guidance in these reflections.

REFLECTIONS ON TEN ARTICLES

Articles on Firm Growth

1. Davidsson, P. (1991), 'Continued entrepreneurship: ability, need, and opportunity as determinants of small firm growth', *Journal of Business Venturing* **(JBV), 6 (6), 405–29 (438 GS/PoP citations – 20 per year – ranking fourth among JBV articles from 1991; reprinted in three different reprint volumes)**
This article is based on my doctoral dissertation study. The enigma that triggered the study was that economic and management theories seemed to take the willingness to grow for granted, whereas you only had to talk to a handful of small business owner-managers to realize that growth was not necessarily high on their wish list. Thus, the research question addressed was incredibly broad by today's standards: Why do some (owner-managed) firms continue to grow and develop, while most others stagnate at a relatively modest size? This is obviously a theoretically interesting question, which is also of great policy relevance and of

interest to business owner-managers. Therefore, the minute after I had formulated the question, I said to myself 'This must have been done to death already'. Luckily, this was not the case. Arguably, the most important contribution of the study was that I addressed this question at a higher level of abstraction. Rather than using a laundry list of different kinds of variables – as was common at the time – I argued that all the specific influences could be regarded as aspects of three overarching factors: ability, need and opportunity (see Davidsson, 2004, pp. 36–9). Further, I argued that while objective versions of these factors influence outcomes, it is perceived ability, need and opportunity that guide action. Applying this more abstracted approach was probably the important timing issue in this case – the field was ready for it, especially after Low and MacMillan (1988). I tested the model aggregating 72 manifest variables to this limited set of latent constructs, and tested direct and mediated effects through a then novel structural equations modeling technique, partial least-squares (PLS) analysis, arriving at the conclusion that all three factors mattered as expected, although need seemed more important than the other two.

There were no co-authors. In those days Swedish supervisors did not put their name on works emanating from their disciples' theses (I did not do so myself until 2007). However, there were important others. In retrospect, I can see that my taste for a higher level of abstraction was subtly indoctrinated in me by my supervisor, Karl-Erik Wärneryd. In his very encouraging assessment of my work, the external faculty opponent at my public defense, Clas Wahlbin, made one critical remark that I took on board: I should stick to the high level of abstraction in the empirical analysis. So I reran all the analyses for the journal version; in the dissertation I had engaged in a more detailed jungle of relationships among sub-concepts. I was also lucky to learn PLS from one of its big name pioneers, Claes Fornell (see Fornell and Larcker, 1981).

Hard work and tenacity in this case mostly concerned getting data and other front-end work rather than the publication process. This was dissertation work and, as such, it was not about running some analyses on existing data (that would not have sufficed even if data were available, which they were not). I had to master the literature, which back then meant reading anything and everything you could find relating to entrepreneurship and small firm growth (which still was a manageable set). I applied for money. I undertook a qualitative pilot study (written up by hand, in Swedish, and then typed by a secretary). No measures were available, so I developed the entire questionnaire from scratch, pretested and personally undertook over 70 of the more than 400 telephone interviews. I started developing ideas in late 1985 and the article was published in 1991. Yes, there was some work behind it. Using PLS with Lohmöller's incomplete draft manual had its own challenges.

As regards fit with journal it is hard today to fathom how this publication came about. My supervisor knew about an upcoming special issue in some Europe-based sociology journal. So I sent it there. But they sent it back, because they had changed editors – and plans. So I sent it to another journal? No. I sent copies to perhaps a dozen big names in the field, so that they would know that this work existed. One of them was Sue Birley, who happened to be guest editing a special issue of JBV on entrepreneurship research in Europe at that time. I did not know Sue and was not aware she was editing this issue; she was just one of the 'big names' I wanted to be aware of my work. She apparently thought my manuscript was a good example, so she offered to include it. Timing – serendipitously. I cannot even remember a review process other than some exchange (via snail mail) between Sue and me.

2. **Delmar, F., P. Davidsson and W. Gartner (2003), 'Arriving at the high-growth firm',** *Journal of Business Venturing*, **18 (2), 189–216 (538 GS/PoP citations – 54 per year – ranking fourth among JBV articles from 2003)**

There was a lot of hullabaloo in the mid-1990s in popular media and policy debates – and some in academic outlets – about 'gazelles' or 'high-growth firms' – sometimes portrayed as the next savior of us all. So it was an area where we could get good research funding, and one I found interesting and suitable for me, given my prior work on firm growth. Reading up on the literature I became more skeptical and critical so the original interest in where gazelles came from and how many jobs they created turned into something like the following research question: 'Does this phenomenon even exist (that is, is 'high growth' a stage rather than a type of firm) and, if so, are researchers talking about the same thing when they are talking about high growth firms?' Thus, we aimed at key issues with a phenomenon of high practical and methodological – and possibly theoretical – importance. Our contribution was to use a large, high-quality, customized data set to demonstrate that there are different kinds of 'high growth firms' – depending on what criteria you use you end up with very different groups. As a consequence, you cannot expect to validly aggregate findings across studies.

From my perspective, the hard work part again pertained to obtaining the unique data. Again, it was not about taking a data set 'as is' and running some analyses on it. Based on experiences and contacts from a previous project we worked closely with experts at Statistics Sweden to compile a data set that could do the job (see Davidsson, 2004, chs 7–8).

By matching data in different databases we made sure surviving firms appeared as such even if they changed, for example, ownership or main industry. We also ascertained that we included the highest quality sales and employment data available; originally these were not necessarily to be found in the same database. I wanted to be able to separate acquisitions from organic growth and specifically remember spending hours and hours at a friend's place in Singapore working out a rather convoluted way of achieving this. When I showed my solution to the Statistics Sweden expert he set his mind to coming up with a more elegant solution – which he did.

As regards co-authors I had the initial idea, the experience with Statistics Sweden data and collaboration, and better writing skills. Frédéric had more time, incentive, youthful energy and inclination to learn the latest methods tricks. He did all the analyses, drafted the first version(s) and was the main driver for most of the process. Bill Gartner entered the stage much later primarily for better packaging for high-quality, US-based outlets; something we were still a bit uncertain about. Actually, without Bill showing an interest we may not even have sent it to a journal. At the time of the last round of major revisions I was on sabbatical and had more time, so I could again take a greater stab at giving the manuscript its final shape.

The timing was definitely right: it was a hot topic. And after being rejected by the *Academy of Management Journal* (AMJ) and one or two more top management journals, citation statistics suggest we eventually found the right journal in JBV. So, with a 2003 publication date the publication process required some tenacity; the first version of the paper received a best paper award at the Babson conference in 1998 (although some of the delay was self-inflicted). It was decidedly not an AMJ paper – it was almost humorous to read the reviews; the reviewers did not seem to know quite what to say about this paper which almost completely lacked the front-end theory they expected, although they found the data to be excellent and the findings important. As I recall it, the process with JBV was reasonable. Today, under its present editorial policy, JBV would also be unlikely to accept a paper as weak on theory as this one was. Personally, I believe that papers can make different types of contributions, and that theoretical contributions are not always the most important. Therefore I am looking forward to witnessing the development of the new *Academy of Management Discoveries* journal and the direct and indirect impact it might have on our scholarship.

3. **Davidsson, P., P. Steffens and J. Fitzsimmons (2009), 'Growing profitable or growing from profits: putting the horse in front of the cart?', *Journal of Business Venturing*, 24 (4), 388–406 (76 GS/PoP citations – 19 per year – ranking sixth among JBV articles from 2009)**

The trigger again was the uncritical hullaballoo about high-growth firms and the frequent use – particularly in entrepreneurship research – of growth as the sole dependent variable, interpreted as 'good performance'. So the important question we asked was '(when) is going for growth really advisable (from a financial performance point of view)?' I find this to be a very important question for all stakeholders – and one which prior literature too frequently ignores. The contribution we make is to provide empirical evidence that starting from a situation of low profitability it is probably not a good idea to go for high growth, as well as a resource-based view (RBV)-based theoretical explanation of why this is so. I am not sure timing was a big issue in this particular case – the question is pretty much eternal – but in my own view it was about time that someone addressed this important question head on.

I remember the process of producing this piece of research with joy, for a number of reasons. First, the results are controversial according to some, and therefore interesting (Davis, 1971). Second, it was my first paper based on Australian data and with my new Australian colleagues as co-authors. It was good teamwork. They had started by digging up an existing, four-year Australian data set of high quality, and were puzzled about some early results. I walked into Paul's office and, with my deeper background in small firm growth research, the results made immediate sense to me. In the continued work, I took a lead on theoretical framing, while Paul took the main responsibility for analysis work and Jason added special insight into financials as well as serving as excavator of related gems from prior literature and as a general sounding-board.

We enjoyed success with the conference version at Academy of Management (AoM) in 2005, where we received the award for best empirical paper in the Entrepreneurship Division. So with that evidence we just had to make a light revision and then submit, get the acceptance letter and enjoy eternal glory, right? No. Hard work, remember? We already had high-quality data from Australia, although feedback compelled us to switch to a better measure of profitability. As the results were not immediately accepted by all, we added a second longitudinal data set from Sweden. We also performed subgroup analyses by industry, firm size, firm age, and so on, and could thus considerably strengthen the case for the generalizability of our findings. We engaged in a thorough search for a more sophisticated data analysis method for addressing our particular problem, without finding one. Then we submitted and got rejected – as usual – by AMJ. Based on citations so far, I am happy with the journal fit we have seemed to obtain with JBV. However, I think the finally published version would have had a good chance of being accepted in AMJ, and it was actually the feedback in the rejection letter from AMJ that put us on track for this improved theoretical positioning. In my usual, phenomenon-focused way I had stacked up evidence and arguments from all corners of the Earth to back up our hypotheses and interpretations. That is simply not the AMJ way, and one of the reviewers (or possibly the editor) suggested we could frame the paper entirely within resource-based theory (which in rudimentary form already was somewhere in our random pile of arguments). This I thought was complete nonsense for about a month, until I went back to the feedback with less emotion (and arrogance) and saw that they really had a point. That is how slow a learner I am – one month to appreciate the feedback, and half a career (at least) to learn how to craft a theoretical argument in the AMJ style!

It was very early 2005 that I stepped into Paul Steffens office, and it was rather late in 2009 that we saw the article in print. Both data sets covered the late 1990s. Again, publishing takes time and some tenacity.

4. **Lockett, A., J. Wiklund, P. Davidsson and S. Girma (2011), 'Organic and acquisitive growth: re-examining, testing and extending Penrose's growth theory',** *Journal of Management Studies* **(JMS), 48 (1), 48–74 (15 GS/PoP citations – 7.5 per year – making it rank 16 among year 2011 articles in JMS. No evidence of real take-off yet, but we are still hoping)**

The accumulation of research of growth had demonstrated that it is a heterogeneous phenomenon (see 2 above) and review articles started to ask for theory-driven treatments of antecedents or effects of specific forms of growth rather than more research trying to explain the total rate or amount of growth (Davidsson et al., 2010; McKelvie and Wiklund, 2010; Shepherd and Wiklund, 2009). In this regard, our article is timely because it does just that. We ask: 'Do organic and acquisition-based growth differentially affect the firm's ability to grow (organically) in subsequent periods?' Pretty important, if you ask me, and mysteriously nonexistent in the literature. Our contributions are empirical evidence and a theoretical explanation – building on and extending Penrose (1959) – suggesting that whereas organic growth in one period is hard to sustain in the next period, acquisitive growth opens up new opportunities for subsequent organic growth.

It was good teamwork across the co-authors, albeit a bit slow at times. I created the unique data that allowed the question to be pursued – no prior, large-scale data could distinguish between acquisitions and organic growth (see 2 above). That is where and when my part of the hard work happened. I also came up with the first ideas about linking Penrose's theorizing to our ability to analyze this distinction, although the specific relationships we tested drifted quite a bit over time from my first, crude suggestions (see Davidsson, 2004, p. 43). Later my role was relatively limited, more of a sounding-board nature. Lockett was the Penrose-theory man and he and Wiklund – a competent jack-of-all-trades – alternated as main drivers of the project. Lockett's insights into how to package a manuscript for JMS was probably also important. Girma was brought in as econometric expert.

Again, it takes a bit of tenacity to publish. Admittedly, all the authors did a million other things in the meantime, but here we have a case where there is a good 15 years between first plans of applying for money and creating the data set, and seeing this particular manuscript in print. The data set was ready to use in 1998 (and this is but one out of many publications from it). My first thoughts about Penrose, related to the two forms of growth, must have been from the first years of the new millennium. We probably started working on the paper in 2005 and presented it at conferences in 2007. It was rejected by *Management Science* and possibly elsewhere before we sent a revised version to JMS, and the process there was not exactly an easy one either. But it was worth it. Although my part in later stages was limited and the impact of the paper still uncertain, I am proud to have contributed to it. It is a fine piece of research.

Articles on New Venture Emergence

5. Delmar, F. and P. Davidsson (2000), 'Where do they come from? Prevalence and characteristics of nascent entrepreneurs', *Entrepreneurship & Regional Development* (ERD), 12 (1), 1–23 (471 GS/PoP citations – 36 per year – apparently the highest total number for any ERD article at any time)

Arguably, timing and unique data are the main reasons for the citation success of this relatively simple, empirical fact-finding paper. It is the first publication from the Swedish version of the Panel Study of Entrepreneurial Dynamics (PSED) (Gartner et al., 2004) and although we started data collection after the US counterpart study – in which I also had a role – the more agile Swedish project achieved shorter time to market. Thus, it became one of the first journal articles based on a nationally representative sample of nascent entrepreneurs, predated only by a couple of articles from the less comprehensive, Norwegian counterpart study (Alsos and Kolvereid, 1998; Alsos and Ljunggren, 1998).

The question we asked was essentially: 'What does the population of nascent entrepreneurs look like?' Our contribution was to answer that question. There would seem to be nothing theoretical about that – but I would argue that you cannot theorize well about a phenomenon if you start from an uninformed image of what the phenomenon is. We had to map the terrain first, and I can clearly remember at the time reflecting on how much we learnt from these projects – about the make-up of the population and the business start-up process – before a single paper had been published. So that is the bigger, underlying aspect of 'what is it that the field of entrepreneurship really needs at this point?' in this case – to take part in Paul Reynolds's endeavor to make possible empirical research on representative samples of emerging new ventures in their formative, pre-operational stages. This development was also in line with influential scholars' views of what the field of entrepreneurship ought to be doing in order to make a unique contribution to the broader field of economic and organizational studies (Gartner, 1989; Katz and Gartner, 1988; Shane and Venkataraman, 2000).

The publication process was smooth, starting with encouragement or perhaps even an invitation by the main editor, who had seen the paper presented at a conference. This did not eliminate the need for hard work and tenacity – which had already happened. Paul Reynolds first tried to lure me into the American project *circa* 1992 (cf. Reynolds and Miller, 1992); we started that project in earnest in 1995. Raising money and collecting data for the Swedish project was not easy either. Some would frown upon ERD as the outlet, but it was (and remains) the leading entrepreneurship journal in Europe; it has a more aggregate-level orientation and an appreciation for different kinds of contributions, which fit with the manuscript. It should also be remembered that at the time only one journal in this field – JBV – was Social Science Citation Information (SSCI) listed. The outcome suggests the paper–journal and journal–audience fit was good, which cannot be said, for example, for the many AMJ articles from 2000 that have not even been cited one-tenth as often. Again, it was a good Delmar–Davidsson co-authorship, similar to 2 above. I was so busy in research leadership roles at the time that these manuscripts hardly would have happened without Frédéric taking the driver's seat.

6. **Davidsson, P. and B. Honig (2003), 'The role of social and human capital among nascent entrepreneurs',** *Journal of Business Venturing*, **18 (3), 301–31 (1325 GS/PoP citations – 132 per year – both numbers apparently the highest for any JBV manuscript at any time. Received Greif and JBV awards for best cited – entrepreneurship – paper published in 2003)**

How can 'just another empirical paper' achieve such numbers of citations? The research question 'How do human and social capital influence discovery and exploitation of ideas for new ventures?' is important and arguably even central – but not thrilling. Our contribution is to show that both matter; apparently social capital (SC) more so than human capital (HC), especially later in the process. The results also suggest that further into the process, more specific forms of capital become relatively more important compared with general forms. The main reasons for the extraordinary citation numbers, I would say, are the timing and unique data. The article is probably the first in entrepreneurship in a major journal to frame education, experience, personal networks, and so on, in terms of human and social capital. This was entirely Honig's doing. The majority of citations are probably for this – when colleagues need to say something about HC and/or SC in relation to entrepreneurship, even when this in not a main theme of their paper – Davidsson and Honig has become the standard reference to throw in. I was one of the pioneers of empirical research on nascent entrepreneurs, and this manuscript was probably the first in a major outlet to use longitudinal data of this kind. That probably explains quite a number of citations, too. JBV – the leading niche journal speaking straight to our core community – was the right outlet for this manuscript; I do not believe it would have been more cited – or even cited as much – had it appeared in a higher-prestige outlet of a broader nature.

The paper is an example of successful and enjoyable co-authorship, but it was certainly not a straight, comfortable or easy journey. Again, it's about tenacity and hard work – I am sorry to say that I cannot give any useful advice about shortcuts. I had seen the name 'Benson Honig' pop up here and there; he seemed to be a coming man in the field and on this basis I hired him as 'international affiliate' – more or less sight unseen – to the so-called 'PEG' research program that I was directing at the time. I was right in my hunches; he became one of the greatest contributors to the program. Among other things he started working on two papers based on our Swedish PSED data and offered me co-authorship on both. At the time I did not think of providing the data as contribution enough, so I declined the offer on one of them (Honig, 2001) and participated actively in the crafting of the other, although Benson was the main driver. An early version appeared as a Honig and Davidsson paper at AoM 2000. I was still not thrilled with the paper, which obviously already had more qualities than I saw at the time as it was one of the runners-up for an All-Academy paper award.

As more longitudinal data became available the paper grew ever more interesting. We submitted, and got rejected as usual by at least one of the major management journals (which in those days published very little entrepreneurship research). We then revised and submitted to JBV, where we endured a long and somewhat painful process with three major revisions, if I remember correctly. I think it was the second of these that coincided with my aforementioned sabbatical in Australia. So now I had the time to take a major stab at the paper's positioning, and streamlining our story throughout the paper (Benson was not as driven an academic writer back then as he is today). At this point I suggested we change the author order to Davidsson and Honig, reflecting equal authorship, to which Benson agreed. I had no clue at the time what a no-no this is; to me it was just changing to what I thought had become the true balance of contribution, considering also my work on raising the money and creating the data set. We had no quarrel about this; instead our email traffic signals frustration with reviewers moving the target and suspicion that someone perhaps had a specific interest in delaying the publication of this manuscript. In the end, though, I must say it was an example of a good review process. It definitely made the paper much better, while remaining solidly our brainchild. And the bean-counters of today do not care in the least about how long it took to get it to print, whereas they may have some appreciation for citations statistics.

7. Senyard, J., T. Baker, P. Steffens and P. Davidsson (forthcoming), 'Bricolage as a path to innovativeness for resource-constrained new firms', *Journal of Product Innovation Management* (JPIM) (just accepted for publication)

I include this just-accepted paper to bring us out of the Stone Age in some readers' perception, and in order to illustrate some issues not covered in my discussion of the other papers. Bricolage is currently one of the really 'hot' topics, but all the research to date has been conceptual or case based. This makes the research question '(When and for what) is bricolage any good?' central to the field and the task to put it to systematic testing important (cf. 9 below). Addressing aspects of this is what we contribute in this paper. We present competing hypotheses suggesting either a positive or a curvilinear effect of bricolage behavior on innovativeness. Our results predominantly support the former hypothesis. Undertaking these tests requires developing a survey measure of bricolage, so providing such a measure is part of the contribution.

Timing and journal fit were important for this paper. Yes, in this case we felt at least a faint whiff of the pressure that researchers in some branches of the natural sciences live under all the time – we would very much like to be first with a published, survey measure of bricolage behavior. So when JPIM – a journal with similar standing in innovation as JBV enjoys in entrepreneurship – announced a special issue on innovation under resource constraints, we jumped on it. In a special issue with this focus, we could expect a sympathetic view on bricolage as a phenomenon and emerging theory. In addition, publishing with other articles on the same general theme is likely to boost actual reading and citing of the article. Further, it is not one of the journals that are likely to voice the greatest concerns with a previously untested measure of a core construct. This does not mean we were cruising; it took two rounds of revisions to get the paper accepted. In the end we were pleased with the outcome and with our decision not to take the gamble – and possible rejection and associated delays – with a major management journal.

Again, the team of co-authors is important. Senyard is the doctoral student who wrote the first draft and contributed to all aspects of the manuscript. When publishing on bricolage having Ted Baker on board is not an entirely stupid idea. This is very true even though the review process is blind; the man actually knows something about the topic (for example, Baker and Nelson, 2005). He had a big role in developing the measure and in the paper's theory development. I, again, provided unique data by raising the money and drawing up the overall design of an Australian version of PSED – Comprehensive Australian Study of Entrepreneurial Emergence (CAUSEE) – which, unlike its counterparts, follows both nascent and operational but young firms (Davidsson and Steffens, 2011). Hard work and tenacity rule as usual: I wrote the first grant application in 2005; main data collection started in 2007 after pretests, and my contribution builds on experiences from as far back as 1995 (see 5). Then again, getting the biggest grant on campus from the Australian Research Council – and the biggest in the country by a factor of two in business in economics – did something for my reputation at my new university and in my new country. Journal publications are not the only thing that matters. With Ted Baker I helped develop the bricolage measure; with colleagues at JIBS I also developed the measure of innovativeness (cf. Dahlqvist and Wiklund, 2012). In addition, I also took part in writing the manuscript. Steffens likewise contributed in several ways – including grant application success – and took a big part of the responsibility for statistical analyses.

Conceptual and Methods Oriented Contributions

8. Davidsson, P. and J. Wiklund (2001), 'Levels of analysis in entrepreneurship research: current practice and suggestions for the future', *Entrepreneurship Theory and Practice* **(ETP), 25 (4), 81–99 (485 GS/PoP citations – 40 per year – which if GS captured it correctly would place it on top for articles published in 2001, and among top ten ever in ETP for citations/year)**

This manuscript grew directly out of the authors' own experience with analysis level issues in entrepreneurship research. For example, I had noted the ambiguity in PSED research – was it nascent entrepreneurs or nascent ventures we were sampling and following over time? Different parts of the questionnaires would suggest different answers. In his doctoral thesis, Johan Wiklund had, among other things, worked on entrepreneurial orientation– a construct that is supposed to be a firm-level abstraction but invariably is measured through questionnaire items answered by a single individual. For me personally, it also meant a great deal if entrepreneurship was just about how individuals enrich themselves through business activities or also about how such activities improve the functioning of the economic system and the total wealth it generates. The frustration over the limited success of research focusing on entrepreneurs' personal traits can also be understood in levels terms – the performance of the sampled firm is not contingent solely on a single individual, and the focal person need not invest all their energy in the firm one happened to have in the sample. Further, the increased emphasis on entrepreneurial opportunities, discovery and exploitation processes, and different modes of exploitation (Shane and Venkataraman, 2000) seemed to call for studies focusing neither on the individual nor the firm, but on the emerging new venture itself, through whatever changes in human champions and organizational homes it might encounter during the journey. In this confused state, we thought an important question for the field was 'How can we do better research by paying more attention to levels of analysis?' and our contribution was to suggest some ways to achieve this.

Looking back at it now, it is almost comical how our vantage point in own experiences in entrepreneurship research made us reinvent some wheels. It was not until I rewrote parts of the same arguments for Davidsson (2006) that the editor, Michael Frese, who has a solid background in organizational psychology, saved me from embarrassing myself in front of a psychology audience by pointing out that these issues had been thoroughly dealt with before, and guided me to Rousseau (1985) and Kozlowski and Klein (2000). But this was also rather typical for entrepreneurship research at this time – not seeing that much of what we did was a special case of something more general, where others had put in brain power and developed tools that we could also find a use for. In our defense, their emerging nature and other aspects of the entrepreneurial phenomena create particular problems, so there is valid reason to have an entrepreneurship-specific treatment of these issues in the literature alongside the more general sources.

Timing is interesting in relation to this paper. It was not until a few years later that others dealt in earnest with some of these issues by studying teams and habitual entrepreneurs, thus breaking the strong but unstated one person equals one firm assumption that had guided the design of much earlier research. In the past few years, multi-level modeling and analysis have become 'in', and it is also more recently that citations of this article have really taken off, so it probably was slightly 'ahead of its time'.

As regards co-authors, Johan and I worked really well together on all aspects of this type of paper (see also Davidsson and Wiklund, 2000), bouncing ideas and rounds of writing back and forth. Apart from Johan and myself, research assistants played a role. It is one of the few papers for which I have used paid research assistants (which almost seems to be a national sport in my new home country, alongside cricket, rugby league and Aussie rules). I generally prefer to have one or all of the authors do all essential parts of the research, including literature review and data analysis. Another important person in this case was Mike Wright, who took the initiative to transform ideas presented at an ad hoc international gathering at JIBS into an ETP special issue. The fact that I also co-edited this special issue and that there was no open call and no external reviewing meant that the demands for hard work and tenacity were lower than usual. Today, such a process would not be deemed acceptable, and rightfully so; things work differently these days. This said, I am not going to apologize for being one of the originators of an issue colleagues have found particularly useful; every article in this special issue counts GS citations in the hundreds.

9. Brown, T., P. Davidsson and J. Wiklund (2001), 'An operationalization of Stevenson's conceptualization of entrepreneurship as opportunity-based firm behavior', *Strategic Management Journal* (SMJ), 22 (10), 953–68 (297 GS citations – 25 per year –within the top third for SMJ articles published in 2001)

Stevenson's ideas regarding entrepreneurial management (Stevenson and Gumpert, 1985; Stevenson and Jarillo, 1985) probably peaked in popularity around this time, so arguably, the timing was right. Stevenson's ideas appeared a great deal in teaching and textbooks, but had never been systematically tested. So we thought providing an instrument that made such testing possible was an important task (cf. 7). Hence, our research question was 'Can Stevenson's ideas be operationalized?' and our contribution was to provide such an operationalization which had been separately validated on a number of sub-samples, and demonstrate how it partially overlapped and partially was distinctive from the notion of entrepreneurial orientation (EO).

Although important, this is admittedly a contribution at one corner of entrepreneurship rather than at its core, and the uptake of our measure has been nowhere near that of EO. So the high citation numbers are a positive surprise, which likely derives from good journal fit. As far as I can remember, this was the first time I very carefully positioned a manuscript for a particular journal, including pointing out in the letter to the editor why SMJ – based on it addressing corporate rather than individual entrepreneurship and SMJ having been the outlet for earlier Stevenson and EO manuscripts – was the right home for this article. The general standing of SMJ has no doubt a major role in driving citation numbers in this case. Possibly, colleagues refer to the article not so much for the particular measure, but more generally for its effort to develop, document and validate an operationalization of an important construct.

The co-authors had distinctive roles. Terrence Brown came up with the idea; he had wanted to include it in his dissertation project but was made to put it off until his postdoctoral years. He and I developed and pretested the item bank, and the surviving items were included in a large, multi-purpose survey study (providing strong data, especially in terms of sample size, response rate and opportunities to analyze a range of subgroups separately for validation purposes). I believe I took a lead in statistical analysis as well as writing, with Terrence and Johan assisting. Johan came in rather late in this process. Importantly, he penned a strong section on the steps of development and validation of the scale, and he probably had a significant role in crafting a revision. As regards hard work and tenacity it takes quite an effort to develop a useful measure and a survey study of this magnitude, but the review process in SMJ was a surprisingly easy ride. The data were collected in 1998 and the article was published in 2001. This includes lead times for which SMJ was notorious at the time.

10. **Zahra, S., H. Sapienza and P. Davidsson (2006), 'Entrepreneurship and dynamic capabilities: a review, model and research agenda', *Journal of Management Studies*, 25 (4), 917–55 (561 citations – 80 per year, second highest of JMS articles published in 2006. Received the JMS best paper award for 2006)**

This conceptual paper makes rich and varied contributions to the literature on dynamic capabilities, among other things by explicating links to entrepreneurship and outlining how it can be studied. I have not systematically investigated what it is being cited for, but I know which of its questions and contributions I think is the most important: 'How can we define dynamic capabilities in such a way that it can be the subject of useful theorizing and empirical testing?' In my view, dynamic capabilities (DC) is one of those intuitively appealing concepts in management studies which have caught on and found widespread use, but which on closer look turn out to be very, very messy – perhaps even unhelpful for any serious scholarly work and progress. Another is entrepreneurial opportunities, which I am currently working on in a manuscript that might become one of my more important works or end up unread and uncited in *Journal of Entrepreneurship & Bicycle Repair* (I got this generic name for journals you do not want to be seen in from Norris Krueger). We will see. The problem with DC is that the way it had been variously defined in earlier literature – by no small names – it either had a definitional connection with a specific type of environment or it conceptually overlapped what should supposedly be an *explanandum* performance – or both. We tried to clean up the act. I think we did so fairly well, but I cannot claim any role in this contribution.

Another important factor in publication and citation success in this case is probably journal fit. At the time, JMS had just started to become recognized as belonging in the very top tier. The link to entrepreneurship was a good fit with the journal, and our implicit or explicit critique of some predecessors was possibly a less contentious issue in JMS than in some of the alternatives. Further, the editorial team was helpful, without granting any particular privileges; they clearly wished to see a strong manuscript of this kind in their journal.

The paper has a strong team of co-authors (who are also good friends) but this did not make for an easy journey in this case. Shaker Zahra initiated the paper and for the first draft we had a decentralized writing process – where I contributed parts on DC, entrepreneurship and growth, and Harry, among other things, engaged with the learning literature – which Shaker pulled together into a first submission. As things developed I had actually contributed very little of the contents that remained in the paper, and I was not entirely happy with the first two or three versions of the paper. The reviewers saw potential but were not entirely happy either, so there were rounds of substantial revisions through which I still did not feel I could contribute meaningfully, so I actually suggested I be dropped from the paper. My co-authors encouraged me to stay on, though. I am not sure my recollection is correct, but I think the editor (Mike Wright, again) decided that we did not make any more progress with the reviewers' help, and he saw enough potential in the paper to conditionally accept it, trusting that we would be able to work out remaining issues between editor and authors. At this stage I believe Shaker had run out of steam, become too absorbed by other things or thought the paper was essentially good enough already. So Harry and I worked intensely to give the paper its final form, trying to weed out inconsistencies and streamline our narrative. This is a lesson about tenacity – one advantage of being a team is that it is not always the case that the same person can be the main driver at all stages of the process. In the end, I am glad I stayed on; I am proud to have had a minor role in this fine paper which won the JMS Best Paper Award for 2006.

SOME CONCLUDING REFLECTIONS

I have emphasized, above, the identification of an important research question, and hence making a strong contribution, as the primary factors behind publication success. However, a good research question in itself, even when addressed through a good study, does not automatically lead to publication success. You need skillful packaging as well, and sometimes you need to settle for not quite the journal you first imagined. But there is an asymmetry. Whereas addressing an important question may trigger reviewers' and editors' best efforts to help you get the packaging right, skillful packaging without important content will not normally be well received or suffice for publication success. Occasionally it does – these are the papers in top journals that get very few citations. I would rather have the citations than the prestige journal. One of my current favorite boasting points is that according to Google Scholar both of my JBV papers from 2003 – both of which were rejected by AMJ – outcite every AMJ paper published that year. This said, it is also the case that many third-tier, or below, journals hardly attract any readership or use at all, and publishing in these journals seems to fill little purpose beyond adding lines to CVs and perhaps transferring some funds from libraries to publishers.

I have also discussed and illustrated the supplementary roles of hard work, good data, tenacity, fit with the journal, co-authors and timing. I realize that my emphasis on an important research question and strong contribution, in combination with the time it takes to see it through to publication, can be discouraging to some. How does one deal with this in a maturing field where the big questions are likely to have been addressed already, and when the pressure is on to get X number of articles published at tier Y or higher within Z years?

Well, not everybody is going to succeed, but there is light at the end of the tunnel. First, we are not going to run out of important questions. Great entrepreneurial successes tend to open up additional opportunities for other entrepreneurs. In the same vein it tends to be the case in research that progress opens up new avenues. Second, journal publication and academic hiring are two-way streets. Journals cannot reject everything – they need hard-working researchers to offer to publish good work in their journal, otherwise they cannot stay in business. Similarly, if the expectations of every dean and every hiring/promotion committee add up to requesting many more top-level publications than there is room for in the journals they care about, then something is going to have to give. Business schools cannot operate without employees, so all but the most attractive employers will have to adjust or lose good prospects to those who are just ahead of them. We know how markets work, right? Further, one can be more focused and systematic than I have been in trying to get one's publications through the pipeline. A little bit of planning and strategy might help, although I am personally unable to follow such advice. Working in the direction of faster publication processes are also efforts by editors to speed up the process and avoid unnecessary delays. A case in point is JBV, which under Dean Shepherd's editorship strongly emphasizes short turnaround cycles.

The process from idea to finished product is likely to be faster if one starts with existing data rather than collection of primary survey data. The problem with traditional, secondary data sets is that if a data set is publicly available, how can it possibly allow the investigation of important, central research questions that have not already been addressed? Probably they cannot. Possibly they can, if you combine more than one data source. The greatest potential, however, may be to find available data that have previously not been used for research purposes. Here, the sky is the limit – data are collected by many organizations for many purposes, and electronic traces in abundance are left everywhere. Just recently I had a postdoctoral fellow finding over 20 years of relatively complete, multi-level data for an entire industry, which had previously not been tapped as a resource for research. It may take some creativity –

and perhaps hard work – but I am sure there is a lot of potentially useful data lying around out there. As regards survey data I am skeptical of its potential under time pressure. Large surveys are versatile in terms of what questions they can address, but expensive and often multiple waves are needed. So, apart from getting a share of surveys that are already ongoing, there may be limited potential under time pressure, one possible exception being instrument development. Various forms of laboratory research – experiments and simulations – seem to hold more promise, and also have the capacity to deal with the multidimensional heterogeneity that plagues real world data.

Finally, I have emphasized co-authorship. One way of boosting your publication record is to develop unique skills, for example, in simulation techniques or 'next generation' data analysis methods. This would make you someone to invite as co-author on a number of papers; you need not be the lead on everything. Further, if you invite your colleagues to co-author 'your' paper, they are likely to invite you in return. I am not suggesting meaningless name-swapping, but genuine collaboration. Apart from when it deteriorates to committee work in the bad sense, collaboration will improve the quality, and hence the publication prospects, of each individual piece of research.

I cannot offer you heaven, but I hope my reflections will be perceived as somewhat useful by junior researchers in our field. If nothing else, I hope some of the insights into particular publication processes can provide entertaining anecdotes. Perhaps the insights that 'big names' in the field also get rejected on a regular basis, and that eventually well-cited papers did not get there very easily, can provide comfort in some situations. Because this is the case; even those who occasionally or even regularly make it into *Academy of Management Review* (AMR), AMJ, *Administrative Science Quarterly* (ASQ) and so on, have received quite a collection of rejection letters as well. Getting into these journals is difficult for anyone, with any research question, at any time. If we can do it once in a while, with our most important work, we are doing really well – whatever your dean says.

NOTE

1. To be fair, through the 1990s I engaged in quite a bit of dissemination directly to policy makers, and it is not entirely without amusement or pride that I note that with around 100 GS citations each, some of our main reports – in the Swedish language! – fare better in this regard than do many entrepreneurship articles published in respected journals during the same era (Davidsson et al., 1994; 1996).

REFERENCES

Alsos, G.A. and L. Kolvereid (1998), 'The business gestation process of novice, serial and parallel business founders'. *Entrepreneurship Theory and Practice*, **22** (4), 101–14.

Alsos, G.A. and E.C. Ljunggren (1998), 'Does the business start-up process differ by gender? A longitudinal study of nascent entrepreneurs', *Journal of Enterprising Culture*, **6** (4), 347–67.

Baker, T. and R.E. Nelson (2005), 'Creating something from nothing: resource construction through entrepreneurial bricolage', *Administrative Science Quarterly*, **50** (3), 329–66.

Brown, T., P. Davidsson and J. Wiklund (2001), 'An operationalization of Stevenson's conceptualization of entrepreneurship as opportunity-based firm behavior', *Strategic Management Journal*, **22** (10), 953–68.

Dahlqvist, J. and J. Wiklund (2012), 'Measuring the market newness of new ventures', *Journal of Business Venturing*, **27** (2), 185–96.

Davidsson, P. (1991), 'Continued entrepreneurship: ability, need, and opportunity as determinants of small firm growth', *Journal of Business Venturing*, **6** (6), 405–29.

Davidsson, P. (2004), *Researching Entrepreneurship*, New York: Springer.

Davidsson, P. (2006), 'Method challenges and opportunities in the psychological study of entrepreneurship', in J.R. Baum, M. Frese and R.A. Baron (eds), *The Psychology of Entrepreneurship*, Mahwah, NJ.: Erlbaum, pp. 287–323.

Davidsson, P. and B. Honig (2003), 'The role of social and human capital among nascent entrepreneurs', *Journal of Business Venturing*, **18** (3), 301–31.

Davidsson, P. and P. Steffens (2011), 'Comprehensive Australian Study of Entrepreneurial Emergence (CAUSEE): project presentation and early results', in P.D. Reynolds and R.T. Curtin (eds), *New Business Creation*, New York: Springer, pp. 27–51.

Davidsson, P. and J. Wiklund (2000), 'Conceptual and empirical challenges in the study of firm growth', in D. Sexton and H. Landström (eds), *The Blackwell Handbook of Entrepreneurship*, Oxford, UK: Blackwell Business, pp. 26–44.

Davidsson, P. and J. Wiklund (2001), 'Levels of analysis in entrepreneurship research: current practice and suggestions for the future', *Entrepreneurship Theory and Practice*, **25** (4), 81–99.

Davidsson, P., L. Achtenhagen and L. Naldi (2010), 'Small firm growth', *Foundations and Trends in Entrepreneurship*, **6** (2), 69–166.

Davidsson, P., L. Lindmark and C. Olofsson (1994), *Dynamiken i svenskt näringsliv (Business Dynamics in Sweden)*, Lund: Studentlitteratur.

Davidsson, P., L. Lindmark and C. Olofsson (1996), *Näringslivsdynamik under 90-talet (Business Dynamics in the 90s)*, Stockholm: NUTEK.

Davidsson, P., P. Steffens and J. Fitzsimmons (2009), 'Growing profitable or growing from profits: putting the horse in front of the cart?', *Journal of Business Venturing*, **24** (4), 388–406.

Davis, M.S. (1971), 'That's interesting', *Philosophy of the Social Sciences*, **1** (2), 309–344.

Delmar, F. and P. Davidsson (2000), 'Where do they come from? Prevalence and characteristics of nascent entrepreneurs', *Entrepreneurship & Regional Development*, **12** (1), 1–23.

Delmar, F., P. Davidsson and W. Gartner (2003), 'Arriving at the high-growth firm', *Journal of Business Venturing*, **18** (2), 189–216.

Fornell, C. and D.F. Larcker (1981), 'Evaluating structural equation models with unobservable variables and measurement error', *Journal of Marketing Research*, **18** (1), 39–50.

Gartner, W.B. (1989), 'Who is the entrepreneur its wrong question', *Entrepreneurship Theory and Practice*, **12** (2), 47–64.

Gartner, W.B., K.G. Shaver, N.M. Carter and P.D. Reynolds (2004), *Handbook of Entrepreneurial Dynamics: The Process of Business Creation*, Thousand Oaks, CA: Sage.

Hambrick, D.C. (2007), 'The field of management's devotion to theory: too much of a good thing?', *Academy of Management Journal*, **50** (6), 1346–52.

Honig, B. (2001), 'Learning strategies and resources for nascent entrepreneurs and intrapreneurs', *Entrepreneurship Theory and Practice*, **24** (Fall), 21–35.

Huff, A.S. (1999), *Writing for Scholarly Publication*, Thousand Oaks, CA: Sage.

Katz, J. and W.B. Gartner (1988), 'Properties of emerging organizations', *Academy of Management Review*, **13** (3), 429–41.

Kozlowski, W.J. and K.J. Klein (2000), 'A multilevel approach to theory and research in organizations', in K.J. Klein and W.J. Kozlowski (eds), *Multilevel Theory, Research, and Methods in Organizations*, San Francisco, CA: Jossey-Bass, pp. 3–80.

Lockett, A., J. Wiklund, P. Davidsson and S. Girma (2011), 'Organic and acquisitive growth: re-examining, testing and extending Penrose's growth theory', *Journal of Management Studies*, **48** (1), 48–74.

Low, M.B. and I.C. MacMillan (1988), 'Entrepreneurship: past research and future challenges', *Journal of Management*, **14** (2), 139–61.

McKelvie, A. and J. Wiklund (2010), 'Advancing firm growth research: a focus on growth mode instead of growth rate', *Entrepreneurship Theory and Practice*, **34** (2), 261–88.

Penrose, E. (1959), *The Theory of the Growth of the Firm*, Oxford: Oxford University Press.

Reynolds, P. and B. Miller (1992), 'New firm gestation: conception, birth, and implications for research', *Journal of Business Venturing*, **7** (5), 405–17.

Rousseau, D.M. (1985), 'Issues of level in organizational research: multi-level and cross-level perspectives', *Research in Organizational Behavior*, **7** (1), 1–37.

Senyard, J., T. Baker, P. Steffens and P. Davidsson (forthcoming), 'Bricolage as a path to innovativeness for resource-constrained new firms', *Journal of Product Innovation Management*.

Shane, S. and S. Venkataraman, S. (2000), 'The promise of entrepreneurship as a field of research', *Academy of Management Review*, **25** (1), 217–26.

Shepherd, D. and J. Wiklund (2009), 'Are we comparing apples with apples or apples with oranges? Appropriateness of knowledge accumulation across growth studies', *Entrepreneurship Theory and Practice*, **33** (1), 105–23.

Stevenson, H. and D. Gumpert (1985), 'The heart of entrepreneurship', *Harvard Business Review*, **63** (2), 85–94.

Stevenson, H. and J.C. Jarillo (1990), 'A paradigm of entrepreneurship: entrepreneurial management', *Strategic Management Journal*, **11** (7), 17–27.

Zahra, S., H. Sapienza and P. Davidsson (2006), 'Entrepreneurship and dynamic capabilities: a review, model and research agenda', *Journal of Management Studies*, **25** (4), 917–55.

5. From idea to publication: managing the research process

Robert Blackburn and Friederike Welter

INTRODUCTION

There are volumes of books and articles on research methods for business (for example, Bryman and Bell, 2011; Easterby-Smith et al., 2008) and some with a focus on entrepreneurship (for example, Curran and Blackburn, 2001; Davidsson, 2008). However, the actual process of converting a research idea into publication and the stages in this process are complex, subject to a variety of challenges but ultimately rewarding. In this chapter we map out the journey from idea formulation through to publication and draw upon our experiences in doing so. An underlying assumption of the chapter is that there are specific issues, in terms of the knowledge base, theory development and methods, intrinsic to the field of entrepreneurship in this journey and hence lessons that can be learned from previous experiences.

One of the great advantages of being an academic is the relative freedom to pursue research agendas of your choice. Yet, researchers have, for some time, been under pressure to disseminate their outputs to both academic and practitioner audiences (for example, Harzing, 2011; Hills, 1999). There is also a growing emphasis on academics to increase their engagement with practitioner and policy organizations and develop research agendas, employ appropriate methods and produce results that will achieve an impact on the economy and society. For researchers in the field, these diverse parties of interest present significant pressures but also opportunities. Entrepreneurship research, by its very nature, is embedded in mindsets and real-world activities, and involves interaction with a variety of stakeholders and interested parties: support organizations, funding bodies, state policy agencies and, of course, entrepreneurs themselves. Hence, there are numerous academic and practitioner outlets for your work, plus a growing range of open access media through the Internet.

Clearly, this expanding landscape provides lucrative opportunities for research activity. However, generating an idea that 'has legs', in the sense of a publication that contributes to theory and/or practice and has impact among audiences, involves going on a journey. While we are not being overly prescriptive in saying that *every* publication is a result of the journey we discuss in this chapter, being aware of the elements can help reduce uncertainty, ensure that research projects have a sound foundation, are approached with rigour and, thus, lead to publications that are more likely to be of high quality and have impact. This is also set within a context of striving to help raise the quality of the approaches used in entrepreneurship research and help overcome the view that it is a relatively new field that needs to establish rigour alongside other business and management fields (for example, Short et al., 2010).

As a starting point, we accept that undertaking research is a messy process in which your original plans are frequently challenged, or you encounter unforeseen events that seemingly threaten the survival of the whole research project. Sharing experiences and discussing the stages of the research process may help others reduce the risks involved in their research journeys and increase the chances of producing significant and interesting research in the field.

Figure 5.1 outlines the basic stages in the research process from ideas generation through to dissemination: these stages are relatively straight-forward and form the basis for the structure of the chapter. Yet, we would also be the first to contest the adoption of formulaic, routinized and staid approaches to doing research, particularly in a field of study that is dynamic, contradictory and which questions many of the underlying assumptions of mainstream management theory and practice. Figure 5.1 is, therefore, only a broad framework depicting the research process: given the breadth of approaches in the field of entrepreneurship, its interpretation, application and use depends on your own judgement and those who you work with to produce imaginative outcomes. You will also often have to revisit stages as your research undergoes an iterative, rather than linear, process of development.

IDEA GESTATION: WHAT IS INTERESTING OUT THERE?

The first step in the publication process is what we may term 'ideas generation'. You have to identify an idea or topic and subsequently convert this into a research question, or series of questions. This initial phase of the research process involves the linking of a research idea to

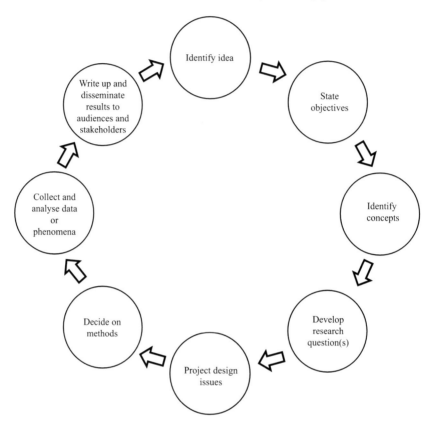

Figure 5.1   Schematic stages of the research process

extant literature, theory and empirical work, in order to provide clarity of objectives. Ultimately, research activity should critically review contemporary thinking and conventional wisdom; contribute to the knowledge and theory of field of study; and, where appropriate, have an impact on policy and practice.

The origins of research ideas in the field of entrepreneurship are multifaceted. There are innumerable topics that the field embraces (Katz, 2003; Xheneti and Blackburn, 2011) and it is delineated from many other fields by its dynamism (Zahra and Wright, 2011). Researchers of entrepreneurship also engage with numerous discourses: with entrepreneurs and people, private and business orientated, and institutions surrounding them through various ties. Ideas may emerge from previous experiences in the field, the reading of the 'grey literature' (newspapers, trade and professional publications), a major government report, or a finding from a key stakeholder, such as a bank. The conventional view that all good research projects emerge from academic journals and books is only partially the case in a field of endeavour that is dynamic, in the sense of the pace of change, and burgeoning, in terms of scale of activity.

We have a range of experiences of ideas generation in developing research projects: from the sharing of a germ of an idea with fellow academics, encounters with government officials and politicians, support agencies, bank managers, business consultants and aspirant entrepreneurs and business owners themselves – to identify but a few – that have provided an invaluable stimulus to project ideas generation.

BOX 5.1   AN EXAMPLE OF IDEA GENERATION

In 2000, Robert was involved in presenting research on the experiences of young entrepreneurs, and their high levels of business churn, to staff of an international bank. In subsequent discussions with a senior bank official, he picked up on an interesting fact: less than around 10 per cent of all business bank account closures ended in debt. This was something of a surprise given the high profile 'failure' stories presented in the media and much of the literature. A more detailed search of the literature found that, at that time, we knew relatively little about the business 'exit' process but what did exist tended to be normative rather than evidence based; hence a gap existed. However, as with any gap, its existence may be for perfectly sound reasons, such as its triviality, or insignificance within the context of how this fits within an understanding of the business life-cycle and entrepreneurs' life-journeys. In other words, we had to decide whether this was an 'itch worth scratching' (Booth et al., 2008). Would there be an audience for our work? Following further literature searches and discussion, a decision was made to study those who had recently 'exited' their enterprise, and detailed research questions were developed. In classifying what happened to 'exiting' entrepreneurs, the research found that around 60 per cent went on to run another enterprise. As a result, the project provided a range of practical and theoretical contributions (see Stokes and Blackburn, 2001; 2002). Key contributions to academic thinking and theorizing highlighted a need to separate out what happens to the business

> from the 'exiting' entrepreneur. The research project was also instructive in that some practical fieldwork issues were discussed around actually finding people who have exited from their enterprise and the possible biases of different sources.

It is critical that a simple idea or inspiration to develop a project undergoes a literature and 'sensibility' check in order to avoid reinventing the wheel. This should involve not only looking through the appropriate journals, but also books and the 'grey literature'. While the latter is often frowned upon by many academics as ephemera, issues that are picked up in the media are often more immediate and can stimulate ideas for more considered, theory-informed academic research. This may call into question some of the more restrictive 'systematic' literature review approaches, so popular in contemporary research methods courses, that select only top-flight academic journals and are based on the reading of abstracts (Easterby-Smith et al., 2008). While being systematic in your research method is important, we would suggest that at the ideas formulation stage, all the literatures that you believe to be relevant should be gleaned in your review and only later should this then be narrowed to the specific area of investigation. This helps you to think beyond the boundaries of what academics are already investigating and prevents the field from becoming overly narrow, boring and, ultimately, suffering from ossification. This is especially the case for entrepreneurship research which tends to be a permeable rather than tightly focused field of study.

BOX 5.2   FROM CONTRACT RESEARCH TO DEVELOPING YOUR OWN RESEARCH PROJECT

One of Friederike's main research fields developed from contract research. The German Federal Ministry of Economics was interested in learning more about small and medium-sized enterprises (SMEs) in the so-called Viségrad countries (the Czech Republic, Hungary, Poland and Slovakia). Friederike's employer won the contract; she had recently joined the institute and was asked to work on the project team. At that time (1993–94) little was known about the emergence, nature and problems of SMEs in the newly emerging market economies. A literature review provided few insights, so it had to be combined with a survey in the four study countries and personal visits to interview entrepreneurs and policy-makers who were eager to learn from the Western researchers. Over time, several projects followed, all with a focus on different themes around entrepreneurship and small businesses in emerging countries, and, over the years, a close network of colleagues and friends in those countries with a common research interest emerged. They conducted empirical research in countries where entrepreneurs often operated under turbulent and sometimes, as in Belarus, outright hostile conditions.

But which theories could be used to explain entrepreneurial behaviour in such conditions (Welter and Smallbone, 2003; 2011)? Why were there so many portfolio and serial entre-preneurs (Smallbone and Welter, 2001a)? Was it possible for informal petty traders to develop more substantial businesses over time (Welter and Smallbone, 2009)? Could entre-preneurs change the contexts in which they operated (Small-bone et al., 2011; Welter, 2011)? Which role did governments play in fostering entrepreneurship in these countries (Small-bone and Welter, 2001b)? Once we had embarked on this field, ideas seemed to generate themselves, often emerging from previous projects where we saw a gap in our know-ledge. Also, our interest in theoretical approaches increased, in particular as we perceived a need to search for theories which could explain entrepreneurial behaviour in non-Western contexts; and this ultimately led us to write a whole book about our results and experiences (Smallbone and Welter, 2009).

Discussing your preliminary ideas with colleagues and sharing them at workshops and in brainstorming sessions is also a worthwhile pursuit; not only can these activities help unearth work that may have already been undertaken on the topic, but they will also help clarify thinking. Nor should you confine your ideas discussion to entrepreneurship researchers exclusively; 'outsiders' can raise difficult questions and issues that may be germane to your initial idea but, because they are outside the conventional field of entrepreneurship, have not yet been picked up by entrepreneurship researchers. Moreover, outsiders can ask the awkward 'so what' question which helps you think of the contribution that the research can make: its target audiences and publication routes.

Too often, researchers are singing to their own choir rather than affecting those outside their immediate domain. This is a particularly important point for entrepreneurship researchers; we need to be able to engage with disciplines and fields outside the area, and impress upon them the significance and growing maturity of the field. Thus, airing your ideas early on will effectively test their feasibility, helping to jettison any erroneous ideas and, thus, increasing their chances of success, reaching interested audiences and making a contribution to theory, knowledge and practice.

Ideas can be pioneering or replicating/verifying/contradicting what we already know. Others may be 'hole-filling'. Most of the time, your initial ideas might seem little more than a specific problem, but once the issue is problematized, a series of tangential issues will emerge. This next stage involves shaping your ideas further and honing the specific research question(s) that you seek to investigate. This process is often iterative and chaotic as you delve into different literatures to help you develop your own foci. However, exploring, sharing and problematizing your ideas are all part of the process of developing an agenda that is worthwhile and adds to the knowledge. It is not unusual for entrepreneurship researchers to work outside their 'knowledge' comfort zone as it is a field that draws upon and feeds into many mainstream disciplines. This only underlines further the need to ensure that the process you go through from idea to publication is as systematic as possible without being overly restrictive.

FROM RESEARCH IDEA TO OBJECTIVES, CONCEPTS AND RESEARCH QUESTIONS

Defining Research Objectives

Having explored the broad topic of interest and considered its various antecedents in the literature, the next stage is to develop a focus. No matter how interesting or gripping a research idea or topic is, in order for it to contribute to theory, knowledge and practice, the boundaries of the research project have to be delineated. This involves stating the objectives of the research, recognizing the underlying concepts that you will be drawing upon, as well as defining your research questions. From our own experience, we suggest a procedure to help you set out the objectives for your research as this also will influence the possibilities for publications later on.

We suggest that you actually write down the objectives of the research. These objectives will be work in progress and act as a catalyst for reaching a more definitive set of objectives.

- Writing your objectives down actually stimulates thinking among the researchers involved and raises any initial points for clarification. Achieving 'buy-in' from your colleagues and other stakeholders is crucial at this early stage – writing down drafts of objectives and receiving feedback helps to refine the research as well as ensure that those involved feel some ownership over it.
- Written objectives should flush out any erroneous ideas and concepts that are of little or no importance to the research project. This is important as, too often, research in the field is undertaken by merely applying theories developed from elsewhere, without sufficient consideration to its usefulness in understanding entrepreneurship.
- Setting out the research objectives should help you prioritize what is important and influence the timetable of the research. In other words, this should stimulate your thinking about project design.
- Objective-setting will bring home to all involved the resources needed (and hence constraints) to achieve the objectives. Although this has been tangential to our discussion so far, ultimately all research has a cost: both an opportunity cost, in the sense of pursuing one project rather than an alternative, and the actual fieldwork cost in terms of salaries, fieldwork expenses, data collection/purchase and so on.
- The objective setting process may help you identify which aspects of the project are more likely to be publishable and which are of more relevance to a client. A research report, conference or journal paper, or book are different forms of dissemination and will require different levels of commitment. Here, also, it is important to discuss any ethical issues as well as the intellectual property ownership of the project outcomes with the external sponsor, if appropriate.
- This process will help in the allocation of roles between the members of the research team or, if you are undertaking a much smaller project, help you work out the practical implications for your own activities. As part of this discussion, you should be able to consider the competencies and motivations of those involved. It is especially important to map out these roles and identify any gaps in knowledge or the scientific capabilities of the team.

What are the Key Concepts?

Identifying the main concepts that the research will involve is crucial at this stage. These may be regarded as the basic elements used in theory. In some instances, a concept will be straightforward, such as 'business performance', while in others it may be less easily defined and subject to debate in the literature, such as 'entrepreneurs' or 'cognition'. However, entrepreneurship researchers should not shy away from attempting to identify and define the concepts of relevance to their research. Simply borrowing from other disciplines and applying it to the study of entrepreneurship can be flawed. An appreciation of the actual context of the phenomenon under study is crucial and, as such, it is important that mainstream theories are questioned and critiqued rather than simply applied, if the field of entrepreneurship is to develop (Zahra, 2007).

Failure to address these issues early on may only lead to problems emerging later in the research process. The significance of identifying and sharing the underlying concepts to be used in the project are important when working in a team. When working in international teams, you may face additional challenges at this stage. Box 5.3 provides two examples from our own research, in both cases projects which studied a difficult concept, namely, trust. Communicating across the research team is crucial and this involves additional exchanges compared with working with a colleague within your institution or working alone. The examples also show the multiple interpretations of trust and its application in the entrepreneurship literatures (see Welter, 2012).

BOX 5.3   STUDYING TRUST ACROSS CULTURES AND IN INTERCULTURAL TEAMS

In a cross-cultural study of trust and its role for entrepreneurship in Estonia, Germany, Italy, Russia and the UK, the teams applied the same guidelines, which were jointly developed in English and then translated into the respective languages. This posed additional challenges in researching trust across cultures; differences in research cultures in the various countries might have an impact on how questions are phrased and how the concept of trust is interpreted. Team members might interpret questions differently because of their individual experiences and background. Training sessions were conducted in all projects to ensure that interviewers involved similar understanding of the research topic and the guidelines (Welter and Alex, 2011).

In another example, a piece of research by Robert and colleagues involved examining the relationships between accountants and entrepreneurs, and specifically the role of 'trust' gained from the provision of compliance services to businesses as a vehicle for extending the range of services (Blackburn et al., 2010). For entrepreneurs, questions were developed on the nature of the trust they have with their accountants. From the accountants' perspective, questions were raised regarding the viability of developing non-compliance services for small firms. In attempting to answer what are ostensibly simple questions, it was important to undertake some conceptual ground-clearing, particularly around the notion of trust. This was important not only to help steer the research questions, but also to ensure that all members of the research team understood the underpinning parameters of the research, especially given fieldwork was being undertaken in both the UK and Australia. Hence, a questionnaire was developed which included the specific dimensions of trust to ensure that interviewers covered each element of the concept in their interviews. These underpinning dimensions were discussed in detail so that the team understood the precise routes to follow in the face-to-face interviews while at the same time allowing the interviews to flow.

Developing the Research Question

Having identified your research objectives and related concepts, the research question or series of questions will need to be developed. This will help set out the boundaries of the research topic through the specificity of the question, or questions. This stage will inevitably involve making decisions about the research project; what to include and exclude. In some instances, this process will involve discussions with the sponsor, or key stakeholders, to ensure that there is a shared understanding of the focus of the research. This underlines the case for a clear, unequivocal written statement of the objectives of the project. The actual process of undertaking this exercise is as important as the outcome of the objectives.

The research question(s) you develop may take various forms. These may constitute detailed research propositions, hypotheses or broader questions and statements, depending on your philosophical stance. Although we are not being prescriptive regarding the methods you adopt, we would advise all researchers to have a research question, or series of research questions in mind prior to thinking about fieldwork. While this position may lead to us being accused of being overly positivist and trespassing on the methodological freedom so desired by some qualitative researchers, this is not our intention. We would, however, defend the need to have some questions irrespective of your epistemological position and intended research method. These questions or propositions will help with your ongoing literature trawl, refine your objectives and, ultimately, influence your actual fieldwork questions and methods. This process of problematizing your research idea, its objectives and subsequent questions is quite demanding but very stimulating and, ultimately, rewarding. It is more often than not an iterative process. In entrepreneurship research especially, this process can be very creative and involves using your imagination in order to mark your research out from the too often run of the mill research projects found in the field.

BOX 5.4   SHE IS BLOND AND GOOD-LOOKING, AND SHE IS AN ENTREPRENEUR

Friederike has been studying the image of entrepreneurship and women entrepreneurs in Germany (Achtenhagen and Welter, 2003; 2007; 2011). Our interest arose from discussions we had asking ourselves how media depicted entrepreneurs. Both of us brought complementary interests to the project – one specializing in media and entrepreneurship, the other focusing on entrepreneurship and women. We designed the methodology and did the first ever comprehensive study of German daily newspapers, over a period of ten years. What started as a self-funded research project grew into a successful proposal to a German ministry, was of high interest to journalists and practitioners, and we were able to publish several articles – currently, we have submitted another proposal which, once accepted, will allow us to update our analysis and to study temporal changes.

PROJECT MANAGEMENT AND TEAM BUILDING

Although this chapter and this book focus on publishing, we think a few words on project management and team-building are appropriate, given that much of the research on entrepreneurship involves teams and is increasingly international (for example, Chetty et al., 2013). Both of us have written numerous project proposals over the years and have acquired experience in managing large-scale inter-cultural teams, which also helped us substantially with ideas generation and the dissemination of the results internationally. However, we also know the pitfalls and challenges that come with project management and the task to build and guide an effective team.

Academics often fall into the role of project management, rather than willingly or deliberately embrace it. It is also our experience that researchers tend to both underrate the demands of this role and under-estimate its significance in project completion. Of course, much depends on the scale of the project and the number of partners. However, you should not forget that before you can publish from research projects, they need to be implemented and managed, and this is about all those little things you never ever think about beforehand! Project management could involve:

- organizing, for example, project meetings, study visits, visa if you collaborate with international colleagues;
- liaising with funding bodies, including regular reporting;
- training and coaching new team members in just about everything, from financial rules to statistical package training (for example, STATA and SPSS), qualitative coding and interview techniques;
- building a team. Finding partners and 'maintaining' the team, involves foreseeing any potential problems, thinking through con-tingencies and, if the worst happens, settling disputes within the team.

The latter is a key task of scientific project management. As a project leader, it is important that you know yourself and be yourself with others in the team. This includes knowing your own strengths and weaknesses, both technically and in terms of managerial skills. You will need to be an effective communicator, and be able to understand the bigger picture of the project and demonstrate leadership. Being *au fait* with the resource requirements of the project is critical; this will require an understanding of the time requirements needed from those in the team and may involve a grasp of financial procedures where a budget is linked to a project.

Other issues include considerations of intellectual property matters and a dissemination strategy. A self-competency mapping exercise may prove useful here. This does not have to be unnecessarily formalized, but even the most basic assessment will help you in constructing your research team.

BOX 5.5   THE IMPORTANCE OF SOFT SKILLS

Friederike's research teams in the projects she led consisted of seven to 15 researchers, from at least four different countries, all with their own personalities, different backgrounds and experiences. Our collaboration has a number of success factors: we have, by now, a track record of successfully working together for more than a decade; we went through a trial-and-error process of team-building and also threw partners out of the team at one point; all of us learnt who to trust and how to communicate across cultures, how to work together, and – very important – we never forgot to have fun together.

Similarly, Robert tends to work on projects that involve teams of researchers; these may be based within a single research centre, or across a range of institutions and countries. His experience suggests that, although a project may be very well specified on paper, the implementation of the project is what matters if outcomes are to be successful; having a well-crafted proposal is not worth the paper it is written on if it is not effectively operationalized. For example, where possible, even on cross-border projects, Robert insists on holding a 'kick-off' meeting where clarity is reached in terms of the research objectives, the roles of those involved and any misunderstandings are thrashed out. While other forms of communications are important – telephone calls, emailing and document exchange – and can be performed easily and frequently, there is no substitute for meeting the research team in person, getting to know members, deciding who will do what and sharing any concerns. This, in itself, helps build trust among team members, especially if they have not worked together before, and enhances the chances of a successful research outcome. In some cases the problem may be a random event such as: a member of staff leaving the team, the promise of being able to access a particular group of entrepreneurs collapsing, or fieldwork problems because of a border closing. Having everybody on board means that when such challenges occur the team leader can readily explain what is happening and negotiate with specific members of the team to help think through constructive and imaginative practical solutions without compromising the timetable and outcomes of the research.

In other words, it is people who do research, and leading and pulling together a team, making sure that they all have an understanding of the goals and know the responsibilities of each member of the team, is critical to success. We have learned many lessons the hard way both in terms of managing a project team as well as dealing with sponsors and other stakeholders. Undertaking research involves risks and, often, pioneering research tends to be riskier because of the use of untried methods, or working in uncharted territory. Although you may strive to have contingency plans for all eventualities, there is no way that you can prevent unforeseen circumstances or mistakes. When these occur, it is better to be prepared to acknowledge them and find workable solutions among the team and sponsors. Also, set clear and simple rules for collaboration; 'maintain' your research team, which involves identifying who is responsible for every single (and in your eyes often simple) problem; identify who settles disputes within and among national teams. When liaising with the funding bodies, for example, it is best to not argue about a problem but rather to suggest flexible and sometimes unorthodox answers the funders could agree to.

In short, given that entrepreneurship research is increasingly global and involves teamwork, an appreciation of the dynamics of teamwork is important if the field is to develop. We cannot provide all the answers, nor offer a blueprint for how to construct a team. Neither can we suggest appropriate team structures. However, we have shown examples of the issues that can emerge and emphasize that both communication and having shared goals are critical in team approaches to research.

DATA COLLECTION, FIELDWORK AND ANALYTICAL APPROACHES

Entrepreneurship research is highly innovative and pluralist in its methodological approaches spanning mixed methods, qualitative (for example, Neergaard and Ulhoi, 2007; Perren and Ram, 2004) and quantitative methods (for example, Davidsson, 2008) as well as international case studies (for example, Chetty et al., 2013). It is the fieldwork stage that makes entrepreneurship research particularly distinctive from many other disciplines. However, whatever approach you adopt, it is critical that it is undertaken rigorously, is transparent and stands up to scrutiny by peers. The most important point in your fieldwork plan is that it is appropriate to the research objectives that you have set out to investigate. However, as editors of journals, all too often we find papers submitted that are technically sound but unimaginative or have drawn upon a database or used an analytical technique that is inappropriate.

With the absence of already existing data, the empirical investigation of entrepreneurship at the micro level often involves engaging with entrepreneurs. These are sometimes reluctant individuals and you as a researcher have to persuade them that your interest is actually of interest to them! This is more of an art form than a science as such. Although step-by-step approaches are useful, you will have to be flexible and adopt a 'can do' attitude without compromising the fundamental objectives of the research or introducing biases into the fieldwork responses. Overcoming the often low response rates in entrepreneurship research (Curran and Blackburn, 2001), and hence its validity, is an ongoing battle but one that we must continue if the credibility of the research is to be enhanced.

BOX 5.6   WHERE TO FIND THE ENTREPRENEURS?

In the earlier discussed example from Box 5.1, finding sufficient numbers of entrepreneurs who had 'exited' from their enterprise within the previous two years to allow analysis proved challenging. Initially, the bank was able to provide contact details but because of data protection laws, this involved a long process. Many entrepreneurs had also simply moved on and their contact details were, therefore, outdated. This led the researchers to rethink their recruitment strategies and expand the sources of potential participants. This included contacting all researchers who were already undertaking fieldwork for other projects and asking them to pass on details of any of their interviewees who had 'exited', as well as drawing upon a Dun and Bradstreet database.

Overall, 388 completed questionnaires were analysed, together with the results from 20 face-to-face interviews. The advantages of drawing upon a range of sources also brought benefits in terms of reducing the bias effects of a single source for a sampling frame.

Fieldwork is even more difficult in international and cross-cultural studies. For example, in emerging market economies, it is difficult to use secondary data because it simply does not exist, which introduces the need to generate external funding for fieldwork and data collection. Convenience, snowball and random sampling can be used and have dominated our early projects. However, this generated some difficulties when we started to publish from these projects, because reviewers were not happy with our 'haphazard sampling methods', as one reviewer once put it. We also discovered that not every survey technique worked everywhere. Finally, depending on the topic of the study, you may face additional difficulties with respondents who may be puzzled or question why you are interested in such an issue. This may be on the grounds of 'why is this important?' or, more suspiciously, 'is this person from the ministry or an undercover reporter?' Be prepared to be questioned when you are collecting data in the field, as entrepreneurs by their very nature are curious individuals who, quite rightly, can ask you some difficult questions.

BOX 5.7   RESEARCHING CROSS-BORDER INFORMAL ACTIVITIES

In a project where we researched the role of trust in cross-border entrepreneurship in Belarus, Moldova and the Ukraine, the sensitive nature of the trust topic posed a particular challenge, especially as the specific activities that were the focus of the interviews often occurred outside the law. Researchers had to work hard to establish relationships with potential interviewees. In practice, a variety of approaches were used: the researchers came from the respective country themselves, which allowed them to draw on a common cultural understanding and which created an initial level of trust with their interviewees. In the case of cross-border traders, researchers in Belarus, for example, observed respondents on the Polish side of the border in local markets, railway stations and in cross-border trains. As soon as they had identified potential cross-border traders, they would offer to help with the transport of goods (Welter et al., 2012). This was considered helpful by potential interviewees as border regulations stipulate upper limits for goods imported by individuals. Many traders circumvent these regulations by drawing on an elaborate system of transport workers. Interviewers were thus winning the goodwill of their respondents and facilitating a successful interview.

Having collected data, this then has to be analysed and used as evidence in your argument. This evidence needs to be set against your research objectives and specific questions or hypotheses.

BOX 5.8   READING AND INTERPRETING FIELDWORK DATA

Business growth, the processes underpinning growth and how to encourage growth continue to be a focus of study for researchers in the field (Wright and Stigliani, 2013). In a comparison of growth in SMEs in the USA and the UK, a number of practical challenges were encountered, but also some conceptual assumptions were brought into question (Blackburn et al., 2008). Finding a definition of high growth was relatively easy compared with applying this to fieldwork in the USA and the UK. Using change in turnover as the measure of business growth, firms achieving real turnover growth of 60 per cent over the previous three years were initially selected for interview. However, the fieldwork research was problematic in that it started at the beginning of a major recession – a recession that started in the USA before the UK. In addition, although businesses may have met the 'fast growth' criteria from one source (the interviewee or company records), cross-checking this in interviews was sometimes problematic. However, the project demonstrated that even in adverse fieldwork conditions, through teamwork and effective communication, creative solutions can emerge and high-quality, influential outputs can be produced. The fieldwork also demonstrated the importance of which year, or even which point in the year, you choose as the starting point; one year either way can include or exclude the business from the study. Although any definition of fast growth can be criticized, one of the key points to emerge from this research was indeed the fragility of growth and that it is episodic rather than occurs in a linear fashion (for example, Brush et al., 2009).

We will not dwell on the actual variety of techniques of analysis available to researchers in entrepreneurship in this chapter but focus, instead, on the approaches to publication that you have at your disposal.

DISSEMINATION, PUBLICATION STRATEGY AND AUDIENCE ENGAGEMENT

Although we put dissemination at the end of our chapter, this is the most important activity for academics. Having a ground-breaking piece of research is not worth the effort if you are unable to disseminate your results and let the world know what you have found.

One of the lessons we take from our own projects is the difficulty in publishing once the project is finished. Where external project funders are involved, you may need to clarify any intellectual property issues. In the case of contract research, you often need to obtain permission from the funding agency and we would recommend that you seek this early on in the project-scoping phase. In the case of international projects, only some of the team members might be interested in following up the project and continuing to work together on publications, which normally take their time to develop.

Ideally when you start setting up the project you should write out a dissemination plan, including a timetable that goes beyond the project life. This should cover: the outlets through which to publish and/or present, which audiences are interested, who takes the lead on which publication and, ideally, a time frame. For example, in Friederike's projects we had agreed that national teams were responsible for publishing in national outlets and they were the lead authors for those articles, while the project leader was the main person responsible for international publications. Before you start to write up your results you should identify your audience (this may have been considered at the ideas formulation stage, but other interesting findings may have emerged) and consider why your findings are of interest to them. Put another way, the world is awash with readings on entrepreneurship and you need to realize that you are competing for airtime.

So how do you progress from a project report (we use this example because we are both familiar with the difficulties of publishing from project reports) to a journal publication? Projects report are generally policy or practitioner oriented, and often less theory-driven than is warranted in journal publications. In that regard, you have to start from scratch and rewrite for an academic audience. It is particularly important to identify the academic contribution in a journal article, while a project report has to end with practical and/or policy implications. Such policy recommendations are not always the best implications to merely transfer to your journal articles and they do not necessarily reflect the academic contribution your research could make. Conversely, there has been a recent tendency for academics to focus dissemination on scholarly publications as a means to secure career progression. Depending on your project, it might be equally important that you know how to write for a practitioner-oriented audience or how to 'sell' your results to policy-makers. After all, achieving impact is important and may help you secure recognition among the wider world of academia. This is especially the case with an applied field such as entrepreneurship.

CONCLUSIONS

In this chapter, we have discussed the research journey from idea generation to publication, or at least the first steps on the sometimes long way towards publication. For some of you, this may seem a daunting journey, especially having read the many risks, challenges and pitfalls that we have outlined. No entrepreneurship research journey is typical and each reader will no doubt be able to reflect on their own experiences. However, we also hope that we have been able to show you the benefits of doing research, of continuously generating new ideas and writing new project proposals, and of contributing to theory as well as influencing practitioners and policy-makers. This is fun! And we hope that you will enjoy the research journey as much as both of us.

REFERENCES

Achtenhagen, L. and Welter, F. (2003), 'Female entrepreneurship in Germany: context, development and its reflection in German media', in J.E. Butler (ed.),

New Perspectives on Women Entrepreneurs, Greenwich, CT: Information Age Publishing, pp. 71–100.

Achtenhagen, L. and Welter, F. (2007), 'Media Discourse in entrepreneurship research', in H. Neergard and J.P. Ulhoi (eds), *Handbook of Qualitative Methods in Entrepreneurship Research*, Cheltenham, UK and Northampton, MA, USA: Elgar, pp. 193–215.

Achtenhagen, L. and Welter, F. (2011), '"Surfing on the ironing board" – the representation of women's entrepreneurship in German newspapers', *Entrepreneurship & Regional Development*, **23** (1), 763–86.

Blackburn, R., P. Carey and G.A. Tanewski (2010), 'Business advice to SMEs: professional competence, trust and ethics', Association of Chartered Certified Accountants (ACCA) Research Report no. 119, ACCA, London.

Blackburn, R.A., J. Kitching, M. Hart, C. Brush and D. Ceru (2008), 'Growth challenges for small and medium-sized enterprises: a UK–US comparative study', Report for HM Treasury and BERR, URN 09/63.

Booth, W.C., G.C. Colomb and J.M. Williams (2008) *The Craft of Research*, 3rd edn, Chicago, IL: University of Chicago Press.

Brush, C.G., D.J. Ceru and R. Blackburn (2009), 'Pathways to entrepreneurial growth: the influence of management, marketing, and money', *Business Horizons*, **52** (5), 481–91.

Bryman, A. and E. Bell (2011), *Business Research Methods*, 3rd edn, Oxford: Oxford University Press.

Chetty, S.K., J. Partanen, E.S. Rasmussen and P. Servais (2013), 'Contextualising case studies in entrepreneurship: a tandem approach to conducting a longitudinal cross-country case study', *International Small Business Journal*, Online-first.

Curran, J. and R.A. Blackburn, (2001), *Researching The Small Enterprise*, London: Sage.

Davidsson, P. (2008), *The Entrepreneurship Research Challenge*, New York: Springer.

Easterby-Smith, M., R. Thorpe and P.R. Jackson (2008), *Management Research*, 3rd edn, London: Sage.

Harzing, A.-W. (2011), *The Publish or Perish Book: Your Guide to Effective and Responsible Citation Analysis*, Melbourne: Tarma Software Research.

Hills, P. (ed.) (1999), *Publish or Perish*, Dereham: Peter Francis.

Katz, J.A. (2003), 'The chronology and intellectual trajectory of American entrepreneurship education: 1876–1999', *Journal of business Venturing*, **18** (2), 283–300.

Neergaard, H. and J.P. Ulhoi (2007), *Handbook of Qualitative Research Methods in Entrepreneurship*, Cheltenham, UK and Northampton, MA, USA: Edward Elgar.

Perren, L. and M. Ram (2004), 'Case-study method in small business and entrepreneurial research mapping boundaries and perspectives', *International Small Business Journal*, **22** (1), 83–101.

Short, J.C., D.J. Ketchen Jr, J.G. Combs and R.D. Ireland (2010), 'Research methods in entrepreneurship: opportunities and challenges', *Organizational Research Methods*, **13** (1), 6–15.

Smallbone, D. and F. Welter (2001a), 'The distinctiveness of entrepreneurship in transition economies', *Small Business Economics*, **16** (4), 249–62.

Smallbone, D. and F. Welter (2001b), 'The role of government in SME development in transition economies', *International Small Business Journal*, **19** (4), 63–77.

Smallbone, D. and F. Welter (2009), *Entrepreneurship and small Business Development in Post-Socialist Economies*, London: Routledge.

Smallbone, D., F. Welter and X. Jianzhong (2011), 'From Mao to market – entrepreneurs as institutional change agents in China', paper presented at the 56th Annual ICSB World Conference, Stockholm, 15–18 June.

Stokes, D. and R.A. Blackburn (2001) 'Opening up business closures: a study of businesses that close and owners' exit routes : a research report for HSBC', Kingston Business School, Kingston University.

Stokes, D. and R.A. Blackburn (2002), 'Learning the hard way: the lessons of owner-managers who have closed their businesses', *Journal of Small Business and Enterprise Development*, **9** (3), 17–27.

Welter, F. (2011), 'Contextualizing entrepreneurship – conceptual challenges and ways forward', *Entrepreneurship Theory and Practice*, **35** (1), 165–84.

Welter, F. (2012), 'All you need is trust? A critical review of the trust and entrepreneurship literature', *International Small Business Journal*, **30** (3), 193–212.

Welter, F. and N. Alex (2011), 'Researching trust in different cultures', in F. Lyon, G. Möllering and M. Saunders (Eds), *Handbook of Research Methods on Trust*, Cheltenham, UK and Northampton, MA, USA: Edward Elgar, pp. 50–60.

Welter, F. and D. Smallbone (2003), 'Entrepreneurship and enterprise strategies in transition economies: an institutional perspective', in D. Kirby and A. Watson (eds), *Small Firms and Economic Development in Developed and Transition Economies: A Reader*, Aldershot: Ashgate, pp. 95–114.

Welter, F. and D. Smallbone (2009), 'The emergence of entrepreneurial potential in transition environments: a challenge for entrepreneurship theory or a developmental perspective?', in D. Smallbone, H. Landström and D. Jones-Evans (eds), *Entrepreneurship and Growth in Local, Regional and National Economies: Frontiers in European Entrepreneurship Research*, Cheltenham, UK and Northampton, MA, USA: Edward Elgar pp. 339–53.

Welter, F. and D. Smallbone (2011), 'Institutional perspectives on entrepreneurial behavior in challenging environments', *Journal of Small Business Management*, **49** (1), 107–25.

Wright, M. and I. Stigliani (2013), 'Entrepreneurship and growth', *International Small Business Journal*, **31** (1), 3–22.

Welter, F., D. Smallbone, A. Slonimski, O. Linchevskaya, A. Pobol and M. Slonimska (2012), 'Enterprising Families in a Hostile Environment for Entrepreneurship', JIBS Working Paper Series No. 2012-1, Jönköping: Jönköping International Business School.

Xheneti, M. and R. Blackburn (2011), 'Small business and entrepreneurship (SBE): an analysis of publications and implications for the development of the field', in B. Lee and C. Cassell (eds), *Challenges and Controversies in Management Research*. Abingdon: Routledge.

Zahra, S.A. (2007), 'Contextualizing theory building in entrepreneurship research', *Journal of Business Venturing*, **22** (3), 443–52.
Zahra, S.A. and M. Wright (2011), 'Entrepreneurship's next act', *The Academy of Management Perspectives*, **25** (4), 67–83.

6. Doing a research literature review

Hermann Frank and Isabella Hatak

INTRODUCTION

The first thing researchers must do if they want to publish quality academic research is to conduct a literature review. Regardless of whether this task is approached as a first-time or experienced researcher, both are doing it for the same reason: to increase their awareness and understanding of current work and perspectives in the research field so that they can position their own research clearly on the academic map of knowledge creation, either by identifying research gaps or by problematizing the state of the art as an alternative to the prevailing stopgap strategy (Alvesson and Sandberg, 2011). Therefore, literature reviews as ways of creating knowledge maps which are not only differentiated at a descriptive level but also at an evaluative level are also necessary for identifying a research topic and for formulating an interesting research question that builds on established knowledge.

However, the importance of literature reviews is not matched by a common understanding of what a literature review is. This becomes apparent by the fact that many reviews are only thinly disguised annotated bibliographies, thus offering severe problems: as the literature review constitutes a key element of all parts of a research project report (for example, introduction, discussion and conclusion), or in the case of a pure literature review even represents the research project, its quality determines the value of the whole research activity. Quality in reviewing literature means an appropriate balance between depth and breadth, rigour and consistency, clarity and brevity, and effective analysis and synthesis (Hart, 2009).

However, literature reviews can not only vary in quality, but also in terms of their aims, the extent of work (the complexity of the research problem which the review attempts to address) and their structure. Moreover, they vary in whether they aggregate or configure information, the types of knowledge considered and the heterogeneity and homogeneity of the studies included (Gough et al., 2012). Nevertheless, literature reviews also have common principles and similar processes. As they, like any form of research, can be undertaken well and badly, literature reviewers need to be aware of the many practical and methodological challenges in order to tackle reviewing, which has many facets, successfully. In fact, it requires thoughtful organization and planning from the beginning and, thus, a deep understanding of the review-related procedures and skills.

This chapter gives an overview of types of literature review and of the process of reviewing literature. Moreover, it gives hints for doing successful literature reviews in research and illustrates the benefits associated with research literature reviews. The first section defines what is meant by a research literature review and differentiates between contexts, that is, literature reviews as part of conceptual/empirical papers and pure literature reviews. The second section examines types of research literature reviews, and differentiates between narrative literature reviews and meta-analyses. In the third part, details are provided on the specific steps to take in preparing and writing a research literature review and on ways to strengthen the research literature review. The fourth part outlines the significance and purpose of literature reviews in research. The final section provides a brief conclusion.

DEFINING AND CONTEXTUALIZING THE RESEARCH LITERATURE REVIEW

Definitions

Reviewing literature differs significantly from the review of a book on a topic. Whereas the review of a book might aim at making the public aware of the novel's content and contributing to contemporary literature debate, a research literature review is seen as a specific method because it is systematic by using explicit, rigorous and accountable methods and should lead to reproducible results (for example, Fink, 2010; Gough et al., 2012; Hart, 2009). If it is done properly, a research literature review can provide an academically enriching experience.

It is therefore helpful to break the complex phenomenon 'research literature review' down into two parts: first, the finished product of the research literature review, that is, literature reviews can be seen as an end in themselves, and, second, the process that is involved in conducting a review of the literature: in the course of defining research literature reviews, LePine and King (2010, p. 506) put emphasis on the first part: research literature reviews are manuscripts that provide extensive reviews of the existing theoretical and empirical literature relevant to a given topic or content area and where the intended contribution of the manuscript is grounded primarily against the backdrop of this review material. The purpose of these comments is to discuss these types of manuscripts and to offer guidance for developing their potential so that the promise for novel theoretical insight and the implications for advancing theoretical understanding become clearer.

Fink's (2010, p. 3) definition, on the other hand, focuses on the process involved in conducting a review of the literature:

A research literature review is a systematic, explicit, and reproducible method for identifying, evaluating, and synthesizing the existing body of completed and recorded work produced by researchers, scholars, and practitioners.

Also Hart (2009, p. 13) sees the research literature review, understood as a

selection of available documents (both published and unpublished) on the topic, which contain information, ideas, data and evidence written from a particular standpoint to fulfil certain aims or express certain views on the nature of the topic and how it is to be investigated, and the effective evaluation of these documents in relation to the research being proposed

as an essential part of the research process. From these definitions, it can be deduced that the research literature review is a method-guided replicable process leading to specific results.

Contexts

The process of reviewing literature and the presentation of its results depend on the context. Basically, we can differentiate between two contexts: literature reviews as part of conceptual papers/empirical papers and pure literature reviews as part of review-centric papers (see Figure 6.1).

In the case of a literature review as part of a conceptual/empirical paper, the literature review is embedded in a more comprehensive context, for example to justify a certain research topic, to fill a research gap, to apply a new research method or to stipulate the development of a new theory. Here, reviews of literature

are normally positioned at the start of an article and so not only are important in themselves but also are influential in setting expectations about what is to come. A literature review that is creative, thoughtful, and thorough leads to positive first impressions, and these are likely to influence how the remainder of the article is perceived. Conversely, a weak literature review sets initial

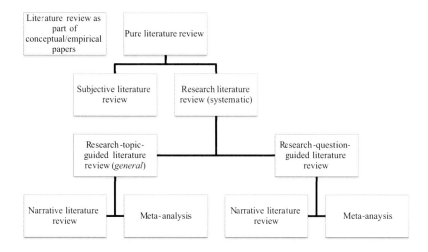

Figure 6.1   Systematizing literature reviews

expectations negatively, reducing the persuasiveness of later arguments and increasing scepticism of the author's research skills. (Reuber, 2010, p. 105)

In the second case, a pure literature review is carried out that is addressing the current state of knowledge regarding a specific research topic (for example, opportunity recognition) or research question and proposing options for further research.

But, aside from the strategy underlying the literature review process, what are the differences between a conceptual/empirical paper, which also includes a literature review, but whose function rather is the promoting of the paper's objectives, and thus arousing interest which substantiates the meaningfulness of the research, and a pure literature review; in other words, what are the distinctive aspects of pure literature reviews?

According to Baumeister and Leary (1997), pure literature reviews allow for addressing broader research questions than a single empirical study, which has to specialize on a niche in order to increase the likelihood of getting published. In essence, pure literature reviews can address questions of a broader scope by focusing on patterns and connections among a variety of empirical findings.

Another point is *post hoc* theorizing. Authors of empirical studies are often pressured by journal reviewers to limit the claims of their study to avoid speculation, thus reflecting the limitations of single data sets. In view of the call for valid generalizations, the role of pure literature reviews is clearly recognizable: as journals are riddled with under-interpreted results, pure literature reviews are needed for bridging the interpretation gap because they can integrate several dozen empirical findings.

Third, pure literature reviews are not limited to a priori hypotheses. We were all taught the importance of delineating hypotheses in advance, that is, prior to collecting data, because formulating assumptions on the basis of data analysis, that is, after data collection, can lead to random results. In the case of pure literature reviews, such concerns are not relevant as the problem of capitalizing on chance is much lower given the number of studies analysed. However, problems could arise if a large number of studies would have drawn wrong conclusions. Nevertheless, in the case of pure literature reviews, hypotheses can be formulated following the reviewing of literature – in fact, it is required that literature reviews theorize on the basis of a variety of studies, thus, implying that pure literature reviews can go the extra mile regarding the level of abstraction compared with single empirical studies.

Another point relates to the conclusions; it is hard to publish inconclusive results, therefore authors try to make their contributions as strong as possible. However, this is not the case for pure literature reviews. In fact, literature reviewers can present such inconclusive results, while at the same time increasing the probability of getting published. Basically, a pure literature review can generate three types of conclusions (Baumeister and Leary, 1997, p. 315):

- Convergence – the field consists of many studies with converging evidence with the effect that the current state of knowledge is supported.
- Best guess – this is the case when some studies have flaws, but evidence points to the same conclusions.
- Contradictory findings – single studies show consistent results, but there are contradictory findings.

Finally, pure literature reviews involve methodological diversity which is highly desirable as there is no single perfect method. Convergence of evidence across multiple research methods entails that the given hypothesis is the most parsimonious conclusion. A hypothesis confirmed by 50 studies that all apply the same method may be shakier and simply wrong compared with a hypothesis supported by five studies with five different methods. In the majority of cases, single empirical studies adopt a single-method-approach (Baumeister and Leary, 1997, p. 316).

Therefore, the value of pure literature reviews depends on its approach. In contrast to research literature reviews, where all sources are systematically examined and what has been done is described and justified, subjective reviews tend to be idiosyncratic as, in the course of producing them, neither the selection of articles is justified nor is there differentiation between good and poor studies. Moreover, as the results of subjective literature reviews are often based on partial analysis of the available literature, their findings may be inaccurate or even false (Fink, 2010, p. 15).

With regard to research literature reviews we can distinguish between two types: research-topic-guided/general literature reviews and research-question-guided literature reviews (for example, Gough et al., 2012; Saunders et al., 2009). A general literature review provides an overview of a specific research topic in rather general terms without guidance of a research question. Its application depends on the dynamics of the research field. A research-question-guided literature review approaches research with a research question and is independent of methodical and theoretical changes in research areas. Both types can be further divided into narrative reviews and meta-analyses, which are regarded as providing high-quality evidence (Tranfield et al., 2003).

DIFFERENTIATING BETWEEN NARRATIVE LITERATURE REVIEWS AND META-ANALYSES

Narrative Literature Reviews

Narrative literature reviews are appropriate for describing the history or development of a problem and its solution (see Figure 6.2). If a research field is characterized by heterogeneous studies in terms of theory, methods, samples, and so on, narrative literature reviews are hugely useful. They can pursue the following objectives (Baumeister and Leary, 1997, p. 312):

- A highly ambitious goal of a narrative literature review is theory development. In such a paper, the researchers' intention is to propose a novel conceptualization or theory regarding a certain phenomenon. In essence, the literature review provides a context for describing, elaborating and evaluating a new theory, or indeed the theory may be found by integrating the reviewed material.
- Compared to theory development, theory evaluation is a slightly less ambitious but more common goal of narrative literature

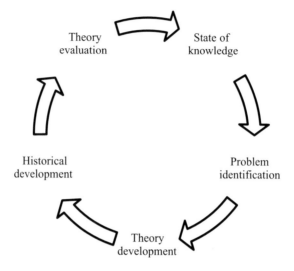

Figure 6.2   Narrative literature reviews

reviews. Here, the researcher reviews the literature relevant to the validity of an existing theory (or two or more competing theories) instead of offering a new theoretical perspective. In this regard, the published literature provides a database from which the researcher can draw conclusions about the value of existing conceptualizations. Top journals most commonly publish reviews that aim at constructing theories, but every now and then also reviews that evaluate theories are published. In order to be successful, researchers aspiring to write such reviews must therefore realize that they cannot just compile and describe the existing literature but rather have to develop and test theory, or as Baumeister and Leary (1997, p. 312) put it: 'In important respects, such an article resembles a report of a laboratory experiment: It describes empirical evidence that evaluates a theoretical hypothesis. Each piece of evidence covered in the manuscript draws its value from how it helps build or evaluate the overarching theory.'

- A third goal of narrative review is to survey the existing literature on a particular topic. Such reviews can provide useful overviews and integrations of a research area, and therefore can be valuable for grant proposals or teaching. However, as they are not intended to offer novel ideas, new interpretations or sweeping conclusions, thus contributing minimally to theory, the leading journals are generally reluctant to publish manuscripts of this kind. This point is illustrated by Academy of Management Review (AMR) editor Kilduff's conduct (2007, p. 700), who desk-rejects papers that 'simply review the existing literature, sometimes summarizing the literature in propositions but failing to offer distinctive contributions to theory beyond what has already been written by others'.

- A fourth goal of a narrative literature review is problem identification, which is about revealing problems, weaknesses, contradictions or controversies in a particular research area. The researcher may suggest solutions to the problems identified, but is more concerned with informing the field that some difficulties exist. Therefore, such reviews typically raise more questions than they answer, identifying research gaps and leaving it to future researchers to close them. Still, as identifying problems in the existing literature can serve a valuable scientific function, such reviews appear in journals as short articles or critiques rather than as full-length articles.

- Finally, a less common goal of a narrative review is to provide a historical account of the development of theory and research on a particular topic. Although such reviews, which are typically organized chronologically, aim primarily at tracing the history of an idea or a theory, they typically include comments on the impact and shortcomings of contributions to the research field.

Against this backdrop, we can conclude that the nature of a review, which primarily provides a systematic analysis and synthesis and therefore does not pursue the goal of theory development, differs from literature reviews presenting new theories. Regarding narrative reviews with the primary goal of theory development, there are three types of contribution that are encouraged by top journals (LePine and King, 2010):

- Clarify/challenge existing theory: articles that make this type of contribution are often grounded in literature reviews that reveal significant inconsistencies in a theory. As these reviews may also illuminate assumptions that may not be acknowledged and cause confusion in the way a concept is interpreted and applied, they have the potential to motivate researchers to engage with the topic in new ways. To be precise, the review should have a high probability of launching new ways of thinking in an existing theoretical conversation. An example of this type of contribution is the organizational diversity concept, which was seen as a unitary concept, but on the basis of Harrison and Klein's (2007) literature review is now understood as being composed of three distinct types, thus allowing for the gaining of a better appreciation of the mixed findings from the previous research and for making meaningful advances in the theoretical understanding of diversity and related phenomena.

- Initiate search for new theories: a second type of contribution encouraged by top journals is reviews that provide evidence that existing theories are significantly deficient in their ability to explain a particular phenomenon and that a fundamental shift in thinking is needed. In essence, if a researcher is well informed about a powerful theory which has not yet been applied to a certain phenomenon, the opportunity to reconceptualize this phenomenon arises. As an example, Sitkin and Pablo (1992) argued that contradictions in research predicting risky behaviour could be attributed to the practice of considering the direct effect of a variety of idiosyncratic individual, organizational and problem-focused factors, and that these contradictions could be resolved by positioning risk perceptions and propensity as mechanisms that explain why these factors influence risky behaviour. This reconceptualization provided the basis for research's focus on understanding these more direct determinants of risky behaviour and, as a result, a much more cohesive understanding of this important behaviour has evolved.

- Synthesize recent advances and ideas into fresh new theory: literature reviews that make this type of contribution often integrate different theories or theoretical perspectives to provide a theoretical structure that was not there before. This often occurs through the positioning of a central construct within a constellation of antecedents and outcomes in ways that not only generate communication among researchers but also encourage research activities aimed at resolving the theoretical puzzles and empirical questions raised by the literature review. An example is trust research, where Mayer et al. (1995) used commonalities as to the diverse literature on trust to derive a definition for the concept and to distinguish it from closely related concepts which they subsequently positioned as antecedents, moderators and consequences of trust in their theoretical model.

Finally, we can conclude that reviews that simply summarize the existing literature without generating distinctive theoretical insights are outside the scope of top journals' mission and, as a consequence, they will not likely be reviewed favourably and may even be desk-rejected. However, if theory development is not the goal of a narrative literature review, its value can be significantly increased by pursuing more than one objective, thereby making it publishable in a top journal.

An excellent example of a multi-goal and multifaceted narrative literature review is the article by Jones et al. (2011) which provides a comprehensive overview of two decades of international entrepreneurship research. Based on an inductive approach (as against a deductively determined framework of analysis) different thematic fields emanating from the premise that international entrepreneurship is a heterogeneous field of research were categorized. Beginning with 323 selected articles (books, book chapters, conference papers and so on were excluded) the authors identified 51 first-order themes. Themes were defined as the basic concepts that reveal the subject matter of each article analysed. These themes were then refined, classified and synthesized to develop an ontological structure of international entrepreneurship research. The 51 first-order themes (for example, traditional internationalization) were grouped based on their similarity to second-order (for example, patterns and processes) and third-order themes (thematic areas; for example, internationalization). This finally led to three types of international entrepreneurship research ('entrepreneurial internationalization', 'international comparisons of entrepreneurship' and 'comparative entrepreneurial internationalization'). The findings were visualized in the form of a thematic map. In addition, this literature review incorporated a historical reconstruction of the development of international entrepreneurship research.

Jones et al. (2011) acted on the assumption that young domains (for example, international entrepreneurship research) can benefit significantly if there is a common awareness of the issues and nature of the phenomena researched and of inconsistencies as well as of knowledge structures inherent in extant research. Such awareness can be fundamental to the development of theories within a research domain and even for its paradigmatic unity. Therefore, the study offers a rich set of issues identified (for example, that firm size and age may not be of primary relevance for international entrepreneurship research) and a significant number of concrete potential areas for future research (for example, most international entrepreneurship research assumes that there are relevant differences between international new ventures and domestic new ventures, though this assumption could be challenged). Furthermore, this 'inventory review' rests upon on a comprehensively documented and traceable methodology with regard to literature search and literature selection. Decisions on search and exclusion criteria are based on definitions found in international entrepreneurship literature. Decisions concerning classification and grouping of articles are based on the agreement of the researchers, ensuring validity.

The focus on the reconstruction of the thematic landscape of international entrepreneurship research, its historical development during the two decades analysed, the disclosure of issues and fields of future research as well as the sophisticated methodological approach led to an exemplary piece of research published in a top entrepreneurship journal, although theory development was not its major goal. In sum, if the narrative literature review resembles a method-guided replicable process leading to specific results it can be published in a top field journal (for example, *Entrepreneurship Theory and Practice, Journal of Business Venturing* or *Journal of Small Business Management*) – even if its goal is not theory development. However, in that case its value has to be significantly increased by pursuing more than one objective.

Meta-analyses

As well as a narrative literature review, a meta-analysis is an important and valuable form of literature reviews. It can be defined as an analysis of analyses; in other words, it is a statistical analysis of a large collection of results of the analysis from individual studies for the purpose of integrating the findings. A meta-analysis is therefore useful if there are many studies available which test the same set of hypotheses (Fink, 2010).

By analysing a large collection of individual studies, a meta-analysis can come to the following conclusions/suggestions: if the outcome of a meta-analysis is that the results of the reviewed studies testing the same hypotheses are heterogeneous, then a search for moderators can be suggested by the literature reviewer. Moreover, it can be established from meta-analyses that a relationship is strong, but often the mediation processes are still unknown. Finally, a meta-analysis may show that some relationships are more important than others, thus implying that theories have to cope with this information and incorporate the size of relationship into their theories (Frese et al., 2012). A best-practice example is Rauch et al.'s (2009) meta-analysis exploring the magnitude of the entrepreneurial orientation (EO)-performance relationship and assessing potential moderators affecting this relationship. Analyses of 53 samples from 51 studies with an N of 14 259 companies indicated that the correlation of EO with performance is moderately large ($r = .242$) and that this relationship is robust to different operationalizations of key constructs as well as cultural contexts. Internal and environmental moderators were identified, and results suggest that additional moderators should be assessed. Another best-practice example is Unger et al.'s (2011) study, which meta-analytically integrates results from three decades of human capital research in entrepreneurship. Based on 70 independent samples (N = 24 733), the authors found a significant but small relationship between human capital and success (r_c = .098) indicating that future research should pursue moderator approaches to study the effects of human capital on entrepreneurial success.

However, meta-analyses are confronted with a 'garbage-in-garbage-out-problem'; as studies with varying quality levels are part of the meta-analysis, its results may lack validity. Further problems can arise from the differences in operationalizing variables. Therefore, operationalizations should be at least homogeneous for the dependent variable – otherwise, a meta-analysis does not make sense (Rosenthal, 1995; Rosenthal and DiMatteo, 2001).

Summing up, both narrative literature reviews and meta-analyses are systematic and reproducible methods as they rely on explicit search strategies, unambiguous criteria for selecting high-quality studies and a standardized review process. However, they differ in the dealing with findings and conclusions of each study included in the research literature review. Whereas meta-analyses apply statistical techniques for combining study results, narrative reviews rely on experience and evidence in their interpretations (Fink, 2010, p. 233).

CREATING THE RESEARCH LITERATURE REVIEW

The Research Literature Review Process

So, how can you produce a systematic, explicit, comprehensive and reproducible research literature review? First, you need to identify your research interest in terms of a specific research topic or an interesting research question (problem formulation stage) and decide on the best sources and search terms (literature search stage). Next, you must evaluate the information's quality (data evaluation stage), analyse the research included in your literature review (data analysis stage), and interpret and synthesize the results (interpretation and synthesis stage). To be more precise, writing a research literature review is developmental, with each of its steps (see Figure 6.3) leading to the next (Cooper, 1998).

The following is a brief explanation of the illustrated steps in the course of doing a research literature review (Fink, 2010, p. 5): first, the reviewer has to select a specific topic or a research question, which has to be precisely stated, as it guides the review. There are reviews which cover

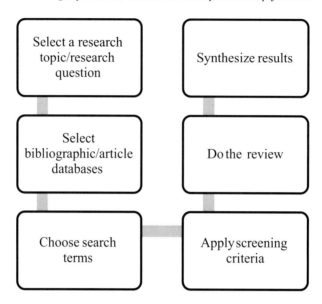

Figure 6.3   Steps

several hundred articles, and others which examine only two or three dozen articles, depending on the chosen topic or on how narrow or broad the research question is formulated and therefore on the chosen review type (general versus research-question guided literature review), respectively. For example, if the goal of a narrative literature review is theory development, then the focus is not merely on the literature review, but rather the theory development occupies centre stage so that including a smaller number of papers in the review is acceptable. If the research area under review is immature and only few publications are available, then the literature review should be heading for theory development. On the other hand, the journal to which the reviewer wants to submit the research literature review determines the amount of articles to be reviewed. Some journals that specialize in literature reviews require drawing on 100 publications as a minimum within the elaboration of research topics or research questions.

Second, the reviewer has to select bibliographic or article databases, websites and other sources. In this regard, bibliographic databases are of high importance for the review as they contain full reports of original studies that can provide data to map the research topic or answer the research question. In many cases, only peer-reviewed journal articles are considered for research literature reviews. Therefore, we can recommend EBSCO and ABI/Inform as examples of databases providing relevant articles in entrepreneurship research. In addition, we highly recommend conducting manual searches of journals that publish research on entrepreneurship: *Academy of Management Journal*, *Journal of Applied Psychology*, *Journal of Business Venturing*, *Entrepreneurship Theory and Practice*, *Journal of Small Business Management*, *Small Business Economics* and *Strategic Management Journal*. Moreover, with regard to Rauch et al.'s (2009) meta-analysis, the review can be strengthened by an additional review of proceedings of conferences covering entrepreneurship topics, such as Academy of Management (AoM), Babson College-Kaufman Foundation Entrepreneurship Research Conference, RENT Research in Entrepreneurship and Small Business of the European Institute for Advanced Studies in Management, International Family Enterprise Research Academy (IFERA) and International Council of Small Business (ICSB). Finally, referring to Rauch and Frese's (2007) meta-analysis, it is useful to contact several research groups that are active in the research area examined, and ask them for relevant data and unpublished papers. Such a strategy allows for an analysis of both published and unpublished data, which is an important desideratum of meta-analyses (Hunter and Schmidt, 2004).

Third, the reviewer needs to choose search terms which are the words and phrases used to get appropriate articles. They have to be based on the words and phrases that frame the research topic or the research question, respectively. In fact, this is a trial and error process, but in order to choose appropriate search terms it is helpful to have an a priori overview of the topic. For example, within their meta-analysis of the relationship between entrepreneurial orientation and business performance, Rauch et al. (2009) used the search terms 'entrepreneurial behaviour', 'strategic orientation', 'strategic posture' and 'entrepreneurial orientation', which is consistent with the labelling of the entrepreneurial orientation construct found in previous literature reviews, for locating relevant studies in databases (namely, PsycInfo; EconLit; Social Science Citation Index; ABI/Inform).

The fourth step is about applying practical and methodological screening criteria. Preliminary literature searches always yield many articles, but not all of them are relevant. Practical screening criteria such as language in which the article is printed, the setting of a study and its funding sources, and methodological screening criteria such as the scientific quality of an article need to be applied to include relevant articles and exclude irrelevant articles from the review. In order to sharpen the focus on high-quality research, several researchers should be involved in this step. For example, Rauch et al. (2009) included only those articles in their meta-analysis that reported sample sizes, measurement procedures and zero-order correlations or equivalent calculations. Their initial screening left them with 134 publications potentially relevant for the scope of their meta-analysis. As some of the articles could not be located or used entrepreneurial orientation to predict individual-level performance or were used for multiple publications, the number was then further reduced to 51 studies that reported in all 53 independent samples with a total of 14 259 cases for their meta-analysis. Such an extensive reduction in studies in the course of doing a meta-analysis is not uncommon. For example, Unger et al. (2011) identified 444 empirical studies dealing with the relationship between human capital and entrepreneurial success, out of which 70 could be included in a meta-analysis.

Fifth, the researcher has to do the review. The creation of a reliable and valid research literature review requires the usage of a standardized form for abstracting data from articles, the training of supporting reviewers, the monitoring of quality of the review and the pilot testing of the review process.

Finally, the results of the research literature review need to be synthesized. In the course of a narrative literature review, interpretations of the review's findings are made on the basis of the reviewer's experience and the quality and content of the reviewed literature. Statistical methods are used within a meta-analysis in order to combine the results of two or more studies (for meta-analytic procedures, see Hunter and Schmidt, 2004).

In order to ensure validity regarding these steps, it makes sense to start the literature searches with broad conceptual definitions associated with their research topic. For example, if the research topic is 'conflicts in organizations', we recommend adopting a more general approach towards the topic 'interpersonal conflicts'. With regard to the literature search stage, the reviewers should apply a broad and comprehensive search strategy which also includes informal contacts with researchers of the field (for example, for generating new search terms, getting access to journal articles not yet published). Regarding the data evaluation, it is important to make the decision for inclusion or exclusion of studies on the basis of a priori, conceptual, methodical and methodological evaluations – not on the basis of the studies' results. In the context of categorizing the methods applied in the reviewed studies, we recommend applying as many design characteristics as possible and linking them with the studies' results. As to data analysis, the analysis of studies adopting different methods, which yield the same results, is preferred in terms of validity compared with studies employing the same method. In order to increase the validity of the conclusions it makes sense to check whether the adoption of two different data analysis strategies leads to the same result, thus signalling validity. In the course of synthesizing research, reviewers should provide details on their synthesizing procedures (Cooper, 1998).

Active Reading

In order to successfully complete the steps described above, researchers should be willing and able to read ACTIVEly (for example, Hart, 2009, pp. 54, 94; Saunders et al., 2009, p. 62):

- **A**sk questions before, during and after reading (Is this text relevant for answering the research question of the review? How does the message of the paper fit to the review structure? Is the argumentation convincing? Is the text of major or minor importance for the review?)
- **C**onnect literature to other pieces of literature (As they read, active readers make note of connections they are able to make throughout the literature. They put down their highlighter and make marginal notes or comments instead.)
- **T**rack down information (Active readers track down information as they read. They look up vocabulary words, answer questions, and do research as needed while reading.)
- **I**nfer (Successful readers make inferences based on their reading. As they read papers, they make inferences, and write them here.)
- **V**isualize (Successful readers visualize, or make pictures in their heads as they read. They also develop a symbol system to categorize ideas, questions, and connections.)
- **E**mbrace (Successful readers summarize their discoveries about the literature – reading and summarizing does not mean that they simply look at the contents; rather, it implies adopting a meta-perspective.)

Capacities needed for active reading are the capacity to evaluate and the capacity to relate it to other sources included in the review (Saunders et al., 2009).

Strengthening Research Literature Reviews

What are attributes that characterize strong research literature reviews? First, authors can increase interest in their paper if it is clearly linked to ongoing conversations in the field and to publications in the journal to which it is being submitted. Therefore, we suggest citing articles published recently in the target journal, especially in the introductory chapter of the paper. If you cannot find any articles on your topic in the target journal, then you should ask yourself whether your paper is suited to this journal. If so, then you might invent a new field which can be an opportunity if you have a really strong argument – otherwise, it might be a tough challenge. To gauge fit, it makes sense to familiarize yourself with the journal to which you want to submit your paper, for example, by reading editorial notes. 'Fit' is a necessary condition for your research to be interesting and relevant. However, it is also essential to identify a gap with your research, describe it and inform the reviewer why it is important to fill it and how you are going to fill it in terms of theory, methods, data and so on (Reuber, 2010). Another option can be to problematize assumptions underlying theories, in the course of developing new influential theories (Alvesson and Sandberg, 2011). Also the selection of a research topic or research questions has strengthening potential as they shape the literature review: therefore, you should be as specific as possible when identifying your research topic or developing research questions, and position them in the current literature directly and succinctly. In this regard, you should also highlight that your research topic or your research questions are not only motivated by a gap in the literature, but also by a 'real-world' issue, thus stressing the importance of the topic or question for research and/or practice. Moreover, it is important to recognize that doing a research literature review is different than writing a literature review. Doing a research literature review is an ongoing process and should be wide ranging to allow for gaining a wide and up-to-date understanding of the topic. However, writing a research literature review needs to be tightly focused and purpose driven. Thus, instead of describing the learning process, its outcome has to be included in the research literature review (Reuber, 2010). Evidence-based conclusions, which encompass a deeper logic with an emphasis on rigour in formulation and relevance for practice, can lead to practical recommendations, thus strengthening the systematic literature review (Tranfield et al., 2003). Furthermore, a review can be strengthened by centring it on one or a few key constructs. For example, you can analyse the construct of 'familiness' and subsequently develop your paper's title on the basis of this construct (for example, Frank et al., 2010). As the coverage in your research literature review signals to reviewers how well you know this body of past research, we suggest searching for key articles in the field, as they offer an anchor for a comprehensive body of literature and can also help in positioning your own research. Another important point is how recently the articles were published. As a paper with references older than three years is likely to be desk-rejected, make sure your literature is up to date and include a few pertinent in-press articles which signal that you have assimilated new knowledge in your paper. Furthermore, a research literature review can be strengthened by being critical and reflective – a simple enumeration of papers cannot provide new insights. In order to support your research questions and also to help you concisely summarize the literature, you need to think about the extent to which you are going to portray prior research as complementary (for example, partly overlapping) or in tension (for example, leading to different expectations). Finally, as only some of your readers will be expert in your particular topic, you need to have a clear logical progression when you are laying out your arguments. Therefore, it can be helpful to have a colleague read over your literature review before you submit it to a journal, thereby preventing myopia and identifying weaknesses (Reuber, 2010).

Common Mistakes in Doing Research Literature Reviews

What are common mistakes that researchers commit when undertaking research literature reviews? One error is inadequate development of the introduction. There are several reasons why authors may skimp on presenting their conceptual and theoretical ideas early, however, it is usually necessary for a research literature review to present a full and vigorously integrative theoretical framework early in the paper. Only a few readers can wade through a lot of pages without learning what the point is. However, there are two options for overcoming this problem: one is to present the full theoretical conceptualization up front, using it as a focal point for the research literature review; the other is to provide an early, brief 'bottom-line' preview of the theory, postponing its full elaboration until after the literature has been reviewed. Both options provide readers with sufficient context to make sense of the content cited in the review.

Another common mistake is inadequate coverage of the cited literature. This inadequacy stems from an uncertainty about how much detail to give. A common form of inadequacy is to cite an article's conclusion without describing the method and specific results. As the purpose of a research literature review is to provide a basis for accepting a conclusion without taking someone's word for it, evidence has to be presented at the operational level, not just at the abstract level of theoretical conclusions. However, if the author describes the operational details but fails to relate them to the theoretical issues (lack of integration), this is equally destructive to the value of a research literature review. All reviews have to explain how the selected papers fit together – a research literature review is an integrative endeavour.

Another common flaw in research literature reviews is the lack of critical appraisal. It is essential for the literature reviewer to point out weaknesses of reviewed papers. However, not every study can be criticized and the reader of the research literature review does not need to know every flaw in every study. As the reader should know how strong or how weak the overall evidence for each main point is, group or section critiques can be applied. After describing the methods and results of a group of studies relevant to some point, the author should briefly indicate the major flaws in the methods. In the next step, the consistency of the findings should be addressed. Then the author should consider the methodological diversity. Finally, the author should provide a summary regarding the strength of the evidence.

A simpler error is the failure to distinguish between assertion and evidence. In a research literature review, the evidence is precisely in the presentation of past research so that the nature of this evidence must be explained carefully and fully. Literature reviewers should therefore inform their readers whether a cited source proved or merely asserted something. Another problem is selectivity in a research literature review. Although research literature reviews are less subject to capitalizing on chance, they are probably more susceptible to the danger of confirmation bias. What are solutions to selectivity? Ideally, a literature reviewer should avoid advocating a certain theoretical position, unless it is the result of the review, and selective critique. Another strategy is to search for counter-examples or domains of evidence that would seem to contradict the main conclusions and patterns. Another weakness of research literature reviews is to focus on researchers rather than on research. Starting paragraphs in a research literature review with the names of researchers is problematic, and often an indicator that the reviewer lacks integration capabilities. Therefore, downplaying the names of researchers by putting citations in parentheses is the rule.

A final mistake is to stop at the present. Editors want research literature reviewers to make explicit statements about future research based on their findings. It is therefore important to point out remaining unresolved issues and questions, and what needs to be done (Baumeister and Leary, 1997, pp. 316–20).

Dos and Don'ts for Doing the Research Literature Review

There is a basic list of rules that should be observed when doing a literature review (Hart, 2009, p. 219; Saunders et al., 2009); see Table 6.1.

Table 6.1   Rules that should be observed when doing a literature review

Dos	Don'ts
Make yourself aware with the rules for the chosen research literature review type	Inform the reader about your review system
Identify and discuss relevant key studies on the topic by clear assessment criteria for the selection	Include methodological procedures for search, selection and exclusion
Include as much up-to-date material as possible	Include procedures for thematic analysis
Read actively	Discuss outdated materials
Try to be reflective, examine your own bias	Use concepts without definitions
Use extracts and examples to justify analysis and argumentation	Accept any position at face value or believe everything that is written
Be analytical and evaluative	Only produce a description of the content you have read
Have a system to manage the information the review produces	Drown in information by not keeping a record of materials
Make the review worth reading by making it systematic and coherent	

The research literature review as an academic work must provide a clear and balanced picture of current leading concepts, theories and data relevant to the research topic or research question that is the subject of study. By making use of explicit, rigorous and accountable methods leading to reproducible results, it should reach sound recommendations using coherent argument that is based on evidence.

BENEFITS AND VALUE OF RESEARCH LITERATURE REVIEWS

So now that we have outlined the types of literature reviews and the process of doing research literature reviews, the question that arises is what are the benefits of reviewing literature for researchers?

Research literature reviews provide researchers with the opportunity to see the whole picture of a stream of research, for example, its historical background, its relevant theories, concepts and terminologies, and the current context in which the research is embedded, by referring to contemporary debates, issues and questions in the field (Baumeister and Leary, 1997). As the body of knowledge is increasingly fragmented (Tranfield et al., 2003), such an overview enables researchers to develop a research focus, that is, to find their research niche – specialization is an important prerequisite for a successful career in research. However, a too narrow specialization can have a negative effect on researchers' careers, as it hinders flexibility, further development, cooperative activities, and so on. With regard to career development, being aware of the knowledge structures, the methodological traditions and challenges of a research field can be a decisive career factor – thus, research literature reviews can also benefit the embedding of the researcher's own research in a larger context.

Practical reasons also exist for doing research literature reviews. For example, literature reviews are used in proposals for research funding – they describe related research in the field and show how the proposal writers' proposed work extends or challenges this, or address a gap in work in the field. With this in mind, research literature reviews can also serve as content for teaching. In general, they also provide supporting evidence for a practical problem or issue which the proposal writer's research is addressing, thereby underlining its significance. Owing to the compiling of knowledge about the research field including its contemporary issues and questions, research literature reviewers also qualify for acting as reviewers of journal papers and conference papers.

To sum up, literature reviews enable researchers to do better research and teaching. When the research literature review 'is relevant, comprehensive, and coherent as a compelling narrative that partitions and puts in order essential past accomplishments while identifying important challenges and future opportunities' (LePine and King, 2010, p. 506), it is likely to be highly cited. As a systematic, explicit, comprehensive and reproducible synthesis of work in a research field (Fink, 2010, p. 15), research literature reviews not only have the potential to inspire new discussions and directions for future research, but also impact positively on the researchers' motivation for doing theoretical research!

CONCLUSION

In this chapter we have explored the literature review both as a product and as a process. We have differentiated between different types of literature reviews and illustrated the basic steps in the research literature review process. Throughout the chapter, guidelines and suggestions have been put forward which encourage you to consider the way you approach literature searches, the reading, the management of the process, the purposes of the review and the integration of the literature into your writing. Owing to the availability of literature covering issues such as selection of databases, selection of search terms and developing screening criteria, our considerations did not focus on these technical aspects which are elaborated in the cited books.

We conclude with ten rules regarding the reviewing of literature which we have extracted from this chapter:

- A literature review must be a key element of all parts of a research project or in the case of a pure literature review even constitutes the research project.
- Writing a pure research literature review has to be different from writing a literature review as part of conceptual/empirical papers.
- A research literature review has to be a method-guided reproducible process generating specific results.
- Focus on high-quality research.
- Be aware of the mass of information; a systematic approach from idea to paper is needed.
- Reading texts for research literature reviews requires an active and critical approach and a meta-perspective.
- Research literature reviews should significantly impact and contribute to future research.
- Research literature reviews for top journals require theory development or theory evaluation.
- Theory-development literature reviews require a more reflective approach towards literature.
- Research literature reviews should enable a better research and teaching.

Whereas in a variety of research areas (for example, medical research) research literature reviews belong to the methodical standard repertoire, such comprehensive reviews are just emerging in the field of entrepreneurship. However, against the background that the entrepreneurship research literature has been growing significantly over the past decade, it is especially important to provide systematic and valid overviews on the different areas of entrepreneurship research. In fact, both students and junior faculty benefit from research literature reviews provided by faculty members or done by themselves, as such method-guided replicable review processes help them to better position their own research and gain experience with a specific research method.

REFERENCES

Alvesson, M. and J. Sandberg (2011), 'Generating research questions through problematization', *Academy of Management Review*, **36** (2), 247–71.

Baumeister, R.F. and M.R. Leary (1997), 'Writing narrative literature reviews', *Review of General Psychology*, **1** (3), 311–20.

Cooper, H. (1998), *Synthesizing Research: A Guide for Literature Reviews*, 3rd edn, Thousand Oaks, CA: Sage.

Fink, A. (2010), *Conducting Research Literature Reviews*, 3rd edn, Los Angeles, CA: Sage.

Frank, H., M. Lueger, L. Nosé and Suchy, D. (2010), 'The concept of "familiness". Literature review and systems theory-based reflections', *Journal of Family Business Strategy*, **1** (3), 119–30.

Frese, M., A. Bausch, P. Schmidt, A. Rauch and R. Kabst (2012), 'Evidence-based entrepreneurship (EBE): a systematic approach to cumulative science', in D. Rousseau (ed.), *The Oxford Handbook of Evidence-Based Management*, New York: Oxford University Press, pp. 92–111.

Gough, D., S. Oliver and J. Thomas (2012), 'Introducing systematic reviews', in D. Gough, S. Oliver and J. Thomas (eds), *An Introduction to Systematic Reviews*, London: Sage, pp. 1–16.

Harrison, D.A. and K.J Klein (2007), 'What's the difference? Diversity constructs as separation, variety, or disparity in organizations', *Academy of Management Review*, **32** (4), 1199–228.

Hart, C. (2009), *Doing a Literature Review*, 8th edn, London: Sage.

Hunter, J.E. and F.L. Schmidt (2004), *Methods for Meta-Analysis: Correcting Error and Bias in Research Findings*, revd edn, Newbury Park, CA: Sage.

Jones, M.V., N. Coviello and Y.K. Tang (2011), 'International entrepreneurship research (1989–2009): a domain ontology and thematic analysis', *Journal of Business Venturing*, **26** (6), 632–59.

Kilduff, M. (2007), 'Editor's comments: the top ten reasons why your paper might not be sent out for review', *Academy of Management Review*, **32** (3), 700–702.

LePine, J. and W.A. King (2010), 'Editor's comments: developing novel theoretical insight from reviews of existing theory and research', *Academy of Management Review*, **35** (4), 506–9.

Mayer, R.C., J.H. Davis and F.D. Schoorman (1995), 'An integrative model of organizational trust', *Academy of Management Review*, **20** (3), 709–34.

Rauch, A. and M. Frese (2007), 'Let's put the person back into entrepreneurship research: a meta-analysis on the relationship between business owners' personality traits, business creation, and success', *European Journal of Work and Organizational Psychology*, **16** (4), 353–85.

Rauch, A., J. Wiklund, G.T. Lumpkin and M. Frese (2009), 'Entrepreneurial orientation and business performance: an assessment of past research and suggestions for the future', *Entrepreneurship Theory and Practice*, **33** (3), 761–87.

Reuber, A.R. (2010), 'Strengthening your literature review', *Family Business Review*, **23** (2), 105–8.

Rosenthal, R. (1995), 'Writing meta-analytic reviews', *Psychological Bulletin*, **118** (2), 183–92.

Rosenthal, R. and M.R. DiMatteo (2001), 'Meta-analysis: recent developments in quantitative methods for literature reviews', *Annual Review of Psychology*, **52** (1), 59–82.

Saunders, M., P. Lewis and A. Thornhill (2009), *Research Methods for Business Students*, 5th edn, Harlow: Pearson.

Sitkin, S.B. and A.L. Pablo (1992), 'Reconceptualizing the determinants of risk behavior', *Academy of Management Review*, **17** (1), 9–38.

Tranfield, D., D. Denyer and P. Smart (2003), 'Towards a methodology for developing evidence-informed management knowledge by means of systematic review', *British Journal of Management*, **14** (3), 207–22.

Unger, J.M., A. Rauch, M. Frese and N. Rosenbusch (2011), 'Human capital and entrepreneurial success: a meta-analytic review', *Journal of Business Venturing*, **26** (6), 341–58.

7. Ethics and publishing in entrepreneurship research

Benson Honig

INTRODUCTION

Scholarship in entrepreneurship relies upon research, publication and practice. As a result, ethics in entrepreneurship research is an increasingly important component of the field. As more and more universities, colleges, communities, secondary and, even, primary schools 'get into the act', the issue of ethical values becomes both central and relevant to scholars in the field. Our field continues to prosper and, as a result, we can observe that entrepreneurship research, education and training are growing rapidly in universities and colleges throughout the world (Honig, 2004; Katz, 2003; Kauffman Foundation, 2008; Kuratko, 2005; Solomon, 2007). This trend is fuelled in part by a recognition that entrepreneurship can play an important role in economic growth (Kuratko, 2005; Schumpeter, 1934; Shane and Ventkataraman, 2000), and in part by assertions that entrepreneurship research and education can play an important role in developing more and/or better entrepreneurs (for example, Gorman et al., 1997; Katz, 2007; Pittaway and Cope, 2007). This chapter examines the ethical implications of this assumption, as well as examining ethical relationships regarding what we do as scholars and as researchers in order to earn our living, justify our existence, and assist with the often grand aspirations associated with our field and profession.

THE INSTITUTIONALIZATION OF ENTREPRENEURSHIP PUBLICATION AND PEER REVIEW

Young scholars today are no doubt familiar with the adage 'publish or perish' – an apt description of modern academic life. However, scholars should be aware that this was not always the case; in fact, the model of social science publication as we know and practice it is actually a relatively recent invention. To better understand the present and possible future direction of peer review, I present a short summary of this important history.

Universities had their origin in the medieval era, when they were typically associated with religious instruction, not publication, and it was not until the advent of the German Humboldtian model, following the Reformation, that academic freedom and publication became synonymous with contemporary higher education (Martin, 2012). The importance of academic freedom – independence between the universities' boards of directors and their power to hire and fire – became a feature of North American universities beginning in the 1900s, and achieving prominence only in the post-World War II years.

The American Association of University Professors (AAUP) began recommending academic tenure in the 1940s. Academic tenure has two goals: (1) to provide economic incentives to proceed with the profession and (2) to ensure freedom of academic expression. Approximately 35 per cent of US university instructors hold tenure-track appointments, of which 25 per cent have tenure (AAUP, n.d.). The economic incentive for tenure is rationalized by suggesting that there are few returns to investment for a PhD education, relative to working in industry with a graduate degree (perhaps an MBA). Tenure is a necessary incentive in order to encourage young, bright intellectuals to enter academia, as without it, the huge risk involved in 'publish or perish' would outweigh the benefits.

The notion of academic freedom developed in Germany during the nineteenth century and is based on the de-politicization of academic life (Fuchs, 1963). Because the duration of many research projects is long, and the political consequences remote, tenure provides scholars with a free environment within which they can pursue their intellectual interests without worrying about job security. However, the university model, in terms of tenure, publications and three-step rank, is primarily an American innovation. In many European universities, 'permanence' is granted instead of tenure, as labor market regulation is more strictly regulated. This may happen as early as the first or second year of employment. In fact, in some European countries (for example, the Scandinavian countries), doctoral students are considered as professorial colleagues.

The history of the peer review process is surprisingly absent from academic discourse, despite its obvious pre-eminence and the implications for prestige, notoriety and, even, success. The development of peer review appears to be somewhat idiosyncratic, faced with the frequently conflicting values of objectivity, efficiency and quality. Academic journalism itself is historically rooted in early newspapers that had one editor who made all the critical decisions regarding what went 'in' and what was left on the cutting room floor. Medical journals, for example, maintained a single editor as gatekeeper well into the nineteenth century, as did weaker publications in the USA, the UK and France (Burnham, 1990). It should be easily recognized that having one individual make a critical decision such as whether a paper should be published, or not, when tenure and careers were at stake represented a very dangerous and potentially conflicting position. For example, early non-journalistic publications were typically associated with an academic center, serving as an organizational mouthpiece, but were also limited to a single editor who considered himself expert in all areas related to the center/journal topic. Thus, work that supported the philosophy of the center director was much more likely to be published – constraining, to a certain degree, innovation and progress. Only as fields of study became too large and the specialization of knowledge too specific and extensive did these editors relinquish some editorial control and seek out external review advice (Burnham, 1990). Finally, with the increase in submissions, accompanied by specialization outside the capacity for editorial boards, the need for systematic editorial review processes emerged in the 1940s (Burnham, 1990). Thus, it was primarily after World War II that peer review journals, tenure and the peer review process as we know them came into being.

As the model for tenure diffused in North America, so did the accompanying pace of peer review academic journals, to accommodate the growing needs of junior faculty to demonstrate productivity to tenure and promotion boards. One consequence of this phenomenon is the ever-increasing emergence of new and highly specific journals, frequently with niche titles, appealing to a very small and narrowly focused academic community. For example, the field of 'entrepreneurship', which emerged at the Academy of Management in 1971, began with two or three prominent journals. Today, there are well over 50 academic journals that publish entrepreneurship papers. However, very few of the 50 are widely read, most having little or no registered 'impact factor', meaning that articles are rarely cited or referred to. This is an important point for new scholars, in that publication in many of the 'great unread' journals may not lead to the kind of academic career many people imagine or seek out. Unfortunately, the history of when peer review articles became prominent regarding promotion and tenure is not particularly clear, as stated by one scholar: 'As far as I know, no one has done a study of when the distinction between refereed and non-refereed articles came to be important in various kinds of situations, most notably in academic promotions and in funding' (Burnham, 1990, p. 1327). Further complicating this issue is the rise of new 'e-journals', many of dubious quality, sometimes designed to require hefty submission or publication fees tailored to those in lower-tier institutions who need to demonstrate publication and research, in environments that are not seriously evaluating the quality or content of those contributions. Editors of some of these journals might be considered as having dubious motives. For example, I was recently invited onto one such board, composed of scholars who had no publishing record and from countries not typically associated with research in entrepreneurship. Their 'manuscript publication fee' was US$250. Before declining this questionable honor, I asked the editor if they were willing to consider paying me a handsome honorarium to use my name (of course, I would decline the membership at any price, I was trying to make a point). My supposition is that we will see many more such initiatives in the coming years.

Although the contemporary university migrated from Europe, that was not true of the modern business school. Joseph Wharton, a businessman, learned German, investigated the Prussian system of education, and went on to found Wharton in 1881; by 1887 the German trained dean, Edmund James, laid the foundations for contemporary business education. However, the MBA was an American invention, with first Dartmouth in 1900, followed by Harvard (1908) and then Stanford (1925) (Mintzberg, 2004). The USA has continued to lead, and even dominate, in the field of management for over a century; the Association to Advance Collegiate Schools of Business (AACSB) accreditation organization was established in 1916, and the growth of named schools, chairs and considerable resources seems to continue unabated.

While the model of academic rank and tenure is primarily a North American invention, there has been considerable isomorphism worldwide, with a commensurate focus on peer-review publication. For example, the Research Assessment Exercise in the UK that first began in 1986 is a systematic five-year review of every public higher education facility in the UK. Universities are rated according to the scholarly productivity of their published faculty, and are financially rewarded by the government. The newly introduced Research Excellence Framework (REF) will follow a similar system, but also focus on impact factors, financially rewarding the most research intensive universities (REF UK, n.d.). Australia, too, has followed suit with a research evaluation system. Other incentives occur worldwide, as do requirements for obtaining and maintaining positions in Europe and Asia. For example, a colleague informed me that one Chinese university provides the equivalent of a six-month salary bonus for a single top-tier publication. Perhaps one outcome of this combination of worldwide incentives and requirements has been a massive increase in the number of publications submitted to top-tier journals from locations that previously did not participate in the research publication process. If one considers only a single country – China – and the huge number of professors associated with that system, one can imagine the implications for journals, editors and the peer review system itself. The end result – the increasing difficulty in publishing in top-tier journals, combined with a commensurate difficulty in identifying qualified reviewers – suggests that the peer review system as we know it now will require considerable modification in order to accommodate future demands.

While there has been little change in the peer review process in the past 50 years, I firmly believe that significant changes lie ahead, in part, due to the stresses mentioned above. Many alternatives to the present two-way blind review process are already available, and some have been implemented in other fields. E-journals, where publications are broadcast widely and fully transparent reviews conducted by field-level experts, exist in other fields, such as physics. Open access journals present another alternative to the conventional peer review system, and include both those where the author pays for publication and those where the authors self-post for public viewing (Clark et al., forthcoming). Reputations can still be ensured through adequate citation and quality reviewing, however, the process is expedited and available to virtually any interested scholar (as opposed to those whose universities purchase a particular research journal). Applications for readers and smartphones might be developed to launch new debate, share and critique new work, and generally enhance academic dialogue and innovation. Given the dearth of quality reviewers, it may be necessary to collect small processing fees from potential authors, which are than passed along to the reviewers as a token of compensation, something already practiced in some finance and economics journals. Further, authors might 'earn' credits that would enable them to submit articles only *after* they completed responsible reviews for particular journals. This system would ensure some sort of balance regarding the demands of time placed on experienced scholars. Finally, systems might be implemented to publicly rate the quality of reviews and offer an impact factor similar to citation counts. These might be utilized for tenure and review processes.

ETHICS AND THE PRESSURES OF PUBLICATION IN ENTREPRENEURSHIP

Unfortunately, the global pressure to meet elevated research expectations has resulted in a number of recent high-profile cases of academic misconduct (for example, Honig and Bedi, 2012; Storbeck, 2012; also http://retractionwatch.wordpress.com and www.elsevier.com/wps/find/intro.cws_home/article_withdrawal). These cases call into question the presumption that scholars all over the world acquire similar 'research ethics' during graduate training, and in particular question whether there is a shared ethical view regarding what is acceptable, and what is not, in terms of navigating academic careers. Errors in plagiarism, analysis and data fabrication are increasingly evident (Tsui and Galaskiewicz, 2011). Ethical norms vary culturally. For example, in China, individuals (called 'gunmen') are routinely paid to sit Graduate Management Admission Test (GMAT) and Graduate Record Examinations (GRE) examinations.

Without a doubt, the pressures on top-tier publication in management, as well as in entrepreneurship, continue to mount. Top journals now accept less than 12 percent of submissions, meaning that approximately 90 percent of any scholarly work will find rejection at the leading journals. As entrepreneurship positions are increasing worldwide, the necessity to publish in top-tier entrepreneurship journals continues to drive a considerable range of research activity. Publication provides legitimacy, and in the nascent field of entrepreneurship, scholars are particularly sensitive to the importance and prestige incurred thorough selective peer-review publication. Comprehensive lists typically provide only between two and four entrepreneurship journals rated at the 'highest' quality (Harzing, 2011). Competition for placement in these journals is considerable, with acceptance rates typically less than 12 percent. Note that in the physical sciences, rejection rates are considerably lower, although retraction rates are also higher. Scholars in science typically write much shorter papers, and publish far more papers during an academic year. One study of high-impact factor scientific journals identified a tenfold increase in the retraction of scientific publications due to research misconduct, from a low of 30 in the early 2000s, to over 400 in 2010 (Van Noorden, 2011). PubMed reported 743 English language retractions in the last decade, of which 74.5 percent were for errors and 26.6 percent due to fraud (Steen, 2010). Of course, disagreement regarding what is appropriate and worthy of publication leads scholars to view other perspectives as deficient, thus increasing rejection rates (Hargens, 1988).

Given the considerable growth of the worldwide community of entre-preneurial scholars, the apparent cap on high-tier journals and impact factors should reflect a growing concern regarding issues of access and openness. Pressures and demands regarding top-tier publication may also account for ethical compromises, including academic plagiarism and fraudulent data manipulation (Bakker and Wicherts, 2011; Bouyssou et al., 2006; 2009; Carey, 2011; Honig and Bedi, 2012). In short, given that a growing number of scholars are competing for a comparatively smaller piece of a new field's publishing 'pie', both editors and scholars should anticipate increases in ethical lapses, and take appropriate measures.

Ethical lapses in entrepreneurship scholarship can occur at many points, but can nonetheless ruin careers. Unfortunately, retractions, in management as well as in entrepreneurship, are becoming an increasingly evident example of ethical lapses (Schminke and Ambrose, 2011). A major blogging site now tracks retractions that are consistently on the rise, demonstrating that they are caused by a range of behaviors including plagiarism, data fraud, submission discrepancies and malpractice (Retrac-tion Watch, 2012). In addition, editors have been faced with considerable threats regarding falsified data and plagiarism. For example, one senior colleague privately told me of being invited to co-author with a younger scholar a paper that was already in the review process. The colleague accepted, and was completely broad-sided when s/he was informed by the journal's editor that a significant portion of the paper was plagiarized material taken from a different author's forthcoming paper. Much as for someone who buys stolen property, 'ignorance is no excuse', and reputations can be jeopardized or even ruined by simply agreeing to co-author with someone who may have a different ethical compass.

A good suggestion is to work slowly and carefully with new collabo-rators. Get to know them, learn their values, how detail oriented they are, and what their strengths and weaknesses are. Identify individuals who complement your capabilities, but only continue to work with those that you are confident share your own ethical perspective. Failure to carefully vet a co-author can, by itself, ruin a promising career in entrepreneurship. Consider making written agreements regarding authorship order and responsibilities before beginning your project, so that all scholars are aware of the expectations, as well as the potential rewards (Chen, 2011). Some scholars use the '70–30' rule regarding authorship, a norm that states that alphabetical order is expected unless one person does 70 percent of the work and the other 30 percent – in that case, the authorship would follow the workload. In addition, you should be very careful in properly documenting the source of your ideas, as well as any particular sentence, or paragraph, published elsewhere by you or by others.

Unfortunately, ethical lapses that have been uncovered, or discussed with me, are becoming more evident and more readily detectable, and are of increasingly serious concern. Plagiarism, whether it be a single paragraph, a page, or an entire article have all been reported to me by various editors. It is a severe lapse of scholarly behavior. According to the Academy of Management's code of ethics regarding plagiarism, members 'explicitly identify, credit, and reference the author of any data or material taken verbatim from written work, whether that work is published, unpublished, or electronically available'. Members also 'explicitly cite others' work and ideas, including their own, even if the work or ideas are not quoted verbatim or paraphrased. This standard applies whether the previous work is published' (AOM, n.d.). Thus, plagiarism includes self-plagiarism, as well as taking someone's core ideas without proper citation (Tsui and Galaskiewicz, 2011).

Our ability to systematically examine the digital uniqueness of a written product through programs such as Turnitin, SafeAssign and CrossCheck are increasing the probability that plagiarizing scholars will be discovered (Honig and Bedi, 2012). Academy of Management journals now use CrossCheck, as do *Entrepreneurship Theory and Practice* and other leading entrepreneurship journals. As editors gain experience with this reporting system, we can expect greater transparency and more severe consequences. Editors have also shared ethical lapses that may or may not have been widely broadcast – but appear in their 'rejection pile' of submitted manuscripts. I have been informed of data manipulation, cases where significance of variables has changed in subsequent revisions that contradict statistical probabilities, the arbitrary dropping of cases that do not support a particular theoretical assertion and the outright use of fraudulent or otherwise manipulated data. The consequences of each of these violations differs – in some cases, scholars have been forced to resign in 'shame'. In others, the university has preferred to keep the outcomes under wraps, but censure the faculty member.

As your professional life develops, you, too, will increasingly be asked to conduct reviews. Scholars should be aware that blind review means just that – it is blind before, during and after the process. It is completely unacceptable to congratulate an author of a paper you have reviewed and indicate you were a reviewer. This would suggest that person 'owes you a favor', when, in fact, the review process is meant to be entirely non-transparent and anonymous. Reviewers should never disclose material they have reviewed, should indicate any conflicts of interest they might have to the editor (for instance, the author may be a friend or colleague they recognize) and should avoid re-reviewing an article they previously reviewed (Rupp, 2011).

Ethics in scholarship is rarely a black-and-white phenomenon; it is more typically one of shades of gray. New scholars are encouraged to take their ethical questions to the Academy of Management's 'Ethicist' blog, where they can receive honest and credible answers to a range of questions. For example, may your advisor insist on co-authorship if s/he had little or no contribution (Lee and Mitchell, 2011)? According to the Academy of Management's ethical code regarding exploitative relationships, 'AOM members do not exploit persons over whom they have evaluative or other authority, such as authors, job seekers, or student members'. Other ethical decisions are just as complicated. How can a researcher ensure a respondent will be anonymous? Who owns ideas that are broadly discussed during academic activities – is it necessary to cite a discussion you may have overheard at a conference? While the answers to these queries are conditional, scholars are encouraged to develop their own sense of ethical clarity, in order to maintain a personal standard that they can rely upon when questionable situations present themselves. Only through attention and (self-) respect can an entrepreneurship scholar satisfy his/her commitment and contribution to this dynamic and important field of study.

ETHICS AND THE FIELD: A BROADER PERSPECTIVE ON OUR ACTIVITIES AND ACCOMPLISHMENTS

As scholars, we are mercifully free to pursue research that interests us, for practically any reason. The measure of good scholarship is rarely linked to practicality or societal level outcomes. However, it is worth noting that most of us entrepreneurship scholars are public servants, in that we work for non-profit institutions either directly or indirectly supported by our government. As such, we enjoy considerable privileges, including academic freedom, limited restrictions on our time, independence and authority in the classroom and in the research environments, job security, and the kind of quality of life and social status that many of our peers only dream about. In many ways, achievement in this field is the recognition of long and hard work developing a consistent and active schedule dedicated to the promotion of entrepreneurship, entrepreneurs and, by association and expectation, economic development. In this section, I discuss some of the broader field-level implications that include a scholar's ethical responsibility to the field, the subject and the greater communities we occupy. What we choose to research has ethical implications, and we should not pretend that there are no consequences to our studies.

Unfortunately, while scholars in the field have aggressively developed measures and models that make for good publishable journal articles, there has been only a limited attempt to measure our productivity in terms of social outcomes. One would expect that criminologists be measured by the reduction of recidivism and crime statistics in the environments where they operate. Doctors and health systems are held accountable by measurable standards, including costs, benefits and outcomes. Evidence-based medicine is specifically designed to monitor the relationship between what a doctor does, and the outcomes for the patient (Sackett, 1997). In fact, medical education is one of the outstanding success stories of the contemporary university system. However, in the field of entrepreneurship, we have few if any such measures. The entrepreneurship class that attempts to track entrepreneurial outcomes in actual behaviors is rare. Owing to time limitations, we are far more likely to study entrepreneurial intentions – with the expectation that this might lead to actions. Few studies examine the outcomes of entrepreneurship education, beyond asking students if they appreciated the class and the instructor, shortly after completing a course. This is like deciding who is a good driving instructor according to how much the student appreciated the jokes and conversations taking place during the driving instruction. Instead of asking shortly after the course, we should be either asking many years later, or, more appropriately, measure outcomes (for driving instructors, it would be accident rates, for us, it might be entrepreneurial rates).

Entrepreneurship research suggests the need for entrepreneurs to develop the necessary skills to re-evaluate, adapt and revise activities in a resourceful manner to suit new environmental contingencies (Honig, 2004). Entrepreneurship is both an art and a science (Jack and Anderson, 1999). Pedagogical techniques need to be developed that focus on applied hands-on activities, resulting in experiential learning, in addition to the teaching of general principles and theory (Solomon, 2007). These techniques vary significantly worldwide, and scholarship has, as yet, failed to systematically and comparatively assess the impact of one particular pedagogical innovation over another. In my opinion, this represents both a field-level opportunity, and a field-level ethical challenge. Rather than examine whether or not our teaching is effective in accomplishing particular goals we may have set, we tend to avoid the consequences and assume, rightly or wrongly, that we are teaching useful material of relevance to future entrepreneurs that will positively impact their activities. Further, traditional pedagogy is frequently in contrast to the needs of entrepreneurial education. Academic learning typically consists of presenting information in a consistent and predictable manner.

Students review, digest and repeat previously dictated solutions to specific abstract problems, and demonstrate competence during examinations. While these techniques are well adapted for teaching foundation material, such as providing tools that assist students in analytical decision-making, this method of learning may be ill suited to the complex and dynamic problems typically faced by contemporary managers (Mintzberg and Gosling, 2002) and by entrepreneurs (Honig, 2004). This dilemma suggests that each of us, as well as our field, will eventually be held accountable for the investments made in entrepreneurship research and education. We have an ethical obligation to deliver improvements, and each of us should actively pursue strategies which advance our knowledge and the actual evidence of improved entrepreneurial outcomes.

ETHICS AND ENTREPRENEURSHIP SCHOLARSHIP: CONCLUSION

While no single chapter can do justice to the ethical dimensions of scholarship, I have attempted to point toward some of the more obvious and critical dimensions that new scholars ought to be familiarized with. We began with a discussion of the institutional norms of the field – what is means to be published – and why we have developed what many consider to be an arcane and somewhat arbitrary system of knowledge progression and dissemination. Following that, I highlighted some of the research ethical dilemmas scholars face – including issues we are hearing more about each and every day, such as plagiarism, retraction, manipulation of data, and false and erroneous reporting. I further introduced other issues relating to knowing your co-author, your data, and being well grounded in the knowledge that what you present as your own scholarly contribution is, as best as you can ascertain, an original credible contribution to the field of entrepreneurship. Lastly, I highlighted some of the apparent dilemmas of contemporary entrepreneurship scholarship, in particular, issues related to entrepreneurship education. How is it that, despite spending considerable sums of money, we have little if any evidence that our social investments are appropriate, efficient, and conducive to economic growth and prosperity?

Entrepreneurship scholarship is an exciting field of study. It has the attention of global and local leaders, politicians, economists and social actors of nearly every stripe and persuasion. Considerable resources continue to be expended in advancing this field of study. As entrepreneurship scholars, we surely live in 'good times'. However, with resource munificence come responsibilities. Our field is increasingly being asked to demonstrate that it 'delivers' on expected promises – promises that have attracted many of us into the field in the first place. Only by ensuring that our research activities are carefully monitored to the highest ethical standards will we ever begin to deliver on some of these expectations.

REFERENCES

Academy of Management (AOM) (n.d.), accessed 9 November 2012 at www.aomonline.org/aom.asp?id=14&page_id=235.

American Association of University Professors (AAUP) (n.d.), accessed 28 December 2009 at www.aaup.org/aaup/issues/tenure/benjamintenureimps.htm.

Bakker, M. and J.M. Wicherts (2011), 'The (mis)reporting of statistical results in psychology journals', *Behavior Research Methods*, **43** (3), 666–78.

Bouyssou, D., S. Martello and F. Plastria (2006), 'A case of plagiarism: Dănuţ Marcu', *4OR: A Quarterly Journal of Operations Research*, **4** (1), 11–13.

Bouyssou, D., S. Martello and F. Plastria (2009), 'Plagiarism again: Sreenivas and Srinivas, with an update on Marcu', *4OR*, **7** (1), 17–20.

Burnham, J. (1990), 'The evolution of editorial peer review', *Journal of the American Medical Association*, **263** (10), 1323–9.

Carey, B. (2011), 'Fraud case seen as a red flag for psychology research', *New York Times*, 2 November.

Chen, Z. (2011), 'Author ethical dilemmas in the research publication process', *Management and Organizational Review*, **7** (3), 423–32.

Clark, T., S. Floyd and M. Wright (forthcoming), 'JMS50 Editors reflection: "in search of the impactful and the interesting- swings of the pendulum?"', *Journal of Management Studies*.

Fuchs, R. (1963), 'Academic freedom. Its basic philosophy, function, and history', *Law and Contemporary Problems*, **28** (3): 431–46.

Gorman, G., D. Hanlon and W. King (1997), 'Some research perspectives on entrepreneurship education, enterprise education and education for small business management: a ten-year literature review', *International Small Business Journal*, **15** (3), 56–77.

Hargens, L. (1988), 'Scholarly consensus and journal rejection rates', *American Sociological Review*, **53** (1), 139–51.

Harzing, A.W. (2011), *Journal Quality List*, 42nd edn, Melbourne: University of Melbourne.

Honig, B. (2004), 'Entrepreneurship education: toward a model of contingency-based business planning', *Academy of Management Learning and Education*, **3** (3), 258–73.

Honig, B, and A. Bedi (2012), 'The fox in the hen house: a critical examination of plagiarism among members of the Academy of Management', *Academy of Management Learning and Education*, **11** (1), 101–23.

Jack, S and A. Anderson (1999), 'Entrepreneurship education within the enterprise culture', *International Journal of Entrepreneurial Behaviour & Research*, **5** (3), 110–25.

Katz, J. (2003), 'The chronology and intellectual trajectory of American entrepreneurship education 1876–1999', *Journal of Business Venturing*, **18** (2), 283–300.

Katz, J.A. (2007), 'Education and training in entrepreneurship', in J.R. Baum, M. Frese and R.A. Baron (eds), *The Psychology of Entrepreneurship*. Mahwah, NJ: Lawrence Erlbaum Associates, pp. 209–35.

Kauffman Foundation (2008), *Entrepreneurship in American Higher Education*, accessed 16 October 2008 at www.kauffman.org/items.cfm?itemID=1132.

Kuratko, D.F. (2005), 'The emergence of entrepreneurship education: development, trends, and challenges', *Entrepreneurship Theory and Practice*, **29** (5), 577–97.

Lee, T and T. Mitchell (2011), 'Working in research teams: lessons from personal experieencee', *Management Organization Review*, **7** (3), 461–9.

Martin, B. (2012), 'Are universities and university research under threat? Towards an evolutionary model of university speciation', *Cambridge Journal of Economics*, **36** (3), 543–65.

Mintzberg, H. (2004), *Managers, not MBAs*, San Francisco, CA: Berrett-Koehler.

Mintzberg, H and J. Gosling (2002) 'Educating managers beyond borders', *Academy of Management Learning & Education*, **1** (1), 64–76.

Pittaway, L. and J. Cope (2007), 'Entrepreneurship education: a systematic review of the evidence', *International Small Business Journal*, **25** (4), 479–510.

Retraction Watch (2012), accessed 31 August 2012 at http://retractionwatch. wordpress.com/category/by-author/ulrich-lichtenthaler/.

Retraction Watch (n.d.), accessed 31 August 2012 at http://retractionwatch. wordpress.com/category/by-author/diederik-stapel/.

Retraction Watch (n.d.), accessed 9 November 2012 at http://retractionwatch. wordpress.com/transparencyindex/.

REF UK (n.d.), accessed 9 November 2012 at http://www.ref.ac.uk/background/.

Rupp, D. (2011), 'Ethical issues faced by editors and reviewers', *Management and Organizational Review*, **7** (3), 481–93.

Sackett, D. (1997), 'Evidence-based medicine', *Seminars in Perinatology*, **21** (1), 3–5.

Schminke, M. and M. Ambrose (2011), 'Ethics and integrity in the publishing process: myths, facts and a roadmap', *Management and Organizational Review*, **7** (3) 397–406.

Schumpeter, J. (1934), *The Theory of Economic Development*, Cambridge, MA: Harvard University Press.

Shane, S. and S. Venkataraman (2000), 'The promise of entrepreneurship as a field of search', *Academy of Management Review*, **25** (1), 217–26.

Solomon, G. (2007), 'An examination of entrepreneurship education in the United States', *Journal of Small Business and Enterprise Development*, **14** (2), 168–82.

Steen, G. (2010), 'Retractions in the scientific literature: is the incidence of research fraud increasing?', *Journal of Medical Ethics*, online doi:10.1136/jme.2010.040923.

Storbeck, O. (2012), 'Top-flight German business prof faces severe accusations of academic misconduct', *Economics Intelligence*, 19 July, accessed 15 August 2012 at http://economicsintelligence.com/2012/07/19/top-flight-german-business-prof-faces-severe-accusations-of-academic-misconduct/.

Tsui, A. and J. Galaskiewicz (2011), 'Editorial: Comment to excellence: upholding research integrity at Management and Organization Review', *Management and Organizational Review*, **9** (3), 389–95.

Van Noorden, R. (2011), 'Science publishing: the trouble with retractions', *Nature*, 5 October.

8. Moving from the periphery to the inner circle: getting published from your thesis

Sally Jones and Helle Neergaard

As a doctoral student you will undoubtedly be met with demands for publication – sooner rather than later. Since you will start out as a novice in the race for publication, you will need some advice on how to get a head start. This chapter is a primer for doctoral students in the early phases of working on their dissertation. It sets out to provide some basic guidelines for how to overcome the significant challenge posed by publication requirements. It commences with an auto-ethnographic narrative of the doctoral process. It proceeds to address the differences between the monograph and the article-based thesis, highlighting the pros and cons of each. This is followed by some general advice on how to publish from your PhD. In conclusion it deals with the issue of an academic identity and the emotions involved in the process of development.

THREE YEARS AND 100 000 WORDS

I started my PhD in 2007 in a UK university and completed it in 2010. Three years of total immersion in the field, of total involvement and engagement with my data, analysing, theorizing and summarizing, watching and waiting for themes and findings to emerge from this complex combination of theory and practice; zooming in and zooming out of the field and building my research skills, writing skills and the sense of myself as an 'academic'. My PhD thesis was in the form of a monograph, the more common form of PhD in the UK. In fact, I was not aware of the option of completing a PhD through publication until very far into my PhD. However, I am glad that I pursued my PhD in the monograph form as I believe it has helped me to hone my writing skills; forcing me to construct a narrative (or golden thread) that would develop over

100 000 words and allowing me to 'wallow' in the literature, data production, analysis and, most importantly of all, helping me to develop academic writing skills, with a view to perhaps writing a book at some point in the future (although, as it stands, books are not necessarily well regarded as academic outputs – particularly in the UK – something that I find very confusing as I would consider this the ultimate achievement and would aspire to eventually write a book).

I must admit to being slightly naive in writing my PhD – initially seeing it as an end, rather than a means to an end. It was not until I was into my final year that I realized that, on its own, my monograph was considered a mere exercise, an 'amuse bouche' before the real academic work that would establish my reputation began; this real work being the process of pulling out findings and ideas from my monograph for journal articles. This was not something that I had really considered and the level of competition and expectation came as somewhat of a shock. Was the fact that I had crafted 100 000 words with a narrative flow that told the 'story' of my research journey and contributed new knowledge in my subject area (Gender and Entrepreneurship Education) not enough? Well, no it wasn't. The PhD thesis is merely a calling card, a way of being in the frame. It is the resulting journal articles that will get you through the door so that you can actually share and 'sell' your ideas and contribution to knowledge. So how can this be done?

The challenge of developing 7–8000 word articles from a prospective choice of 100 000 words is immense and should not be understated. How could I provide the context, the richness of detail and the sense of beginning, middle and end, a sense of 'completeness' that is vital to a successful monograph? How would I do justice to my data, give voice to my research respondents and summarize the many findings and theoretical contributions that a monograph inevitably contains?

Well, one activity, which I had thankfully started before completing my PhD, really helped with this and that was presenting papers at conferences. This was a good training ground – forcing me to take a different view on my research and its presentation, making me focus on specific aspects or emerging themes rather than trying to encapsulate the whole thesis in one presentation. This also allowed me to get feedback on my ideas and to get a sense of the areas that were worthy of further development and presentation. This was not an easy process – I presented my first working paper at the International Small Business and Entrepreneurship (ISBE) conference, just a few months after I had started my PhD. To present the very early stages of my ideas to my peers, many of whom I had read and cited, was terrifying but ultimately rewarding. The odd nod of agreement, the suggested extra reading and introductions to others studying and researching in my field were invaluable and, I believe, laid the foundations for developing later, more confident pieces of writing and ultimately to my first paper being published in a well-respected journal in 2012.

Again, the process leading up to getting the journal paper published was not just about me working in splendid isolation, sweating to craft a paper that would encapsulate my research. It was partly about that but it was also about my growing involvement in a community of practice and participating in the wider academic community that I felt wanted to hear what I had to say. This confidence and involvement has been strengthened by presenting papers and work in progress from 2007 to the present, by having conversations with my peers and also by becoming involved in the publishing process by proxy. By this I mean that, towards the end of my PhD, I volunteered to review for a journal in my field. This was a very big step for me and I would not have done this had I not been encouraged by those in my academic community who suggested I 'just get in touch with the editor'.

I now review for several journals and this has provided invaluable insights into what makes a 'good' journal paper. It has emphasized a certain 'form' of readable and engaging paper and has also taught me about the use of language in academic writing. That the main point is to be clear, to have clarity in both the words and structure that you use. Initially, I would have thought that the use of long words and 'academic-ese' would have proved that I was a 'proper' academic writing in a proper academic style. However, once I started to review, it was clear that those authors who use plain, 'unflowery' language inevitably get their message and arguments across better. Also, the signposting used in a paper is very important. The headings used sparingly, to guide the reader through the text, the logical unfolding of the argument. The more papers I reviewed, the more 'obvious' the merits of this approach became.

And yet, I still had 100 000 words to 'chop' or 'slice' up into articles in order to do my three years of intensive research and writing. It was all very well having an understanding of the form and content of a good journal article but how could I write one without watering down my findings or losing sight of the bigger, more complex, picture?

I started by considering my findings/discussion chapter – this, after all, is my contribution to theory and to my field. These are the ideas and theoretical extensions that will supposedly help to move my particular field on. These are the ideas that I needed to tell others about – but what were they and how could I summarize them?

Throughout my PhD, certain words, phrases or ideas started to emerge and these were threaded through my discussion and findings. Phrases such as 'the suspension of disbelief', 'the fictive entrepreneur and student', 'the gendering of discursive space', for example, permeated my attempts to make sense of my data and of my findings. There were also themes linked to the staff and students that I had interviewed and observed. Staff attitudes to entrepreneurship education as a 'fad', female students unanimously labelling themselves 'business owners' rather than entrepreneurs. Here were emergent themes that might help my peers and fellow enterprise educators make sense of what is 'going on' in the classroom and curriculum.

Starting with these ideas or findings first, forced me to really think about the focus of each paper (and I include conference papers here as preambles to journal papers). They helped me to identify the literature to draw upon in situating their importance and contribution to knowledge. Obviously, I could not include all of my literature review in a journal paper, but by focusing on one element of my findings I could draw on the literature that highlighted and explored individual, relevant themes. I could also do a more focused review of any new literature published since I completed my PhD. I did not have to read everything – just to identify new developments in my field that linked to the particular finding or theme that each paper explores. I very often use the theme or idea in the paper title too – to add focus and to make it clear exactly what the paper is 'about'. This also acts as an anchor for me and (hopefully) stops me from drifting away from the main focus of the paper.

There are some who suggest that there is a tendency to slice research too thinly when developing papers from a monograph. However, although my papers are obviously based upon my thesis, much of what I now write is actually a synthesis of those findings, further engagement with newer literature and also, as I work in the area that I research in, on-going ideas, questions and issues that are constantly emerging from my practice as a gender-aware and critical entrepreneurship educator. Therefore, I do not see the papers from my PhD as being 'sliced' out of my PhD. If anything, they are part of a bigger research 'sandwich', a 'filling', which is surrounded with more up-to-date research and my own continuing engagement with and understanding of the theoretical and practical issues highlighted by my PhD.

That said, to date I have only had one journal paper published (although I am currently working on five). It was a positive process (in hindsight, of course). The first set of feedback from the three reviewers suggested that, although I did have something interesting to say, I was not articulating it clearly and concisely. All three reviewers suggested major revisions in different areas, which, at first, almost paralysed me, as my first thought was 'This is an impossible task!' However, after a week away from both my paper and the feedback, I was able to see the points that the reviewers were making and really appreciated that, although some of the feedback was blunt, it was constructive. It was well-meaning and, ultimately, it strengthened my paper and made it much better. The comments introduced me to new theories and concepts that I now draw upon in my developing writing and research, so I am grateful for the time and care that these reviewers gave to my work. Having responded to the feedback, the next set of reviews (from two reviewers this time) still asked for minor revisions. This was actually a relief as I was unsure whether I had addressed the major issues from the previous reviews. Again, the minor revisions improved the paper and it was eventually accepted for publication in the *International Small Business Journal* (ISBJ).

Although it felt like a great achievement, I could not rest on my laurels and relax. I soon realized that getting this journal paper published was not the end of anything but the start – just as getting my PhD was not really the end of anything, it was more about gaining entry into an academic community where I would then have to articulate the ideas, themes and importance inherent in three years work and 100 000 words. However, publishing an article in a high-quality journal does give a sense of personal and academic progression and growth. It is a form of acceptance into an academic community of practice and feedback from your peers that you are included in their conversations and that you have something to say.

This was a single-authored piece and I have only recently started to write with others. This may be a drawback of the single authored monograph, as it does not allow you to write collaboratively. I think it also made me less happy to share my embryonic ideas with others as I was very heavily invested in the work – it felt like any criticism of my PhD and my ideas was ultimately a criticism of me. I also worried that working with others would potentially hold me back as I would have to wait for others to complete work, or that other people would let me down. You do become very self-reliant when writing a monograph and this is a hard habit to break.

But, I am now writing with others and, far from being the onerous, negative experience that I had envisaged, it has proved to be liberating, creative and intellectually stimulating. I am currently working on several papers with co-authors ranging from one other to four others and it really has been a learning experience. The ideas and insights that more than one person can generate have helped me to improve both my approach to writing and also my understandings of other bodies of knowledge such as philosophy and history – which can only make my future research foci and questions richer and more engaging.

Although there are some drawbacks of the monograph, I realize that it was a rare luxury and I am truly grateful to have spent three years immersed in a field of study and in research that I find fascinating but also believe is crucial for the development of teaching and learning in my field. Writing journal papers allows me to engage in conversations with my peers about my research, it allows the spotlight to focus on areas which may provide others insights into their own practices in this area and it ultimately allows me to signpost others to the 'bigger picture' of my doctoral thesis (for those who are interested) but also to be very clear about why what I have spent three years and 100 000 words exploring is important. I would hope that that is what all researchers would wish for; to feel that your hard work, energy and passion has had an impact, has made a difference and has ultimately been worth it.

At first glance, describing the PhD as a period of apprenticeship seems rather appropriate. Indeed, Lave and Wenger (1991) articulate the idea of legitimate peripheral participation and how it helps people who are learning a trade or learning the practices of a particular community to move from novice to expert community practitioner through a process of situated learning; a form of apprenticeship.

Had I chosen to pursue a formal, trade-based apprenticeship I would need to learn from those who had already 'mastered' the trade or profession because, in order to learn how a community of practice works, we need to learn from those people who are already experts and already know how things work. Thus we need to sit with 'Nelly',[1] who works the important machines – the woman who has been part of the company for 20 years, who has seen the company develop and watched others come and go. Nelly knows how everything works and who everyone is. Watch her, observe how she moves, the things she says, take it all in, revel in her 'Nellyness' and aim to go from just sitting with Nelly to being like her. This metaphor illustrates the notion of moving from peripheral participation – from 'lurking', listening to conversations but not being involved in them, reading academic papers and watching presentations. It also helps to articulate the notion of the PhD as an apprenticeship, where you learn the tools of the trade and that a PhD validates you as a member of this community of practice. As such it also mimics a traditional apprenticeship – however, there are numerous differences between a traditional apprenticeship and the academic one. In the traditional apprenticeship, the apprentice starts with the most peripheral assign-ments, which provides a position from which s/he can watch, which tools are used for which assignments, and thus slowly builds an idea of the structuration and meaning of the community of practice. The apprentice advances from observing to participating in increasingly more difficult assignments until s/he becomes fully skilled. Thus, through participation the apprentice advances from being a novice to becoming more and more expert (Neergaard et al., 2012) and learns the 'habits, norms and practices' of their academic community (Golde, 2010, p. 81).

In the academic apprenticeship, there is rarely a period of pure observation. Usually, in Europe, the doctoral student is thrown in at the deep end, although this may be different in North America, where they may be more structured and include coursework and examinations throughout the period of study (Coimbra Group, 2012). Further, although doctoral students work under supervision, often they conduct the practical part of their research on their own, gathering data because the doctoral work has to be independent; it cannot be carried out as a collaborative effort, as then the doctoral student cannot claim it as his or her own. This also means that, as described above, the 'real work' does not begin until the PhD is completed. However, as the article-based thesis is gaining popularity over the monograph owing to the publish-or-perish mantra, this practice is also changing, particularly in those areas that suffer from what could be termed 'natural science envy'.

In some countries, therefore, the doctoral process is becoming more and more structured and school-like, with doctoral students having to follow standardized courses rather than carrying out the scientific practice under expert supervision, thus moving from participatory learning towards more behaviouristic practices. One could also say that the monograph-based thesis can be associated with Lave and Wenger's (1991) communities of practice ideas, whereas the article-based thesis plays the numbers game. So how do you choose which road to travel?

MONOGRAPH- OR ARTICLE-BASED THESIS?

There are two types of theses that you can choose to write, independent of the research strategy chosen: the monograph- and the article-based thesis. The former was predominant in many countries throughout the twentieth century, and in some countries, such as the UK and Australia, it still is. In most other west-European countries the article-based thesis is, however, gaining popularity.

The tradition of the monograph-based thesis is closely connected to two issues: (1) the tradition within the field and (2) the period of time a doctoral student has to complete the thesis. In general, there is strong tradition for the monograph in qualitative research and, for example, within the humanities. In the past, in some countries, such as Sweden, a doctoral student could spend up to eight years undertaking research before submitting. In Denmark a similar tradition ruled, until the end of the twentieth century when new legislation was invoked. So it used to be a quite lengthy process and advancement in universities was based on factors other than purely publication. However, because of the intensified pressure for publication in the social sciences owing to increasing globalization and mobility of researchers, the monograph-based thesis is today rapidly being phased out. This is an area of debate in the UK, where it is suggested that the nature of the doctorate is changing, with consideration of the PhD as 'process' or the PhD as 'product' (Park, 2005). In this scenario, the monograph-based doctorate is positioned as focusing on the process of writing, researching and developing a major piece of academic writing, whereas the articles-based doctorate is positioned as focusing on the 'product' of the research; being aimed at producing articles that are published in highly regarded journals.

While both forms of PhD have aspects of an apprenticeship, given that they both require candidates to learn the language, mores and 'rules of the game' regarding publishing in their particular field, the monograph has the potential to lengthen this apprenticeship. Indeed, the PhD as process versus product debate highlights issues around the academic credibility and expectations of those writing a monograph and those actively pursuing a PhD through publication. Ballard (1996, pp. 13–14) points out that 'PhD candidates are still apprentices in the profession of research in their discipline; and so their theses are judged in terms of current competence and future promise as academic colleagues'. Consequently, you would assume that this would mean both types of doctoral thesis are viewed as equal. However, given the onus on writing rather than publishing this may mean that monographs are not considered to be the 'finished' piece of work or product and their authors may not be seen as having academic credibility, given the need for them to prove this potential by then publishing high-quality articles that evidence their promise as academics. Arguably, those who have completed an article-based doctorate will have already 'proved' their academic worth to the wider community of practice by virtue of already having published journal papers.

Depending on the choice of methodology for the thesis, the research process of each of these two types may be vastly different. However, there are also many similarities. In the following, an overview of each of these approaches is provided. See also Table 8.1.

Table 8.1   Some characteristics/issues related to monograph-based and article-based theses

	Monograph-based thesis	Article-based thesis
Authorship	Single	Single and multiple
Coherence	Strong emphasis on a holistic, narrative arc through the whole thesis	Smaller articles may lead to a sense of disjointedness and less scope to develop strong arguments
Publications	Provides the opportunity to work in-depth and independently	Provides opportunities to write with more experienced authors
	The thesis in its entirety may need to be complete before publication of findings	Potential for quicker publication of findings prior to completing the thesis
	Opportunity to develop and explore more major findings due to the length and scope of the thesis, with the potential for developing more papers than an article-based thesis	Potential for asking more limited research questions and developing fewer major findings due to limitations of the article format
	Greater potential to publish thesis as a book. This may, however, distract from writing journal articles	Author can become more experienced, more quickly in the art of writing journal articles
	It may take longer for the author to create journal articles given that they will have to heavily revise their work to suit a journal article format	Earlier publication can result in gaining advice from experts in the field and gaining earlier entry into the academic community
	Author may feel they are working in isolation and receive little feedback from the wider academic community about their research. This may prove demotivating and the field could potentially 'move on' during the course of writing the thesis	Potential to receive encouraging and insightful feedback from experts that can provide positive reinforcement
	More emphasis on PhD as process	More emphasis on PhD as product
General	Encourages authors to spend a lot of time planning, reading and developing the structure of the thesis before committing to writing	Encourages author to start writing straight away
	Completing such a large piece of writing may feel overwhelming and demotivating	May make the process more manageable by dividing the work into more manageable, time limited parts

Monograph-based thesis	Article-based thesis
A danger that if the author withdraws from the PhD they will have nothing to show for their time and efforts	If the author has to withdraw from the PhD for any reason, at least they have not 'lost' everything and will have had some articles published

The Monograph-based Thesis

The main purpose of the monograph is to present primary research and original scholarship within a limited area of knowledge (Thompson, 2002). In former times, it was regarded as vital for academic career progression; today, it has lost its standing in many of the social science disciplines, with some suggesting that it can result in overspecialization and can disadvantage students who spend so much time immersed in researching and writing their monograph that they 'do not graduate from doctoral programs as skilled teachers, adept at engaging classes of various sizes and different mixes of students and versed in scholarship on student literacies and learning environments' (Smith, 2010). The monograph is single-authored, a characteristic which distinguishes it from the article-based thesis in which one or more articles can be co-authored. The monograph seems to be becoming less popular as the impact of theses as information sources has been generally declining over the twentieth century and journal articles are cited far more than monographs (Larivière et al., 2007), and this is an argument for pursuing an article-based thesis but it also places importance on those who do pursue a monograph-based thesis to actually publish from it.

However, if we view the monograph-based thesis from a process perspective rather than a product perspective, it is not often in a research career that there is an opportunity to immerse oneself so completely for a lengthy period of time, in the way that is necessary in order to produce a monograph. Actually, the only time in a research career that this is expected is during the doctoral candidacy. However, critics of the monograph, mainly publishers and advocates of open source, perceive the monograph as an outlet for excessive specialization appealing only to small audiences.[2] Douglas Armato and others believe that the monograph has to find another form of outlet than the printed version, because of high publishing costs and cuts in library budgets, which means that access to monographs is likely to be even more limited in the future. The following example highlights this development, since the sales of monographs to libraries have decreased tenfold, from 2000 to 200 since 1980.[3]

For doctoral students, there are other considerations too. First, even if you have a supervisor to guide your work, you are more or less on your own in writing the monograph. There is no co-authorship to ease you into the academic writing tradition of your chosen area, nor anybody with whom to share the burden of writing. However, neither is there any question that this is your work and nobody else's. Further, the writing process itself may be less fragmented and therefore more easily managed, and after the PhD is over you actually have the satisfaction of holding a book in your hand. There are challenges, however. These include getting your PhD condensed into articles either concurrently or afterwards. Having worked so long with your topic means that you have been totally immersed and this may be either positive or negative: positive because you have had more time to reflect, so it may become a better publication, negative because you have been totally immersed and therefore may have difficulty in seeing the various avenues available. Sometimes, when you have worked for so long on putting something together, it is difficult to grasp just exactly how it can be cut into smaller pieces. Publishing from a monograph can also seem more difficult because it can be a challenge to separate out the various insights gained and identify those that will form good points for individual articles. It may be helpful, while you are writing up the findings, that you ask yourself: 'What are the three, four or five major points of interest in my thesis. Where are the wow-factors?' Once you have pinpointed these you can start constructing papers around them.

A final challenge is that once you have written a monograph, submitted and defended it, you may feel that you do not want to revisit the topic again for some time. Three years or more is a long time to spend researching the same topic. Nevertheless, this is the time when you have to start converting your dissertation into articles. There are also concerns about whether doctoral candidates are apprenticed 'with' or apprenticed 'to' and supervisors take ownership of the work of those doctoral students they supervise (Walker et al., 2008) or provide only scholarly input or advice; this is a danger of the monograph, namely its 'highly individualistic' research and supervision structure (Pearson, 1996). This would seem to make it all the more important, when pursuing a monograph-based doctorate, to network, attend and present at conferences and seek feedback and advice outside your particular supervisory team.

The Article-based Thesis

As the title illustrates, the article-based thesis usually consists of a collection of articles. However, there are differences in the demands of individual universities with respect to: the number articles required to constitute the PhD; whether these have to have been published by the time the thesis is submitted; and the 'wrapping' required. There are probably as many approaches as there are universities, thus no uniform formula can be provided. However, in the present competitive environment, the article-based thesis is rapidly becoming predominant. Proponents of the monograph may argue that this detracts from the potential depth of insight that can be gained from research, and this may be true if the articles are allowed to become 'islands in the stream' with little connection between the findings presented in each. Nevertheless, strategically speaking, it is possible to undertake precisely the same research in precisely the same way as one would for a monograph, only separating the chapters as individual articles. For example, most doctoral studies involve doing a thorough literature review in order to gain knowledge of what came before, since research does not exist in a vacuum. The challenge here is that literature reviews are notoriously difficult to publish, so it is necessary to make sure that its relevance is argued and positioned well with respect to existing reviews and theoretical relevance. Further, all research needs to include a methodology section and it is possible to make a methodological contribution to research, so that your methodology section can actually also become an article. However, it is quite rare. Thus, it is mainly in the presentation of the findings to which the doctoral student needs to pay attention.

The publications in an article-based dissertation may also contain joint publications, if the author's independent contribution can be clearly indicated. These publications typically include three to five international refereed articles, and they must have been published earlier or been accepted for publication before the doctoral dissertation is sent for pre-examination. The division of responsibilities and credit in joint publications must be clarified at as early a stage as possible, or at the latest when an article is published. Some universities require the doctoral student to be first author on all articles submitted for evaluation, so it is important to work out how to deal with these practicalities.

SOME GENERAL ADVICE ON DEVELOPING PAPERS FOR OR FROM YOUR PHD

The number of papers that you can develop from your PhD finally depends on the number of major findings. Usually, there will be between three and five of these – as well as numerous minor findings, but these are generally by-products and difficult to develop whole papers around. However, as you are writing up or rewriting the major findings, you may discover that they give rise to new angles. If you have authored a monograph, you can choose to turn these into articles, book chapters, or even a book. Some publishers, for example Edward Elgar, will publish an adapted copy of your thesis as a book if they think that the topic has a sufficiently broad appeal and the findings are interesting and novel. Book chapters may be relevant alternatives for, for example, literature reviews, which cannot find a journal outlet, or for publishing methodological material. With regard to articles, there are a number of challenges, which you can encounter. These include (1) choosing a target journal, (2) dealing with being a non-native English writer, and (3) understanding and dealing with rejection.

Choosing a Target Journal

Experts tend to disagree on this issue, but most advocate that you choose a target journal *before* you start to write. The advantage is that you can set up the manuscript according to the journal rules right from the start. This is particularly important if the submission rules are highly regulated, such as for the American Psychologist Association (APA). Failing to comply with the rules – and it could be a very minor issue – could result in a desk reject.

However, the choice of target journal is very dependent on what is the key research topic or theme in your paper and what type of article you wish to write. Choose a journal that speaks your 'language', and that will accept your methodology and your theoretical standpoint. Also, scrutinize your list of references and identify the journals from which you mainly source your material. Then it is likely that these represent the conversation that you want to join. As a doctoral student it is unlikely that you will be published in highly ranked journals (A, A+) unless you are writing together with someone who is used to publishing in these journals. If you do, take advantage of it and learn from that experience, but remember it is really difficult to be accepted and most journals have very high rejection rates, as discussed elsewhere in this book (see, for example, Chapters 1–3). So there is a time-related trade-off between 'Do you want to be published' or 'Do you want to be published in highly ranked journals?' The review process is often lengthy, so there is a question of whether you can wait, and getting published in a highly ranked journal may well take a lot longer. Even if you get past desk reject, reviewers may still reject your paper, so you really also need to have a plan B.

It is not always a case of simply submitting to a different journal exactly the same paper that was rejected. Often, if one decides to send a rejected paper to a different journal there is work to be done on re-crafting the paper to reflect the concerns and conversations of this newly identified journal. This may involve an analysis of the papers in the journal that are engaging with your research focus, reading papers from the journal and citing them in your previously rejected paper. As a reviewer it is sometimes clear that a paper was originally written and submitted to a different journal (and rejected) due to the emphasis on certain citations and conversations, and this indicates to reviewers that the author is not necessarily interested in the aims and concerns of their particular journal but only in getting their paper published – anywhere, regardless of the journal's readership or research focus. This does not often work to the paper's advantage and can result in another rejection. Needless to say, you should not submit your paper to more than one journal at a time as this is considered bad practice and, as reviewers tend to be specialists who review in their specialist area for many different journals, this may be exposed. Similarly, it is likely that simply sending exactly the same rejected paper to a different journal would result in it being sent to the same reviewer who originally rejected it. Both of these practices can lead to further rejection and also often annoys reviewers.

Finally, regardless of the journal that you eventually identify, you have to write a persuasive covering letter to the editor, arguing why they should publish your paper. You may find yourself in the position that you want to introduce a new discussion in a journal. In this case, you need to explain what the novelty of your paper is, and why it would be advantageous for that particular journal to start a new thread of discussion. However, the cover letter has to be written with humbleness, thus, writing that you believe your paper to be excellent is not a persuasive argument – that is why we have peer review, we let other people decide what is excellent. Arguing that you believe that the paper contributes in x, y and z ways to advance our knowledge would most certainly work better. It does not guarantee that your paper will be published because it still has to go through the review process, but it may get you over the first hurdle – that of desk reject.

Dealing with Being a Non-native English Writer

There is pressure on all doctoral students and early career researchers to publish in highly ranked journals and these are likely to be those published in English. Therefore, it is important that non-native English writers publish in English in order to secure academic employment and tenure. However, many students will not have received any formal writing training during their doctoral studies and this can lead to issues around writing style, which can impact on an article's chances of being published.

It is important that authors take care that they do not play the role of the tailors in the tale of 'The emperor's new clothes', dressing up the paper in elaborate and non-transparent language. As noted at the beginning of this chapter, those authors who use plain and 'unflowery' (down to earth) language invariably get their message and arguments better across. Using unusual words can be interpreted negatively as either trying to show your superiority or hiding your insecurity. Thus, you should ensure you use appropriate language. Whether you are a native writer or not, proofread to ensure that (typing) errors do not detract from your message – there is a big difference in writing 'casual' instead of 'causal'.

One approach would be to write your article in your native language and then have it translated into English – however, this may make it more difficult (and more time-consuming) to respond to advice on revisions if the paper goes to review. Also, if the paper is not translated by someone who has knowledge of your particular field or research tradition, this may result in discrepancies and mistakes, which can undermine the academic credibility of your paper. Thus, if you are not a native English writer, it is advisable to write the paper in English from the beginning and get it reviewed by a certified language auditor. If this is not possible then you should at least ask a native English speaker to read your article before it is submitted.

It has been suggested that it is more difficult for non-native English writers to be published in the social sciences than it is for those writing in the field of science or engineering because 'science and engineering articles have a fixed set of rules and writing such articles is nothing more than a mechanical process' (Basaran, 2009 p. 375–6). However, while this may be a common perception, Wright's chapter in this book highlights that there are several accepted 'rules' and approaches to the construction of an entrepreneurship paper that are also recognized as important for the social sciences generally. Such 'rules' and commonly accepted (and expected) approaches to writing for English-language journals can also be learned through engaging with the academic community in your particular country who have faced similar publishing challenges and have succeeded in publishing in high-quality English-language journals. Early iterations of your work can also be 'tested' for the clarity and accessibility of the language by presenting at international conferences conducted in English.

That said, most reviewers do appreciate the pressure that non-native English authors are under pressure to publish in English-language journals and a paper that has obviously been written by an author whose first language is not English will not necessarily result in the paper being rejected. Often reviewers will recognize the author as a non-native English speaker and offer advice on how the paper can be improved so that it is clearer. However, this will usually only happen if the initial idea or focus of the article is considered to be of interest and relevant to the particular journal. A paper that has many discrepancies and makes clumsy use of the English language may be considered beyond repair and be rejected.

For these reasons, publishing an article in a highly ranked journal as a non-native English speaker may seem like an overwhelming task but fortunately there are many useful resources which can support you. Second language writing is an increasingly researched topic, it even has its own journal (*Journal of Second Language Writing*[4]) and several authors have published useful articles and books on this subject (see, for example, Belcher, 2007; Burgess and Martín-Martín, 2008; Cho, 2004; Delamont, 2011; Wallwork, 2011).

Understanding and Dealing with Rejection

Experienced academics can talk about rejection of journal papers in a very understated and blasé way that seems to ignore the emotional impacts of submitting your research to journals. In attempting to get your research published, particularly when submitting to high-quality journals that have a very high rejection rate (such as those outlined in Fayolle's introduction to this book), you are attempting to push the door open to your academic community. Sometimes the door will nudge open a little and you will get a glimpse of what it is like to publish a paper (perhaps if your paper gets to the revise and re-submit stage but is then rejected) and sometimes the door will be resolutely slammed in your face (with a desk reject). However this rejection happens, it will feel like not only a rejection of your ideas but also a rejection of you as a person. For these reasons it is recognized that 'publishing takes an emotional toll on researchers' (Day, 2011, p. 704)

Perhaps one way of dealing with rejection is to see your paper through the eyes of the editor of that particular journal. Does this paper make a clear contribution to the conversations in the journal and to the know-ledge in the field more widely; given the demands of the lack of physical space (that is, pages) to publish in traditional journals, the costs of publishing and the time taken up with the review process, papers that do not immediately make it clear how they meet these criteria are likely to be rejected without going to review. Editors are under great pressure to meet the demands of their editorial boards, their reviewers, their readership and the authors who submit papers. Does your paper really help them to meet these demands by making your contribution to the journal and the field explicit from the very start?

Then there is the issue of the paper being rejected by one reviewer but being suggested as needing major revisions by another, or general disagreement by the reviewers about the weaknesses or strengths of your paper. Again, the reviewers are under intense pressure to complete their review in a timely and constructive manner and, although the editor may consider the subject matter worthy of further exploration, ultimately if you have not made your contribution clear it is likely to be rejected at review stage. Also, reviewers may have different approaches to your particular area or they may be experts in one discrete aspect of your research (such as the industry sector or the research methods employed). Therefore, different reviewers are likely to have different 'takes' on the value and credibility of your research given their own disciplinary (and sometimes interdisciplinary) understandings. There has been no concerted research into this area by scholars in the field of Entrepreneurship and indeed it is a subject that is rarely addressed. However, some scholars in fields such as psychology and management have considered the reasons for and impacts of journal paper rejection.

For example, Fiske and Fogg's (1990) paper offers insights into this process when they write:

> criticism can be serious in several diverse ways. A critical flaw in the design may (in the eyes of the reviewer) make the paper worthless. An omission or ambiguity in exposition may make the reviewer uncertain about the soundness of the research plan. Departing from current practice in a research area may cause the reviewer to infer that the author is not sufficiently qualified in background and experience to attempt such a research study. (p. 592)

They go on to suggest that, in their field of psychology, the most serious criticisms relate to the author's interpretation of the research findings and the conclusions drawn, with the next most serious criticisms linked to the presentation of the conceptual work that was done before the empirical research was started. This links to both the quality of the literature review and the identification of and engagement with an appropriate theoretical basis for the research. Finally there were criticisms in areas that most authors would expect – the results, methodology and research design. Ultimately, Fiske and Fogg (1990, p. 593) suggest that two-thirds of critical comments were linked to presentation issues – that is, the 'exposition and description' of the research, rather than the actual research activities themselves. Other, more minor, criticisms revolved around poor spelling and grammar, issues that are easily preventable through thorough proofreading and/or having the paper read by critical colleagues before submission to a journal. Rereading or proofreading a manuscript that one has worked on for many weeks or months can be very painful but it really is a necessary and straightforward way of setting up your paper for at least being put out for review.

More recent research in the field of management (Day, 2011) recognizes that negative responses to rejection are common and to be expected. They are part and parcel of the day-to-day development and progression of academics professionals. Furthermore, even if a paper is ultimately rejected there are sometimes glimmers of hope to be taken away from the experience. You will most likely be given some insights into how your paper could be improved to make it suitable for publication (even if that is not in the journal it was rejected from). It is important to take note of the reviewers' comments and advice to help you to develop the paper, especially if you have submitted to a highly ranked journal. This is A* quality feedback from an expert in the field who has actually read and engaged with your research, and it is not often that you receive that!

When authors receive positive encouragement but are asked to revise and re-submit they sometimes do not do this, as rewriting can also be a process tinged with negativity – particularly if you feel that the paper will be significantly 'different' from the one you originally conceived. This is understandable but self-defeating, given all the issues discussed above and the fact that a 'revise and re-submit' moves you one stage further along the road towards being published. For those who have written a monograph this is even more important, given that very few people will actually read your research in monograph format and publishing articles is increasingly becoming the main way of disseminating and sharing your work and building your academic profile.

Ultimately, whether you respond in a negative or more positive way to having a paper rejected, you should recognize this as part of the learning experience in the move from academic novice to expert and take heart from the fact that it happens to all scholars and our negative reactions are normal and to be expected (Day, 2011). Indeed, there are eminent professors who, owing to the anonymous peer review process, still have papers rejected. The fact that they *are* eminent professors is testament to their ability to deal with rejection in a way that has not stopped them from continuing to strive to be published despite this. This also suggests that the more rejections we experience, the better able we will be to deal with them in an increasingly constructive way. We should not seek to never have a paper rejected (as this would be impossible or mean we are aiming too high) but should instead seek to manage our responses to having papers rejected and accept this as part of the process of academic development and this is something that potentially never ends as our field is constantly evolving and new ideas are constantly being tested, explored and developed.

MOVING FROM THE PERIPHERY TO THE INNER CIRCLE: A QUESTION OF IDENTITY?

In developing beyond writing your thesis, you will move from being a novice academic to one with more understanding and credibility within your own research community, but this can bring its own issues for doctoral students and early career academics. Becher and Trowler (2001) remind us that 'Being a member of a disciplinary community involves a sense of identity and personal commitment, a "way of being in the world", a matter of taking on "a cultural frame that defines a great part of one's life"' (2001, p. 47, quoting Geertz). This sense of identity as an academic develops over time through the socialization involved in spending three (or more) years developing and writing a monograph (or articles for publication). With this comes a sense of confidence, of finding your own voice and realization that you have something to say that is interesting, tells your community something new and helps to move knowledge in your field on.

However, this sense of cultural and disciplinary identity can be complicated for those trying to publish in the field of entrepreneurship as it is often positioned as interdisciplinary (indeed, there are suggestions that it has to be interdisciplinary, given the breadth of inquiry and theoretical engagement that it encompasses). Some may draw upon the fields of economics, management or organizational behaviour or, like the doctoral thesis illustrated in the opening of this chapter, upon sociology, education and gender theory. However, this interdisciplinarity also greatly increases the potential audience for your publications and this can only be a positive thing. Non-native English speakers will also have to deal with the issue of establishing themselves as academics in two different languages. Issues around rejection and lessons learned can be seen as a form of identity threat on the road to establishing ourselves as 'experts' – or at least capable of meeting the standards set by our academic community. It is acknowledged that this can have different effects on those students positioned as different to the 'traditionally' white, middle-class, male academic (Ivanic, 1998). This is also an issue when academic success is linked to particular outcomes, such as publishing, with the result that 'many younger academics … must negotiate on a daily basis not only their attempts at "becoming" but also the threat of "unbecoming"' (Archer, 2008, p. 385).

So, ultimately, what does being an expert mean? Golde (2010, p. 83) sums this up when he says: 'Experts are able to ask important questions, to competently conduct research, to assess others' work, to understand the important ideas in their field, to communicate what they know and to apply their knowledge and understanding to solve important problems.' This would also seem to be a succinct description of the characteristics we need to emphasize in writing journal articles so they are considered important and interesting enough to be published in the high-quality journals that a successful academic career is built on.

NOTES

1. On-the job training (OJT).
2. www.upress.umn.edu/about-us/history-and-fact-sheet-folder/what-was-a-university-press-1/iii.-the-monograph.
3. www.researchinformation.info/news/news_story.php?news_id=1051.
4. www.journals.elsevier.com/journal-of-second-language-writing/.

REFERENCES

Archer, L. (2008), 'Younger academics' constructions of 'authenticity', 'success' and professional identity', *Studies in Higher Education*, **33** (4), 385–403.

Ballard, B. (1996), 'Context of judgement: an analysis of some assumptions identified in examiners reports on 62 successful PhD theses', paper presented at the Conference on Quality in Postgraduate Research, Adelaide, South Australia.

Basaran, S. (2009), 'The process of writing research articles in English and getting published: a case study', *Sosyal Bilimler Dergisi*, **8** (2), 371–84, accessed 27 June 2013 at http://www.academia.edu/565518/The_Process_of_Writing_Research_Articles_in_English_and_Getting_Published_A_Case_Study.

Becher, T. and P. Trowler (2001), *Academic Tribes and Territories: Intellectual Enquiry and the Culture of Disciplines*, 2nd edn, Buckingham: Society for Research into Higher Education (SRHE) and Open University Press.

Belcher, D.D. (2007), 'Seeking acceptance in an English-only research world', *Journal of Second Language Writing*, **16** (1), 1–22.

Burgess, S. and P. Martín-Martín (2008), *English as an Additional Language in Research Publication and Communication*, Bern: Peter Lang.

Cho, S. (2004), 'Challenges of entering discourse communities through publishing in English: perspectives of nonnative-speaking doctoral students in the United States of America', *Journal of Language, Identity and Education*, **3** (1), 47–72.

Coimbra Group (2012), *Survey on PhD Programme Structures and Administration in Europe and North America: Main Findings*, accessed 11 April 2013 at http://www.coimbra-group.eu/transdoc/uploads/TRANS-DOC%20Survey%20 findings.pdf.

Day, N.E. (2011), 'The silent majority: manuscript rejection and its impact on scholars', *Academy of Management Learning & Education*, **10** (4), 704–18.

Delamont, S. (2011), 'Academic writing in a global context: the politics and practices of publishing in English', *Studies in Higher Education*, **36** (4), 505–6.

Fiske, D.W. and L. Fogg (1990), 'But the reviewers are making different criticisms of my paper! Diversity and uniqueness in reviewer comments', *American Psychologist*, **45** (5), 591–8.

Golde, C. (2010), 'Entering different worlds: socialization into disciplinary communities' in S.K. Gardner and P. Mendoza (eds), *On Becoming a Scholar: Socialization and Development in Doctoral Education*, Stirling, VA: Stylus, pp. 79–96.

Ivanic, R. (1998), *Writing and Identity: The Discoursal Construction of Identity in Academic Writing*, Amsterdam and Philadelphia, PA: John Benjamins B.V.

Lave, J. and E. Wenger (1991), *Situated Learning: Legitimate Peripheral Participation*, Cambridge, New York, Melbourne and Madrid: Cambridge University Press.

Larivière, V., A. Zuccala and É. Archambault (2007), 'The declining scientific impact of theses: implications for electronic thesis and dissertation repositories and graduate studies', accessed 11 April 2013 at http://individual.utoronto.ca/ azuccala_web/Larivier-et-al.pdf.

Neergaard, N., L. Tanggaard, N. Krueger and S. Robinson (2012), 'Pedagogical interventions in entrepreneurship from behaviourism to existential learning', conference proceedings, International Small Business and Entrepreneurship Conference, 7–8 November. Dublin, Ireland.

Park, C. (2005), 'New variant PhD: the changing nature of the doctorate in the UK', *Journal of Higher Education Policy and Management*, **27** (2), 189–207.

Pearson, M. (1996), 'Professionalising Ph.D. education to enhance the quality of the student experience', *Higher Education*, **32** (3), 303–20.

Smith, S. (2010), 'Beyond the dissertation monograph', accessed 11 April 2013 at http://www.mla.org/blog&topic=133.

Thompson, J.W. (2002), 'The death of the scholarly monograph in the humanities? Citation patterns in literary scholarship', *Libri*, **52** (3), 121–36.

Walker, G.E, C.M. Golde, L. Jones, A.C. Bueschel and P. Hutchings (2008), *The Formation of Scholars: Rethinking Doctoral Education for the Twenty-First Century*, San Francisco, CA: Jossey-Bass.

Wallwork, A. (2011), *English for Writing Research Papers*, New York: Springer.

9. Do European scholars have specific problems getting published in Anglo-Saxon journals?

Dimo Dimov

INTRODUCTION

The globalization of the academic environment has led to institutional-ization of the notion of academic performance around the need to publish in high-quality international journals. This has resulted in significant increases in the number of submissions to those journals and, naturally, in increases in their rejection rates which often reach over 90 per cent of submissions. A rejection is a daunting experience for any scholar and naturally raises questions about biases inherent in the system, which might give rise to structural advantages or disadvantages for certain types of authors.

Discourse in the field often distinguishes between European and North American scholars as representatives of different research worlds. In the light of this distinction, the title question of this chapter is not surprising. I have faced it on several occasions and presume that many colleagues would be interested in an answer, even if such answer were not straightforward. In a recent reaction to calls for establishing a 'New European School' of entrepreneurship and to narratives about the distinc-tiveness of European research, Davidsson (2013) tackles directly and effectively the question of possible discrimination against European scholarship in North American journals. His answer in the negative is based on the strong presence of European scholars among the most cited authors in the field, among the authors of published articles in the leading journals in the field, among the associate editors and editorial board members of those journals, among the members of the Entrepreneurship Division of the Academy of Management, among the submissions to the major conferences in the field, and among the recipients of 'best paper' and 'best dissertation' awards. While some bias may exist in regard to the underlying paradigm of research (for example, positivist versus inter-pretivist), the magnitude of the bias should be assessed against the baseline rates of the size and intensity of research discourse within each paradigm.

I believe that the answer to the question lies not in exogenous factors such as bias in the system but in endogenous ones, related to how prepared European scholars are to engage and compete in the market for ideas. The peer-reviewed nature of the publication process, wherein authors strive to withstand the natural scepticism of the research community in regard to the focus, rigour and contribution of their work, means that success in publication is not so much about the stand-alone scientific merits of the study as it is about keeping up with the evolving notion of what constitutes timely and rigorous research and about the art of communicating the merits of the study to the peer community. I can safely assume that all aspiring authors have produced competent pieces of research by following established conventions around research design, data collection and analysis. The question, then, is whether they are ready to move from the static, safe environment of their research offices to the dynamic, competitive arena of publishing.

To answer the question, I examine issues related to socialization, training, focus and communication. By comparing European and North American practices – or, in some cases, simply highlighting the North American practices that do not have widespread equivalents in Europe – I make the point that some European scholars may face competitive disadvantage and steeper learning curves at the points at which they submit their first work for publication. What will also emerge from the comparison is that the question of who is a 'European' scholar is not simply about geographic origin, in line with Davidsson's (2013) recent reflections. Just consider my own case: I am European by origin (Bulgarian), received my training at a European institution (London Business School), am currently based at a European institution (University of Bath), and have spent most of my research career at European institutions. Yet, I am often perceived as a 'North American' scholar.

SOCIALIZATION FOR PUBLISHING

Successful publishing is essentially a tale of persistence and learning. If there is one consistent message that emerges from the accounts of prominent colleagues, it is that they tend to keep a paper 'in play' by sending it to the next journal while at the same time listening and responding to reviewers' feedback, whether by tweaking the paper for the next submission or by modifying their approach to the next research project. I am proud to have my own war story. After completing my PhD and starting my first academic job – at IE Business School in Madrid, Spain – I started working on a project with my then new colleague, Pablo Martin de Holan, on exploration investments by venture capital firms. This was in October 2004 and we were off to a promising start: successful submission to the 2005 Academy of Management Conference. We started the publication process in the summer of 2006, submitting the paper to *Organization Science*. The paper was finally accepted for publication in its seventh journal submission, in February 2012 – almost six years after the first submission and over seven years after the start of the project – in *Industrial and Corporate Change* (Dimov et al., 2012). In the process we received the following sequence of decisions: 'reject', 'high-risk revise and re-submit', 'reject and re-submit', 'reject', 'desk reject', 'reject', 'high-risk revise and re-submit' (after which we withdrew the paper), and 'revise and re-submit'. Needless to say, we have learnt a lot in the process and the original and final versions of the paper bear little resemblance.

This process can be overwhelming for scholars who are not socialized into it early on. As a result, there are three reasons that European scholars may face a competitive disadvantage. The first is a question of mental preparation for what is to come. North American PhD programmes are tightly focused on preparing students for academic careers and the reality and pressure of the tenure process in North American institutions. As a result, students are exposed early on to the trials and tribulations of the publishing process, internalizing the war stories of their PhD seminar leaders or advisers and actively sharing strategies and tactics for navigating the process. They are also encouraged to engage with the process early on, submitting work as early as their first year and working with faculty collaborators. In contrast, many European programmes place little emphasis on publishing; in the UK, for instance, there is an established practice of advising PhD students not to work on side projects or engage in publishing until after completing their PhD. As a result, they come out of the PhD programmes ill prepared for the reality of publishing.

The second reason has to do with expectations and emotions. In North American circles, success in submission means getting a 'revise and re-submit' decision. This represents a significant milestone for a paper, getting a foot in the door of the journal, beyond which a paper develops in productive dialogue with two or three specific reviewers. Against such expectations, rejection is a normal outcome, in which the comments by the reviewers represent valuable feedback for improvement and not a judgement on the scholarly identity of the author. Indeed, it is very comforting to many that the most prolific 'stars' in the field experience rejections regularly. In the face of rejection, many authors actively look for the lessons that they can extract for their future submissions. The expectations play out differently for many European scholars. In the absence of preparation for the publishing process and with the first submission often based on their doctoral thesis – work in which they have become enormously vested – the submission may become an implicit search for approval. As a result, a reject decision may be seen as a personal blow, with the negative emotional surge overwhelming the potential lessons in the review. Although scholars gradually develop 'thick skin' in the wake of several rejections, there is a real risk that first rejections – particularly when made on a major, identity-shaping work such as your doctoral thesis – can lead to dejection and turning your back on the top-tier journals. In this regard, the practice of early submissions not only calibrates the emotional reactions to rejections but also does so in the safe, supportive environment of a PhD programme.

The third reason relates to learning to read, interpret and respond to editorial letters and reviewer feedback. At top journals, these can be overwhelming at first, often being as long as the paper itself. Gradually, you learn to distinguish major and minor points, deal breakers, and points for negotiation or pushback. In the North American practice, PhD students can develop tacit understanding of this by working with faculty collaborators or can simply enlist their help for interpreting the decision letter. I recall from my own PhD experience giving a long rejection letter to a professor who managed to distil it to three key points. I also learnt that 'ambitious' was not a compliment for my work but simply a signal that I was trying to pack too much into one paper. Again, in a European context, where such platform for tacit knowledge exchange is missing, scholars can often be at a loss as to how to respond to reviewers' feedback. In some cases, a revision may simply appear to be too much work, coming on the heels of the total exhaustion following the completion of a doctoral thesis. From such a disadvantaged position, publishing success will take much longer, with many giving up along the way.

TRAINING

In addition to socialization, there are issues related to formal doctoral training in terms of the substantive theories and research methodologies in the field. Doctor of philosophy programmes in North American universities are known for the extensity of their training, with at least two solid years spent on taking PhD courses. These cover not only fundamental research skills such as research design and methodology, but theory-building and disciplinary knowledge. In terms of methodology, the training reflects the latest trends and developments in the field as evident in recent published work. In terms of disciplinary knowledge, there are a series of courses that introduce students to the development and latest stance of the respective field, and help them to identify avenues for further development and points of contribution by developing papers focused on theoretical synthesis and extension. Knowledge of the basic disciplines is then rigorously tested in a comprehensive examination, which is a major milestone in the second year of the programme. Many programmes have first-year milestones such as developing a theory paper on a topic of interest. It is only after passing these milestones that students develop proposals for their dissertation research. These are subject to rigorous assessment (defence), which – in addition to the merits of the research design and methodology – tests the student's ability to frame their research in terms of a distinct contribution to their field of interest as well as to employ the most appropriate methodology for the research question at hand.

My PhD training was of this nature, following London Business School's complete redesign of its PhD programme to follow the 'American' model. This model operates at many other European business schools and is a model to which many other schools aspire in their quest for building research capacity and excellence.

The research training at many European schools, however, is different. While it covers research skills associated with formulating a research design and implementing qualitative and quantitative research methodologies, this is often done within a more generic social science framework, thereby failing to reflect the specific trends and developments in the field. In addition, it largely misses the disciplinary components. Aside from some exposure to disciplinary literature in previous master's training, students review and make sense of the literature essentially on their own. Although this is an important exercise of independent research skills, given the number of journals and volume of academic publications, it is difficult for a non-socialized mind to discern seminal work, theoretical heritage and distil the unique contribution that an article makes. As a result, there is no transfer of tacit knowledge related to the publication process. Students have to discover this knowledge for themselves, once they send their work to journals, via the often dejecting feedback by reviewers that their paper lacks compelling framing, lacks sufficient theoretical development and fails to make a strong theoretical contribution. Provided that there are no fundamental flaws in the design or methodology of the paper, these are ubiquitous reasons for rejecting a paper.

There are two ways in which the lack of disciplinary training bestows a competitive disadvantage. First, it makes it more difficult to plan and articulate a theoretical contribution, the lack of which represents a major ground for rejection. What constitutes a theoretical contribution is a question with which North American scholars grapple from the early days of their PhD training and the answer to which is honed as a tacit skill over many iterations and submitted papers. Often, PhD courses start from some classic paper such as Whetten (1989) and Daft (1995) on the nature of theoretical contribution and tally these against current practice. Whetten's template is particularly useful as it highlights that two often used justifications for the merits of a paper – which work perfectly well for a doctoral thesis and often for less prominent journals – do not really constitute compelling contributions for the top journals in the field. One relates to simply adding another explanatory variable to account for some incremental variance in an outcome of interest. The skeleton of this argument is that we know a lot about X through its relationship with Y and Z, and we can learn even more by adding W to the equation. If demonstrated, this is solid empirical contribution but does not qualify as theoretical one on the ground that our understanding of the existing theoretical relationships in which X is involved does not really change.

The other often-used justification is that no one has studied X or that no one has studied X in the context of Y. The counter-argument that editors and reviewers tend to make, in the absence of further elaboration, is that simply because something has not been studied does not mean that it should be. What they are looking for is a theoretical reason for conducting a study of this novel phenomenon or context. Addressing this point before submission can significantly increase the chances for a positive outcome at the first round. Very often, simply thinking more deeply beforehand about such justification can lead to some promising insights. This is a key outcome to intensive PhD seminars on a given topic. For instance, a novel phenomenon can lie at the boundary of current theory and can have implications for whether and how this theory can be extended. Perhaps the predictions that the theory would make for this phenomenon would not square with the empirical observations, which will prompt a search for how to extend the theory by incorporating new theoretical constructs or relationships. Similarly, in the case of new context, what generates interest are situations when existing theory predicts things to work in the same way in the new context, but they do not; or when theory predicts that things should not work in the same way in the new context, but they do.

The second way to competitive disadvantage due to lack of disciplinary training relates to keeping up with the methodological rigour of the field. Owing to the increased competition for space in the top journals, the stand-alone merits of a research project have become disconnected from the methodological requirements to get into those journals. Again, in North American practice, PhD students develop a good sense of what these requirements are, which can become a particular point of contention during the defence of your dissertation proposal when the discussion often moves from what is sufficient to get the PhD to what is sufficient to ensure a stream of publications that will help one meet the tenure requirements of their future institutions. Thus, you will see that top journals often have higher sample sizes, perhaps as a result of power analysis intended to determine the sample size that would accommodate a more complex theoretical model. Another trend is that top journals have higher standards for analytical or econometric rigour, with explicit attention devoted to using estimation techniques that are well suited for the nature and distribution of the dependent variable, testing the sensitivity and robustness of the results, and eliminating alternative explanations.

Methodological deficiencies are not limited only to quantitative studies; they apply equally to papers based on qualitative data. While it may appear that leading international journals have smaller proportions of qualitative papers compared to less prominent journals, this may be due to differences in criteria on what constitutes 'good' qualitative work as well as to the spread of associated training. Given top journals' emphasis on theoretical contribution – whether deductively or inductively derived – papers that focus on rich description for its own sake are turned down for failing to extract theoretical insights or juxtapose the description against existing theory. These journals value papers in which the selection of cases serves theoretical purpose and the analysis derives insight both within and across cases. Against this benchmark, proper training is less widespread, which explains the relatively smaller number of submissions and acceptances. On the other hand, rich descriptions of single cases represent a strong tradition in European research, interweaved with stronger presence of interpretivist or phenomenological paradigms. The difficulty for an author coming from this tradition lies in catering to a journal mission highlighting the importance of theoretical contribution.

Since these are all issues related to the core research design of the project, by the time a paper is submitted they are impossible to fix without going back to collect additional data. As a result, some of these will be seen as fundamental flaws of a paper. Raising awareness of them will ensure that the next research project will be more strongly designed, attuned with the practices in the leading international journals. The competitive disadvantage of many European scholars is that they have to learn this as they go, at the expense of receiving rejections with constructive but often brutal feedback, while for their North American counterparts such learning occurs much earlier on and in the safer context of doctoral training.

FOCUS

Anglo-Saxon journals – or indeed any other journals – vary in their explicit focus on small and medium-size firms (SMEs) and/or entre-preneurship. There seems to be a divide in the degree to which these terms are seen as central to the editorial mission of the journals. Much of European discourse seems to be about SMEs and, accordingly, any research that focuses on SMEs would be readily classified as entre-preneurship research. In this setting small business management, small business owners and entrepreneurship are treated as interchangeable terms.

On the other hand, entrepreneurship carries a different meaning in other, often North American but not exclusively so, journals. It reflects the seminal work of Venkataraman (1997), Shane and Venkataraman (2000) and Gartner (1985) which aimed to define the conceptual bound-aries of the field. One definition centres on the discovery, evaluation and exploitation of entrepreneurial opportunities, which involves, albeit not exclusively, new businesses. The other reflects a sociological perspective of entrepreneurship (Aldrich and Ruef, 2006; Thornton, 1999) and focuses on the creation/emergence of new organizations.

Journals that explicitly operate in this realm – whether new opportun-ities or new organizations – may inevitably deem SME-oriented research as not falling within their domain unless dealing with new firms or the opportunity-oriented activities of SMEs. Wiklund et al. (2011) make this point explicitly in their recent editorial introduction of the special issue of *Entrepreneurship Theory and Practice* on the future of entre-preneurship research:

> We strongly recommend that entrepreneurship research be unified as a field approached theoretically and empirically in terms of the *phenomenon*. We propose that the phenomenon of 'emergence of new economic activity' lies at the heart of entrepreneurship (where 'economic' has a much wider meaning than 'commercial'). This might seem like an obvious statement, but the past shows us that this has not been the case. ... Rather, the problem is that to a

large extent, the entrepreneurship field has instead been unified by an interest in small, young, or owner- managed businesses, that is, the context, with far less cohesion and agreement concerning what it is about these small businesses and new firms that is so interesting (the phenomenon). Rather, anything related to small, young and/or owner-managed firms can be found under the rubric of entrepreneurship. … As a consequence of this shift from a context- based to a phenomenon-based view of entrepreneurship, clarification of exactly what constitutes this phenomenon is needed. … The potentially most significant implication of this phenomenon-based view is that it allows us to distill what exactly it is that is entrepreneurial about the things that we study and thus, it establishes the boundaries of our field. (p. 5)

The above is a very clear statement about a bifurcation in the field, with some scholars interested in context (SME) and other interested in a phenomenon (emergence of new economic activity). Given that a lot of 'European' scholars are effectively interested in SME research, then a quick answer to the question of difficulty is whether they are simply submitting work to journals with an explicitly stated focus on the phenomenon of entrepreneurship to the exclusion of papers that focus simply on SMEs. This suggests that scholars should pay careful attention to the mission of each journal and should not make inferences based on crude categorizations such as Anglo-Saxon or European versus North American journals. To illustrate this point, I provide below excerpts from the aims of three prominent journals in the field: *Journal of Business Venturing* (JBV), *Entrepreneurship Theory and Practice* (ETP), and *International Small Business Journal* (ISBJ).

The Journal of Business Venturing provides a scholarly forum for sharing useful and interesting theories, narratives, and interpretations of the antecedents, mechanisms, and/or consequences of entrepreneurship. This multi-disciplinary, multi-functional, and multi-contextual journal aspires to deepen our understanding of the entrepreneurial phenomenon in its myriad of forms.

[Entrepreneurship Theory and Practice]'s mission is to publish original conceptual and empirical papers that contribute to the advancement of the field of entrepreneurship. Topics include, but are not limited to: National and International Studies of Enterprise Creation; Small Business Management; Family-owned Businesses; Minority Issues in Small Business and Entrepreneurship; Research Methodologies; Venture Financing; Corporate and Non-profit Entrepreneurship.

The International Small Business Journal (ISBJ) publishes the highest quality original research papers on small business and entrepreneurship.

Several useful insights emerge from these excerpts. First, JBV focuses exclusively on the phenomenon of entrepreneurship, albeit without defining what the phenomenon involves. This, I believe, is purposeful open-endedness that puts the onus on the submitting author to articulate what is entrepreneurial about their research topic by linking their work to previous work in the journal. In contrast, although ETP also focuses on entrepreneurship, it explicitly includes topics such as small business management and family-owned businesses that would be seen by many as not dealing with entrepreneurial phenomena. Nevertheless, the actual timeliness and viability of these topics in the journal is reflected in the research streams and conversations within the journal to which submitting authors need to connect. These are predominantly steered towards entrepreneurship. Finally, ISBJ's aim suggests that 'small business' and 'entrepreneurship' are distinct categories – in line with the above distinction between context and phenomenon – while being open to both.

These differences in focus represent important tacit knowledge of the field. The implication for scholars not aware of them is that with overemphasis on a research context focused on SMEs and no explicit articulation of the 'entrepreneurship' aspects of the submitted paper there may be strong grounds to desk reject a paper for lack of fit. Where scholars focus their research is a question of field identity and career aspirations. Those who aspire to establish themselves in the field of entrepreneurship and to publish in the top journals in that field have to make their research choices accordingly and convey a clear sense of the entrepreneurial phenomenon they examine.

COMMUNICATION

In the publication process, you engage in a conversation with editor and reviewers about the merits of the submitted research paper. The conversation metaphor offered by Huff (1999) is my favourite. I can vividly imagine entering a room full of people already clustered into conversation groups. To join a conversation, I have to pause and listen to its flow, waiting for an opportune moment to interject something that relates to what has been said and that can take the conversation forward. Throwing in comments that are off topic and disconnected from the flow of the conversation is likely to earn me perplexed glances and leave me alone, with people quietly regrouping behind my back.

A journal is a series of conversations, one of which a submitted paper attempts to join. Although the history of a conversation is clear, where the conversation is going is not. This is where an author can leave a creative mark, interpreting the past conversation trail in a new light and steering the conversation in a particular direction. The first impressions of a paper are created by its introduction, which signals to the editor and reviewers whether and why the paper is timely, interesting and appropriate. Perhaps more importantly, the introduction signals to the editor the conversations in which the author is seeking to engage and thus facilitates the selection of reviewers. Clearly, having the right reviewers – those most closely attuned to the topic and message of the paper – is key at this stage. Whether this occurs depends on how the paper is framed.

Consistent with the points made in the previous sections, lack of or insufficient socialization and training can put an author at a disadvantage when it comes to communicating effectively how the paper fits in the literature. To the extent that this has not been practised as part of your PhD training, you face a steeper learning curve when having to grasp the nuances of framing in the 'live' setting of actual submissions. A piece of advice that accomplished scholars often give at professional development workshops is to send a paper for peer review before submitting it to a journal. But the effectiveness of a peer review depends on having peers who have published in the particular journal or in journals of similar standing. There is thus a network effect whereby there is a strong differentiation between academic environments with high concentration of accomplished scholars, training and socialization, and environments where these elements are lacking. This differentiation does not run along the North America–Europe divide, but cuts across it.

Framing a research paper is a creative act of mapping the field of research in a way that highlights its features of interest and exposes gaps in the map. The analogy of maps is particularly useful here. Maps are abstract representations of areas that focus on particular features of interest, for example, political boundaries, physical terrain, temperature, air pressure, rainfall, and so on. In the same way, research in the field can be represented in terms of particular topic, theory, relationship or research setting. Identifying the feature that will be emphasized in the paper represents the 'hook' around which the paper will be wrapped, aimed at arresting the reviewers' attention. In his classic paper on what makes an article interesting, Davis (1971) points to challenging some of the assumptions held by the audience, highlighting a gap between perceptions and reality. In this sense, 'interesting' stands at a fine balance between 'absurd' (challenging too many assumptions) and 'obvious' (challenging too few). Because different audiences have different assumptions, the framing of the paper is about identifying the audiences whose assumptions can be challenged in the realm of 'interesting'. Davis goes on to list a number of templates of the sort 'while everyone thinks that X is Y, it is actually Z'.

For example, in two papers (Dimov and Shepherd, 2005; Dimov et al., 2007) we examined the relationship between the backgrounds of venture capital managers and, respectively, the success of their investments and the nature of their investment decisions. The papers were framed in different ways, using different maps of the field and thus highlighting different gaps. The first focuses on a particular theory – human capital – and makes the argument that while scholars perceive human capital as a monolithic, we show it to be fragmented. In other words, while studies tend to focus on the quantity of human capital, we show that its qualitative nature matters. The second paper, in contrast, focuses on a particular topic – venture capital (VC) decision-making – and makes the argument that while scholars perceive that there exists a single decision-making process across VC firms, we show this process to vary with the nature of the VC managers and social standing of the VC firms.

Deciding on how to frame a paper is a long, iterative process, not unlike the development of an entrepreneurial idea. In this regard, informal chats with colleagues or conference presentations are vital forums for testing initial ideas with relevant audiences. The response and feedback you are likely to get is often of the 'Have you thought of X?' type, which can point to new ways of seeing the paper.

Another issue of communication relates to the language and writing style of the paper. Non-native English speakers face the hurdle of making their paper readable and easy to follow. Even native English speakers need to be aware of differences between American English and other variants. Informal feedback can identify these issues early on and the authors can retain the help of a copy editor to ensure that they do not detract from the paper once submitted. In terms of writing style, some journals have distinct formats that reviewers expect to see, which in turn facilitates the assessment of the paper in the face of the time pressures that reviewers face. Thus, when a paper is not written in the particular style, reviewers may become frustrated by the amount of cognitive effort needed to grasp the main ideas in the paper, which in turn prevents them from providing more developmental feedback.

CONCLUSION

The above reflections suggest that the answer to the opening question is a qualified 'yes'; not all European scholars face difficulties in publishing in top international journals, but some do. These difficulties are in the form of competitive disadvantage and steeper learning curves owing to lack of timely socialization into the publishing process, lack of disciplinary training, research focus that is tangential to the explicit mission of the journals, and underdeveloped tacit knowledge in articulating how a paper fits and makes a contribution to the field. It is important to note that these difficulties emerge from relative standing rather than stand-alone deficiency. With an increasing number of scholars competing for limited spaces in the top journals, the intensity of competition increases and so do the requirements for getting in. Little differences early in your academic training and socialization can grow into large performance differentials later on. A PhD student who is better trained can publish a paper in a top journal before graduating, which will help him or her get a job at an institution with higher research profile. This will in turn expose the person to accomplished peers who can further accelerate his or her publishing productivity. This will in turn attract top-quality doctoral students who will provide further acceleration, and so on.

Although all these difficulties can be overcome the hard way, through sheer persistence and learning, this path is laden with emotional strain and dejection and may not be compatible with the shorter time frames for academic promotion. With the globalization of our academic community, there are many actions that you can undertake to shorten the learning process. Attending doctoral or junior faculty consortia, particularly at the major international conferences in management and entrepreneurship, can help you develop a network of peers that can facilitate tacit knowledge transfer and provide emotional support. Disciplinary training workshops can improve the formulation and design of the research project, which can pre-empt fundamental flaws later on. Paper development workshops can help with framing a paper and articulating its theoretical contribution. Outside of these formal forums, you can reach out in an informal manner to other scholars in the field to build collaborative relationships, which can greatly accelerate learning.

REFERENCES

Aldrich, H.E. and M. Ruef (2006), *Organizations Evolving*, Thousand Oaks, CA: Sage.

Daft, R. (1995), 'Why I recommended that your manuscript be rejected and what you can do about it', In L. Cummings and P. Frost (eds), *Publishing in the Organizational Sciences*, 2nd edn, Thousand Oaks, CA: Sage, pp. 164–83.

Davidsson, P. (2013), 'Some reflection on research 'schools' and geographies', *Entrepreneurship & Regional Development*, **25** (1–2), 100–110.

Davis, M.S. (1971), 'That's interesting: towards a phenomenology of sociology and a sociology of phenomenology', *Philosophy of the Social Sciences*, **1** (4), 309–44.

Dimov, D. and D.A. Shepherd (2005), 'Human capital theory and venture capital firms: exploring "home runs" and "strike outs"', *Journal of Business Venturing*, **20** (1), 1–21.

Dimov, D., P. Martin de Holan and H. Milanov (2012), 'Learning patterns in venture capital investing in new industries', *Industrial and Corporate Change*, **21** (6), 1389–426.

Dimov, D., D.A. Shepherd and K.M. Sutcliffe (2007), 'Requisite expertise, firm reputation, and status in venture capital investment allocation decisions', *Journal of Business Venturing*, **22** (4), 481–502.

Gartner, W.B. (1985), 'A conceptual framework for describing the phenomena of new venture creation', *Academy of Management Review*, **10** (4), 696–706.

Huff, A.S. (1999), *Writing for Scholarly Publication*, Thousand Oaks, CA: Sage.

Shane, S. and Venkataraman, S. (2000), 'The promise of entrepreneurship as a field of research', *Academy of Management Review*, **25** (1), 217–26.

Thornton, P.H. (1999), 'The sociology of entrepreneurship', *Annual Review of Sociology*, **25** (August), 19–46.

Venkataraman, S. (1997), 'The distinctive domain of entrepreneurship research', in J. Katz and R. Brockhaus (eds), *Advances in Entrepreneurship*, vol. 3, Greenwich, CT: JAI Press, pp. 119–38.

Whetten, D.A. (1989), 'What constitutes a theoretical contribution?', *Academy of Management Review*, **14** (4), pp. 490–95.

Wiklund, J., P. Davidsson, D.B. Audretsch and C. Karlsson (2011), 'The future of entrepreneurship research', *Entrepreneurship Theory and Practice*, **35** (1), 1–9.

10. How to publish qualitative entrepreneurship research in top journals

Nicole Coviello

INTRODUCTION

Publishing in a top journal is often a challenge, and this seems particularly so for qualitative research. Nevertheless, six of the last ten winners of the *Academy of Management Journal*'s (AMJ's) Best Article award (to 2011) are – you guessed it – qualitative. Clearly, qualitative studies are important and impactful. How, then, can you improve your chances of publishing qualitative entrepreneurship research in a top journal? Drawing on my experience as an author, reviewer and editor, I offer some guidance with this chapter. I begin with comments on some qualitative approaches seen in entrepreneurship research and then focus on areas in the manuscript and research process that often need special attention. Finally, I share some observations regarding the writing process. Because I study, publish and review entrepreneurship research in fields such as marketing, management and international business, I use examples from across disciplines.

QUALITATIVE APPROACHES – SO MANY TO CHOOSE FROM!

Many (most) of the qualitative papers that cross my desk as an editor or reviewer rely on the case method. There are, however, numerous ways to approach a qualitative investigation. For example, Table 10.1 reports recent publications from the *Journal of Business Venturing* (JBV), and shows that methods can range from in-depth interviews to archival data, phenomenological interviews or using a nation as a 'case'. Other methods include, for example, analysis of narrative, participant observation and ethnography.

Table 10.1   Examples of recent qualitative studies from JBV

Authors	General goal	Method
Khavul et al. (2013)	To develop a grounded theory of the process of institutional change in micro-financing	Fifty-seven depth interviews with representatives of multiple communities, combined with archival data. Guatemala used as a 'case' nation
Cope (2011)	To understand entrepreneurial learning from failure	Interpretive phenomenological research (using phenomenological interviews) with eight entrepreneurs in the UK and the USA, based on their lived experience of failure
Fischer and Reuber (2011)	To explore how the effectual process is impacted by entrepreneurs' using Twitter for social interaction	Depth interviews with 12 entrepreneurs having various levels of entrepreneurial expertise, combined with archival data related to their Twitter accounts
Petty and Gruber (2011)	To explore actual venture capital decision-making as it occurs over time in its natural decision environment	Textual interpretation of 11 years of archival data of a single European venture capital firm

Given the variety of possibilities, if your research question warrants a qualitative method, take the time to identify which approach (or combination thereof) might be most appropriate. Also consider which approach(es) might offer the greatest potential to make a methodological contribution. This is because one way to differentiate your work might involve employing something other than case research.

For a refresher on qualitative methods, I recommend three books. For fairly clinical but highly usable overviews, I like Creswell (2007) and Lee (1999). Another overview that provides interesting historical insight is found in Prasad (2005). I also recommend reading well-done studies from outside entrepreneurship. One example is Elsbach and Kramer's (2003) investigation of how experts assess the creative potential of others. In this AMJ Best Article winner, the authors use a combination of interviews, observation, participation and archival data to provide rich, multidimensional insight to how studio executives and producers in Hollywood assess the 'pitches' of screenwriters. Another example of rich work is Schouten and McAlexander's (1995) marketing classic: three years of ethnographic field work with Harley-Davidson motorbike owners.

If the case method is, in fact, most appropriate for your research, I offer four suggestions. First, recognize that a particular strength of case research is that it generally integrates a variety of data sources (for example, interviews, observation and archival data). As a result, case research may, for example, analyse narrative and take a phenomeno-logical or ethnographic approach. This means that to do justice to your study, you will need an appreciation of both the case method and the other approaches embedded within that method.

Second, if your sole source of data is, for example, interviews of numerous entrepreneurs, do not refer to it as case research. Instead, recognize the method for what it is: depth interviews – a perfectly viable approach in itself. On a related point, to understand the role of interviews in case research, I suggest reading the AMJ Best Article by Graebner (2009).

Third, most case researchers cite Eisenhardt (1989) and some version of Yin (for example, 2008). I suggest that you should also be very familiar with Eisenhardt and Graebner (2007) and the various empirical studies conducted by Eisenhardt (one example is Ozcan and Eisenhardt, 2009). By reading these papers, you will not only understand the richness of Eisenhardt's arguments but see them applied to her investigations. My personal view is that if we were to critically assess the extant case research in entrepreneurship, it would pale in comparison to what Eisenhardt (and Graebner) recommend we do.

Fourth, if you cite Eisenhardt (1989) or Yin (2008), then follow their guidance. Too often, I see references to either of these authors followed up by a poor explanation (and implementation) of site selection, data collection and data analysis. For example, merely stating you have chosen firms by theoretical sampling is insufficient. So too is a simple statement that you have selected polar cases. These decisions need to be explained, as does your process of reaching theoretical saturation. Similarly, if you are using a tool such as nVivo to analyse your data, explain why it is appropriate and how you use it.

COMMON WEAKNESSES – WHAT TO SPEND EXTRA TIME ON!

What needs extra attention in a qualitative manuscript? Useful insights come from Pratt's (2008) study of the evaluative criteria-in-use at top-tier North American organizational and management journals.[1] He found the top three criteria for a qualitative manuscript to be:

- contribution to theory (49 per cent);
- transparent, exhaustive, well-articulated methods (49 per cent);
- good writing – interesting and compelling (46 per cent).

My experience leads me to agree with Pratt's (2008) findings. They are discussed here in the context of issues that seem to require particular consideration for qualitative studies.

The Introduction and Literature Review

The introduction must be clear, concise and compelling. The first two points lead into the third in that if the introduction is clear and concise, it will be easy to read – and if it's easy to read, it will be more compelling. However, your introduction must do more. It must compel the reader to want to read further. Thus, you have very few pages with which to articulate the need for research, its importance and what you expect to contribute.

One way to write the introduction is seen in Jarzabkowski (2008). She separates her introduction and literature review quite effectively. The former is short and focused – no waffle. The latter discusses the extant research on how managers shape strategy, and reviews the potential value of structural theory in understanding the dynamics of strategy shaping. Once her arguments are clear in the literature review, she has a solid basis for her decision to use qualitative methods. A different type of example is found in Hollensbe et al. (2008). They succinctly combine their introduction and literature review to identify their fundamental research question and three reasons as to why their study is important. This leads to a short summary of their method and a statement of contributions. The paper then moves directly into a richly detailed methods section.

The approach of combining the introduction and literature review (as taken by Hollensbe et al., 2008) is common in qualitative research because an exploratory study is unlikely to have a rich theoretical foundation to draw on. However, there will still be some need to create a theoretical frame for your study. To do this, I recommend using the techniques discussed by Pratt (2008). One way is to build a 'data sandwich', that is, where theory is presented before and after the data. My favourite example is Pratt et al.'s (2006) study of professional identity development in physicians. In the background section, they observe that the topic had already been examined with extant theories pertaining to careers and roles, socialization and identity construction. Importantly however, Pratt et al. (2006) clearly identify the limits of each of these theories. This foundation provides the first slice of bread in the data sandwich. They then present their results (the meat in the sandwich) and, finally, 'close' the theoretical frame by showing how their data fill in the missing pieces from each of the literatures. Thus, they add the second piece of bread to the sandwich. In so doing, they integrate and extend all three areas of extant theory.

A second approach from Pratt (2008) involves creating an 'open-faced' data sandwich: where the front end of the paper is set up to allow the theory to (largely) come after the data. Using Coviello and Joseph (2012) as an example, we argue that because we explore a complex social system, it is inappropriate to use a single theoretical lens to frame the study. Instead, we use the combined introduction/literature review to identify the need for research. This is the base of an open-faced sandwich. Later, we add the sandwich toppings with our data and draw on a range of theoretical arguments to inform our findings and develop propositions. For example, we integrate aspects of learning theory, resource-dependence theory, capability theory and effectuation logic, among others.

Methods

When reviewing the methods section of a qualitative study, my key questions are:

- Is a qualitative approach fully appropriate? Why?
- Is the chosen method appropriate? Why?
- Is the methods section believable? Why?
- Are the data collection approaches well-articulated? Sensible?
- Are the analytic approaches well-articulated? Sensible?
- Is the overall approach fully presented and potentially replicable?

Two points arise from the above. First, your methods section needs to be credible. This is demonstrated by the level of detail you provide (hint:

start by answering the 'why' questions from the above list). Second, there is a fine balance between a well-articulated methods section and one that lumbers along, boring the reader. Because I tend to look for solid explanations and detail, I suggest that if your methods section is getting long, try to include a figure that effectively portrays what you did. This will help save space and also, provide some life to a paper that is likely to be text-heavy. One example is seen in Figure 10.1 which depicts how data generated through case research was transformed into the chronological histories of each firm. These were then used to analyse the interactions that formed the firm's network during start-up. Then, the data and chronologies were used to build matrices to help analyse the structural characteristics of each network.

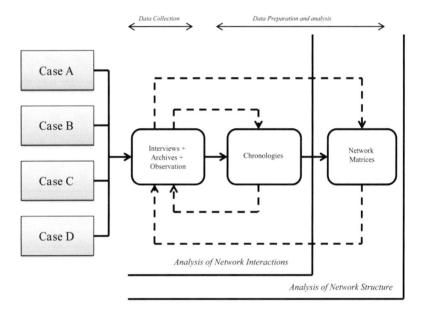

Source: Adapted from Cox (2005) and Fehsenfeld (2004).

Figure 10.1   Depicting a qualitative process of data collection and analysis

Data Analysis

A particularly important – and often weak – part of a qualitative article pertains to data analysis. It is important to discuss how to get organized for analysis and then, what to do with your analysis. In addition, it is important to consider whether or not your qualitative data can be meaningfully made quantitative.

Getting organized

There are a number of paradoxes associated with analysing qualitative data. For example, I have needed to be creative and open-minded, yet able to spot patterns and close holes. I have also had to allow for rich, messy data to emerge, yet be organized in how I track and report the data.

The first thing I do (pre-analysis) is get organized. I stock up with binders, file boxes, labels, coloured sticky notes, coloured pens and coloured highlighters. Second, as the data comes in, I start reading, noting and highlighting. This helps me develop and refine two things: (1) decision rules (that is, for coding and classifying), and (2) insights (emerging patterns). Important here is that data analysis is not left until the end of data collection. Rather, it starts as the data is generated because induction requires ongoing reflection and learning. Over time, I have developed a 'style' that allows me to understand my colour codes and summary notations. Critical to qualitative research, I can 'track back' from a paper to summary notes to transcripts to tapes/archives. This is because I have carefully noted who said/did what when, and where that data is in each source.

Third, I make use of whiteboards and/or large sheets of paper to build tables, figures and/or maps to visualize what I see as insights emerge. Note, I personally do not find a computer helpful in this activity. Instead, I find that if I can, for example, move sticky notes around various steps in a process or to various boxes in a table – where the process or table is portrayed on a whiteboard – then I can see patterns more clearly *and* I can easily ask others for their input. This process also forces me to synthesize my thoughts, decision rules and insights.

Getting into the data

To help determine an appropriate analytical path for qualitative research, I rely on guidance from one of my favourite articles: Langley's (1999) arguments on 'Strategies for theorizing from process data'. This is a 'must read and use' for all process researchers. I also find the approach discussed in Jonsen and Jehn (2009) interesting, where they describe a triangulated approach to validate emerging themes. That is, triangulation in data analysis rather than data collection.

Bem (2003) argues that data should be examined from every angle. I concur. Achieving this with qualitative data requires patience and creativity. Happily, it is almost always worth the extra effort, and my experience suggests:

1.   Having two sets of eyes is almost always better than one. Thus, if I do not have a co-author, I train, mentor and leverage graduate students to assess my work. Alternatively, I draw on other colleagues who are likely to see patterns that I do not or cannot.
2.   Be prepared to reorganize the data – from the beginning. This is why being careful and organized in your approach to managing data is critical.
3.   If you see a glimmer of a theme, note it. Do not, however, get stuck on it. Sometimes, patterns will reveal themselves if you let them simmer for a while.
4.   Anomalies are interesting in qualitative data because they tend to provide some of the richest insight, both empirical and theoretical. Thus, look hard at them – what patterns do they reflect? Why? Are they highlighting boundary conditions? Do they challenge theory?
5.   Again, analyse your data as you collect it. This way, you constantly iterate through the data, with your analysis informing ongoing data collection. This is the process of reaching theoretical saturation, a concept central to the notion of building theory.
6.   Track everything very carefully. The top journals (and increasingly, all journals) are implementing policies that will require you, if asked, to provide your data and evidence regarding your analysis.

Quantification
Should you 'quantify' qualitative data? Many are reluctant to report numbers (for example, 9 out of 12 firms or 75 per cent) and sometimes, when the editor sends your work to a qualitative specialist, you get just that: someone who has no interest in any form of quantitative analysis.

Personally, I believe that the nature of the research question drives the method for both data collection and analysis. Thus, if I am trying to establish patterns over time, transforming qualitative data into comparable patterns can be sensible. Using Coviello (2006) as an example, three detailed cases were transformed into three 'stories' of how new ventures internationalized, focusing on the events, actions and relationships that were involved with internationalization. Those stories were reconstructed as chronologies, with each relationship analysed and coded for specific characteristics. That then provided the basis for analysing a frequency pattern over time. In addition, the base chronologies were transformed into asymmetric network matrices to analyse changing structural characteristics. Thus, I relied on qualitative data as a basis for all my analysis; analysis that was ultimately, more quantitative in nature. In hindsight, that paper probably suffers from a lack of 'life' (in the form of quotes and stories), but the style suited the target journal.

A better example of balance can be seen in Coviello (2005), while a purely qualitative example is in Coviello and Joseph (2012). In both these studies, I worked with the premise that qualitative research 'starts from and returns to words, talk and texts' (Gephart, 2004, p. 455). However, I also believe that qualitative data allows for the bifocal analysis discussed in Coviello (2005).

The Results

The results section is where you have the best opportunity to draw the reader into your story. Thus, you need to consider the structure of this section and its content.

Structure

You can lead up to the findings, or present them first and then provide the details underpinning them. I prefer the latter approach for the simple reason that by offering an interesting finding, you keep the reader engaged. This is particularly critical for qualitative research because you may need to present numerous levels of findings and a variety of themes. Expecting the reader to wade through all of that in order to get to your results is too much. Thus, quickly capture their attention with the core findings and then elaborate.

Content

I have never forgotten one pre-reader's advice: 'this is so boring Nicole – where is the life in your story?' When I discussed this with my colleague, I learned that I needed to help him feel like he knew the informants. I also needed to try to communicate what it was like to be an informant as well as the investigator. This is very difficult in an article but can be aided by including figures that portray thought processes, messy decisions, and so on. Does this mean you should include photographs, vignettes, and so on? Not necessarily. If a photograph tells a thousand words about your ethnographic experience, then it may be appropriate. If the vignette is an example of the narrative you analysed, then this may be appropriate. I would however, be cautious in including such artefacts when space is at a premium.

The content of your results section is also aided by the use of quotes. Indeed, I have found that even if a reviewer is not a qualitative specialist, he or she will generally expect you to use quotes in your 'story-telling'. As explained by Pratt (2008), quotes can have two purposes: power and proof. 'Power' quotes are where the informant is concise and insightful, or has captured the essence of what the data shows. This type of quote should appear in the body of your paper. In contrast, you might use 'proof' quotes to reinforce a point, using, for example, a number of short quotes from other informants to show similar patterns across your findings. Proof quotes are usually found in summary tables. A word of caution however – review your target journal to understand the norms of presenting power versus proof quotes. My experience at the *Journal of Marketing* (a journal with very few qualitative articles) was that when I relied on tables of proof quotes (to minimize space), the reviewers were unhappy. I quickly rewrote the entire results section to integrate power quotes.

Your Discussion

Probably the most important advice I can give about the discussion section is that you should interpret and assess your findings relative to the extant literature. There are two general approaches that seem to be prevalent. One is for to you separate the results from the discussion. Another way is to interweave the findings and theory by adapting Van Maanen's (1979) advice regarding ethnographies. As seen in Gioia and Chittipeddi's (1991) study on strategic sense-making and sense-giving, you can report the informant's perspective (also known as first-order concept) and then second-order concepts, which are infused with theory. Another variant is offered by Narayandas and Rangan (2004) in their study of buyer–seller relationships.

Regardless of the approach you choose, it is important to remember that this part of a manuscript should be an 'interpretive discussion'. For qualitative researchers, this provides the opportunity to show how the results extend and/or elaborate existing theory, provide new insight to earlier findings and/or offer a completely fresh perspective.

Here is where we also find propositions for future research. My experience is that even with qualitatively induced propositions, most reviewers like propositions to sound like hypotheses; that is, they like directional relationships (where x leads to y). I tend to start by presenting the propositions in a manner consistent with the target journal. Then, I revise them to suit the stylistic preferences of the reviewing team. It is worth noting that the wording of propositions (or hypotheses) is rarely a fatal flaw in qualitative research. This is because they are often the outcome of a study and not used to frame it. Keep in mind, however, that propositions can themselves be fatal if the reviewer sees little in the way of added knowledge.

Your Conclusions

I suggest there are three major things to focus on when writing your conclusions: your contributions, generalizability and the implications of your study.

Contributions

The conclusions section is your opportunity to reinforce the contributions of your study. Your article should have highlighted these in the introduction and now, it is time to remind the reader of what you have done. In writing up contributions, I have found the advice from Locke and Golden-Biddle (1997) helpful. Their grounded theory of 'contribution to knowledge' offers insight to the rhetoric we use (and should use) to think about and articulate contributions.

Keep in mind, too, that the 'development of new theory' is a rare occurrence. Instead, I urge you to carefully think about what your study truly contributes. Are you extending a theory into a new context? Are you elaborating an aspect of theory that has not been well-addressed in the extant literature? Are you challenging theory? Are you integrating it to identify new insights?

Generalizability

You may be challenged regarding the 'generalizability' of your findings. Remember, however, there are different forms of generalizability and, like Pratt (2008), I think there are least two ways of overcoming the generalizability problem. One way is to explain how your context is similar to others (thus implying that your findings might be applied in these similar contexts). For example, in Coviello and Joseph (2012), a number of arguments are provided to suggest that the findings from small technology-based firms might be expected in both larger and more established firms, as well as other science-based ventures. This is not empirical generalization. Rather, it is an example of transferability, also known as analytic generalizability. Another way is to explain how your findings fit with extant theory and/or what insights your findings offer to extant theory. Some authors will find this difficult because they have chosen a qualitative method because they believe their topic to be 'new'. However, more often than not, the topic has emerged in some shape or form in other fields. Thus, it is your responsibility to know and use other relevant literature, often beyond entrepreneurship, to inform your research.

Implications

Even if you think that your work is very exploratory and managerial implications are premature, reviewers will want something! At the same time, remember that the managerial implications from most qualitative work are tentative or preliminary. Craft your arguments accordingly.

Your research implications should be given special attention. This is where you have the opportunity to develop a research agenda. By outlining avenues for investigation, you can guide future research and provide a basis for your own work. Think hard and deep about potential research questions and methods. It is insufficient to say: 'these findings could benefit from a quantitative study'.

WRITING QUALITATIVE RESEARCH: CRAFT AND RE-CRAFT AND … RE-CRAFT AGAIN

As discussed by Ragins (2012), writing is a craft. My first suggestion on how to write a qualitative paper is to read Ragins (2012) because I agree with everything she says. One of her key points is that good writing should be accurate and clear. I have found that clarity in writing requires clarity in thought, and this is helped by good organization. To this point, I emphasized earlier the need to be organized with data collection and analysis. This does not, however, mean that your paper should be written in a standard format per se. Like Pratt (2009), I am uncomfortable with the notion of having a boilerplate (or template) for structuring the write-up of a qualitative study. As one example, although I find the various studies of Eisenhardt (and colleagues) to be exemplars of how to conduct case research, her articles have become somewhat predictable. Yes, her work tackles complex issues with particularly rich and messy data. Yes, readers draw comfort from the familiarity of her template; a template that allows readers to quickly scan (long) articles or locate specific information by turning directly to the relevant section. Paradoxically however, there may be diminishing returns to this approach. As a reviewer, I can immediately recognize what seems to be an Eisenhardt study. Is this good or bad for you, the author? If you are mimicking her style, then you had better also mimic the rigour with which she and her colleagues conduct case research. Otherwise, those familiar with the template will quickly spot the flaws of your investigation.

We are all experienced readers of research. We know papers we like and those we do not. Often, that 'liking' is our response to how well a paper is written. Thus, I spend time with doctoral students to deconstruct the structure and rhetoric of articles. This helps them understand their response to an article. Then, I encourage them to consider why they find a particular style and structure compelling and believable. This process has the benefit of forcing us, as writers, to think about what we are trying to communicate and how it is communicated. Although this is important in all research, I have found that, because qualitative data is rich, deep and messy, extremely careful structure and articulation is required. What does this mean?

- *Tell a story*. That is, establish a clear story line. This is a real challenge with qualitative research when you are faced with masses of data and/or multiple theoretical lenses by which to interpret that data. Thus, write simply and directly. Later, when you think you have a nearly perfect paper, force yourself to make the slides for a 20-minute presentation. This requires you to focus on the essence of your arguments (for the slides), and you will likely see a simpler way to structure the paper and tell your story.
- *Make sensible use of figures and tables*. Not only can these tools help make any article more digestible, they might help you save space. As noted earlier, it can be particularly helpful to use a figure to portray a complex process.
- *Be careful with the words you use to frame your qualitative study*. For example, you might be inclined to use the terms 'positive' and 'negative' but in qualitative research these sound positively positivistic! Others words that are overly positivistic include associated, correlated, tested, significant, independent and dependent. Avoid using these.
- *Write economically*. This is very relevant for qualitative manuscripts; papers that are likely to be too long to begin with. It is also very relevant if you are writing for a top North American journal because they encourage writing that is parsimonious and active. Every point should have a point. There should be no unnecessary words and no superfluous sentences. Thus, I regularly ask: So what? Have I used two words when I can use one? Would a figure or table tell the story better? Is that footnote really necessary? If you cannot do this yourself, then find a co-author or pre-reader who will. It is absolutely necessary. Any off-cuts can go into a separate file for future use.

- *Remember the importance of context to your work.* I make this point for two reasons. First, in a qualitative study, a carefully chosen context can help you isolate, for example, a process or group that is critical for theory development; it can help you observe extreme values. Pratt et al. (2006) is an example of this, as is Coviello and Joseph (2012). Second, good context can be intriguing to the reader. My favourite example here is Elsbach and Kramer's (2003) study of Hollywood pitches. I wanted to read the article, simply because it sounded like a fascinating context.
- *Manage the length of your paper.* If the manuscript length is not around 50 double-spaced pages (including figures, tables and references), you probably have not done justice to the method and data. However, it is likely that your editor will ask you to shorten the paper. This is where the ongoing process of crafting (and re-crafting) can be helpful.

CONCLUSION

My goal with this chapter was to share some of what I have learned about publishing qualitative research. Remember, a qualitative approach is appropriate when the investigation calls for research that is inter-pretive, inductive and holistic. If this is not what your research problem demands, rethink your method. Also, remember that qualitative data collection and analysis is flexible and fluid, emerging as insight emerges. This means two things. First, multiple methods are often used; methods that require human interaction and reflection. Second, the qualitative process needs time; time to conduct the research, interpret your findings, reflect on them and then craft a manuscript of high standard. The end result may, however, be worth the commitment because a strong qualita-tive study can transform your career. It may even be award-worthy.

NOTE

1. For authors trying to publish in US-based journals, I encourage you to carefully read George (2012). Although his focus is on getting published in AMJ, much of the advice is generally relevant and I support his views based on my own experience as an international author and my work as an editor and reviewer.

REFERENCES

Bem, D.J. (2003), 'Writing the empirical journal article', in J.M. Darley, M.P. Zanna and H.L. Roediger III (eds), *The Compleat Academic: A Practical Guide for the Beginning Social Scientist*, 2nd edn. Washington, DC: American Psychological Association.

Cope, J. (2011), 'Entrepreneurial Learning from failure: an interpretive phenomenological analysis', *Journal of Business Venturing*, **26** (6), 604–23.

Coviello, N. (2005), 'Integrating qualitative and quantitative techniques in network analysis,' *Qualitative Market Research*, **8** (1), 39–60.

Coviello, N.E. (2006), 'Network dynamics in the international new venture', *Journal of International Business Studies*, **37** (5), 713–31.

Coviello, N.E. and R. Joseph (2012), 'Creating major innovations with customers: insights from small and young technology firms,' *Journal of Marketing*, **76** (6), 87–104.

Cox, M. (2005), 'New venture networks: interaction, structure and resource dynamics', unpublished Master's thesis, University of Auckland, pp. 67, 91.

Creswell, J.W. (2007), *Qualitative Inquiry and Research Design: Choosing Among Five Approaches*, 2nd edn, Thousand Oaks, CA: Sage Publications.

Eisenhardt, K.M. (1989), 'Building theories from case study research,' *Academy of Management Review*, **14** (4), 532–50.

Eisenhardt, K.M. and M.E. Graebner (2007), 'Theory building from cases: opportunities and challenges', *Academy of Management Journal*, **50** (1), 25–32.

Elsbach, K.D. and R.M. Kramer (2003), 'Assessing creativity in Hollywood pitch meetings: evidence for a dual-process model of creativity judgments', *Academy of Management Journal*, **46** (3), 283–301.

Fehsenfeld, R. (2004), 'New venture network dynamics', unpublished Master's thesis, University of Auckland, p. 55.

Fischer, E. and A.R. Reuber (2011), 'Social interaction via new social media: (how) can interactions on Twitter affect effectual thinking and behaviour?', *Journal of Business Venturing*, 26 (1), 1–18.

George, G. (2012), 'Publishing in AMJ for non-U.S. authors', *Academy of Management Journal*, **55** (5), 1023–6.

Gephart, R.P. (2004), 'Qualitative research and the Academy of Management Journal', *Academy of Management Journal*, **47** (4), 454–62.

Gioia, D. and K. Chittipeddi (1991), 'Sense making and sense giving in strategic change initiation', *Strategic Management Journal*, **12** (6), 433–48.

Graebner, M.E. (2009), 'Caveat venditor: trust asymmetries in acquisition of entrepreneurial firms,' *Academy of Management Journal*, **52** (3), 435–72.

Hollensbe, E., S. Khazanchi and S. Masterson (2008), 'How do I assess if my supervisor and organization are fair? Identifying the rules underlying entity-based justice perceptions', *Academy of Management Journal*, **51** (6), 1099–116.

Jarzabkowski, P. (2008), 'Shaping strategy as a structuration process', *Academy of Management Journal*, **51** (4), 621–50.

Jonsen, K. and K.A. Jehn (2009), 'Using triangulation to validate themes in qualitative studies,' *Qualitative Research in Organizations and Management*, **4** (2), 123–50.

Khavul, S., H. Chavez and G.D Bruton (2013), 'When institutional change outruns the change agent: the contested terrain of entrepreneurial micro-financing for those in poverty,' *Journal of Business Venturing*, **28** (1), 30–50.

Langley, A. (1999), 'Strategies for theorizing from process data,' *Academy of Management Review*, **24** (4), 691–710.

Lee, T.W. (1999), *Using Qualitative Methods in Organizational Research*, Thousand Oaks, CA: Sage Publications.

Locke, K. and K. Golden-Biddle (1997), 'Constructing opportunities for contribution: structuring intertextual coherence and "problematizing" in organizational studies', *Academy of Management Journal*, **40** (5), 1023–62.

Narayandas, D. and V.K. Rangan (2004), 'Building and sustaining buyer-seller relationships in mature industrial markets', *Journal of Marketing*, **68** (3), 63–77.

Ozcan, P. and K.M. Eisenhardt (2009), 'Origin of alliance portfolios: entrepreneurs, network strategies and firm performance,' *Academy of Management Journal*, **52** (2), 246–79.

Petty, J.S. and M. Gruber (2011), 'In pursuit of the "real deal": a longitudinal study of venture capital decision-making', *Journal of Business Venturing*, **26** (2), 172–88.

Prasad, P. (2005), *Crafting Qualitative Research: Working in the Postpositivist Traditions*, Armonk, NY: ME Sharpe.

Pratt, M.G. (2008), 'Fitting oval pegs into round holes tensions in evaluating and publishing qualitative research in top-tier North American journals', *Organizational Research Methods*, **11** (3), 481–509.

Pratt, M.G. (2009), 'For the lack of a boilerplate: tips on writing up (and reviewing) qualitative research', *Academy of Management Journal*, **52** (5), 856–62.

Pratt, M.G., K.W. Rockmann and J.B. Kaufmann (2006), 'Constructing professional identity: the role of work and identity learning cycles in the customization of identity among medical residents,' *Academy of Management Journal*, **49** (2), 235–62.

Ragins, B.R. (2012), 'Reflections on the craft of clear writing', *Academy of Management Review*, **37** (4), 493–501.

Schouten, J.W. and J.H. McAlexander (1995), 'Subcultures of consumption: an ethnography of the new bikers,' *Journal of Consumer Research*, **22** (1), 43–61.

Van Maanen, J. (1979), 'Reclaiming qualitative methods for organizational research: a preface', *Administrative Science Quarterly*, **24** (4), 520–26.

Yin, R.K. (2008), *Case Study Research: Design and Methods*, 4th edn, Thousand Oaks, CA: Sage Publications.

11. Laying the foundations for Asia-focused research through qualitative research

David Ahlstrom and Garry Bruton

INTRODUCTION

There has been a rapid expansion of research based on Asian samples (Ahlstrom, 2012a; Peng, 2005). However, researchers in Asia have often simply repeated research questions raised in the West, particularly from North America or Europe (Meyer, 2006). For example, Tsui et al. (2004) reviewed over 100 articles published from 2000 to 2003 and concluded that only two attempted to introduce a new theory to explain a Chinese phenomenon. In a more recent review of the literature, Jia et al. (2012) assessed about 300 articles published in eight journals between 1981 and 2010 on China. They only found three new concepts developed in these articles: market transition, network capitalism and *guanxi*, which described specific, indigenous Chinese phenomena. It should be noted, though, that researchers continue to argue about the validity of *guanxi* or connections as indigenous to China or East Asia (Chen and Chen, 2012; Mao et al., 2012).

Utilizing primarily past work and conducting replications is a suitable approach at times, particularly when a theory is well developed and additional studies with new moderators such as a different cultural setting would help to improve the theory (Ahlstrom et al., 2010; Christensen and Carlile, 2009; Tsang and Kwan, 1999). For example, much research has shown that in the case of social influence, the commonly understood principles of influence and persuasion do work about the same in a variety of cultural settings (Wosinska et al., 2001), though certain influence principles may be more effective (Morris et al., 2001) or preferred (Fu and Yukl, 2000) than others. Thus, in a well understood and studied paradigmatic setting, large sample empirical studies are important to further test and improve theory (Tsang and Kwan, 1999; Van de Ven, 2007).

Yet it has been also recognized that the institutional development of most countries in Asia is considerably different from the more developed economies (Bruton et al., 2010; Peng, 2005). Other differences such as culture and historical path dependencies are likely to impact organizations and their performance (Van de Ven, 2004), though debates exist to what extent (Ahlstrom and Wang, 2010; Singh, 2007). For example, there is support for a tendency towards high collectivism in Asia (Hofstede and Hofstede, 2005). This cultural proclivity pushes individuals to focus more on what is best for the larger collective or group rather than for individuals. Thus, it is important for behavioral research in Asia, for example, to adequately incorporate the team environment surrounding interactions between leaders and followers. Thus, the context of Asia is quite important and can impact a study in terms of a number of inputs beyond the simple addition of a single moderator such as culture (Ahlstrom and Wang, 2010).

Moreover, culture is not the only contextual variable that can impact research. Chen (1995) provided an early example of context-sensitive research by comparing the reward allocation preferences of US and Chinese employees. Based on a rich knowledge of the Chinese context, Chen presented hypotheses on the preferences of Chinese employees for reward rules. He hypothesized that for reward allocation Chinese employees would prefer equity rules over equality rules, both in material and socio-emotional terms. Chen found, however, that economic goals, not cultural values, were most important in the preferences regarding reward allocation preferences of the Chinese workers in his sample. Such insight about organizational behavior in Chinese organizations would be difficult without a close examination of context, and particularly how variables such as different types of rewards might be impacted not only by culture but by economic reforms and path dependencies. This implies the need to design research that accounts for context such as culture and the institutional environment, and re-examines constructs for their applicability and validity.

Yet in spite of these and several other exceptions (for example, Huang and Bond, 2012), Asia scholarship still often repeats the scholarly questions from mature economies with little investigation into the problem of whether the right questions are being asked or if terms and constructs are truly equivalent or indigenous (Jia et al., 2012). Researchers have often limited their studies to simply adding moderators to existing theories. The resulting research has tended to perpetuate the dominant theories and avoids departing from the dominant Western research paradigm. This tendency towards homogenization can impair the understanding of contexts that differ significantly from the locations that gave rise to the dominant paradigm (March, 2005; Tsui, 2007). As a result, leading mainstream journals today publish studies with an Asia research focus that are methodologically rigorous, but have not contributed to theory and practice consonant with those efforts.

As Leung (2009) argues, research in identifying unusual cases, and indigenous concepts and theories is a necessary step before we can identify cross-national similarities and differences, and eventually develop integrative or universal theories of organizational behavior or management. Instead of simply repeating the questions from mature Western economies, scholars in Asia or working on Asian research sites need to first understand the substantive issues in Asia in order to ensure that they are asking the right questions (for example, Lam et al., 2012) and perhaps identifying potentially indigenous constructs (for example, Lai et al., 2010; Smith, 2012). The manner to establish those questions and identify or clarify constructs in Asia is fundamentally through the publishing of high-quality qualitative research focused on Asia (Ahlstrom, 2012b; Ahlstrom et al., 2010; Van de Ven, 2004; 2007). With the correct questions for Asia identified, scholars are better able to establish context and add to the validity of constructs, facilitating large-scale empirical research (Ahlstrom et al., 2010; Christensen, 2006; Christensen and Carlile, 2009).

This chapter focuses on broad research strategies in which qualitative research in Asia can be pursued to be successfully published in the leading journals. The discussion is necessarily broad-based as another chapter in this volume has focused on ground-level steps and recommendations to authors conducting qualitative research (Coviello, Chapter 10 in this volume). Initially we examine the concepts, foundations and principals for high-quality qualitative research. We then employ examples of good quality qualitative research published on Asia to illustrate the concepts, foundations and principals discussed. We then discuss the publishing of such qualitative research from Asia.

QUALITATIVE RESEARCH – WHAT IS IT AND HOW CAN IT BE USED?

As discussed in more detail by Coviello in this book (Chapter 10), there is a rich diversity of what is called qualitative research, as it draws on a wide range of disciplines and a variety of research and professional settings (Yin, 2010). The diversity of different disciplines has challenged scholars to arrive at a succinct definition. In simple terms, qualitative data (as part of a qualitative research program) is a type of evidence. Interviews, ethnographies and content analyses, just to name a few, are data collection methods (Yin, 1981). Case studies are often conflated with qualitative research, but a case study is more of a research strategy or research design, though it is usually constructed with qualitative data (Yin, 1981).[1] Creswell (2006) divided qualitative research designs into five major traditions, namely, biography, phenomenology, ethnography, grounded theory and case studies. Other researchers have added finer distinctions to these categories, such as historical analysis (Carr, 1961; Gaddis, 2002), comparative case and cross-disciplinary analysis (for example, Aaker, 2007; Ragin, 1987), and idiographic, in-depth single cases (Moustakas, 1994; Tsoukas, 1989; Yin, 2010). These five qualitative research traditions and their subsets share a set of data gathering and analyzing techniques that can be used to primarily provide description or theory-building theory, identifying questions, and improving on categorization schemes and definitions in the theory building and improvement process.

These various methods share an emphasis on holistic analysis, dynamism in their perspective, and a focus on processes and experience in order to provide a tool for developing an understanding of complex phenomena from the viewpoint of those who are living them. A key value of a qualitative research design is that it more readily allows researchers to uncover new variables and correlations, to disclose and grasp complex processes, and to identify and clarify constructs and variables (sometimes across disciplines) in the process of building theory (Christensen and Carlile, 2009; Yin, 2010). Qualitative research is thus appropriate for much research on the complex and dynamic nature of management and organizational research in a complex and the relatively newer research site around Asia.

Most of the diverse disciplines and research traditions that widely employ qualitative research employ it to provide rich, thick descriptions of a given situation which allows scholars to 'expose theoretical boundaries and push theoretical insights' (Bansal and Corley, 2012, p. 513). The methods in which those thick rich descriptions can come about vary widely. For example, scholars can gather such insight from action research in which the scholar seeks to create some change in an organization (that is, Luscher and Lewis, 2008), ethnographic research in which the scholar seeks to observe closely a given situation but does not seek to create change, as in action research (that is, Lingo and O'Mahony, 2010; Whyte, 1943), case research in which the study of cases of organizations or group behavior are developed (that is, Suddaby and Greenwood, 2005), historical in-depth cases and their application (that is, Ahlstrom and Wang, 2009; Allison and Zelikow, 1999; Hargadon and Douglas, 2001; Lorhke et al., 2012) or phenomenological research (Moustakas, 1994). While there are a wide variety of ways to get the richness, we argue that in each of these methods there are five common features, which we will discuss next.

FIVE FEATURES OF QUALITATIVE RESEARCH

There are five general features of qualitative research, which we list below. We then discuss these features individually in order to help readers develop a better understanding of the foundations of qualitative research before looking at Asian qualitative research in particular:

1. Studying the meaning of business and people's lives under *real-world* conditions.
2. Ensuring that the *views and perspectives of people* are reflected in the study.
3. Examining the *contextual conditions* within which the people or firm exists or to clarify terms, constructs or figures commonly used in studies.
4. Contributing insights into existing or emerging concepts that may help to *explain* human behavior, organizational behavior, and firm strategy.
5. Striving to use *multiple sources of evidence* to triangulate a meaning rather than relying on a single source alone.

Real World Insights

The first feature of qualitative research noted above is that such research examines organizations, groups, and individuals under real-world conditions. The forms of these observations can come through secondary sources such as newspaper articles, annual reports, or the diaries, journals, and writings of individuals; and as will be detailed later even photography is sometimes utilized. The key is that the action occurs and information is generated largely independent of any research inquiry. The goal is to gain insights on the firm or people with minimal intrusion by research procedures. Thus, the researcher does not want respondents to be inhibited by the confines of a laboratory or any laboratory-like setting.

The goal is to obtain real world insights on how firms and people operate and live and not how scholars preconceive it is to operate.

Views of People

The second point is that qualitative research differs from more positivistic research designs because of its ability to represent the views and perspectives of the participants in a study, often in an interpretive fashion (Lincoln and Guba, 1985). Capturing people's perspectives is often, in fact, the major purpose of a qualitative study. Thus, the events and ideas emerging from qualitative research seek to provide meanings to real-life events and phenomena by the people who live them, not the values, preconceptions, or meanings held by researchers (Moustakas, 1994).

Scholars are not limited to simply observing individuals but can also gain insight from interviews of individuals in the setting being studied or from experts in the field being examined as they talk through their problems (Sarasvathy, 2009). However, even when such interviews are employed, the questions asked are designed to be open-ended in order to generate maximum insight and discussion. Thus, researchers do not want respondents to be limited to only responding to a researcher's pre-established questionnaire or to be overly directed by a line of questioning (Bruton et al., 2009; Kressel and Kressel, 2004). Instead the goal is to generate maximum discussion and insight.

Contextual Conditions

A third feature of qualitative research is that the contextual conditions, including the social, institutional and environmental conditions, are examined as part of the qualitative study. Rather than a narrow study of any given issue, the goal is to make the study of the issues at hand rich, wide-ranging and more holistic. Qualitative research is ideal to open up new fields of study (Christensen and Carlile, 2009). Thus, relationships around the issue being examined which occur in new unexpected ways can be further explored and addressed in qualitative research (Christensen, 2006). Scholars need to be aware of the contextual conditions and how they can influence the issues at hand. The result should be that new insights and relationships are identified and sorted out.

In quantitative research there is an effort to control such contextual conditions. Perhaps the best illustration of this effort to control such contextual conditions is in laboratory experiments. Laboratory experiments are useful under certain controllable conditions, though they have come under some criticism for their sometimes unrealistic nature or the use of student samples (Harrison and List, 2004). Field experiments and quasi-experimental designs help to overcome such objections, but nevertheless focus only on a very limited set of variables, which may not fully appreciate the contextual conditions or interpretations of participants (Lincoln and Guba, 1985). Similarly, surveys are constrained by the need to manage carefully the degrees of freedom required to analyze the responses to a set of survey questions; surveys can therefore be limited in the number of questions devoted to any contextual conditions.

However, in limiting the impact of such contextualizing, scholars place constraints on potential insights into new relationships and questions scholars should be asking and examining. As noted earlier, one of the key uses of qualitative research is to help to identify the key questions research scholars need to be asking. Thus, the ability of qualitative research to include such contextual concerns is a key element in identifying the key questions for future research.

Explanation

Qualitative research is not just a diary or chronicle of everyday life. On the contrary, qualitative research is driven by a desire to identify key action and explain how things work and events unfold, often through existing or emerging concepts (Stake, 2010). For instance, one of the oldest qualitative studies is Whyte's *Street Corner Society* (Whyte, 1943). Whyte lived in a downtrodden section of Boston dominated by Italian immigrants for three and half years. One of the first participant-observer studies, Whyte provided insights on what actually occurred in this setting, generating many new concepts about gangs and hierarchies and social interactions in poorer, immigrant societies in North America in a way that could not be obtained through other methods. Until Whyte's study there were assumptions about how poorer immigrant societies lived, but actual knowledge of them was very limited. Thus, Whyte provided the first viable explanation through detailed accounts of how local gangs were formed and organized and the hierarchies in a substratum of society. Scholars in qualitative research may not provide a foundational insight like Whyte's in every setting, but the goal remains to be able to provide an explanation for firms and people in a way that is not widely understood. Ravasi et al. (2004) added that the adoption of a rich, qualitative method for data collection and analysis can be justified by the exploratory nature of the study. Methodologies can attach meaning as participants see it and trace processes as they unfold over time, ranging from research sites of entrepreneurs to gang members (Sarasvathy, 2009; Venkatesh, 2008).

Multiple Sources of Data

Qualitative research strives to collect, integrate, and present data from a variety of sources and theory across disciplines as part of any given study (Aaker, 2007; Yin, 2010). The variety of data will include not only that noted above gathered from the real world (secondary data) and people (points 1 and 2 in the list above) but all other data sources that can be reasonably obtained. The study's conclusions are likely to be based on triangulating the data from the different sources or combinations of cases (Larsson, 1993; Yin, 2008). This convergence will add to the study's credibility and trustworthiness.

In conceptualizing the data for a qualitative study there are multiple levels that can include different sorts of data. To illustrate: to understand a firm in depth a scholar can gather in-depth descriptions from the industry's history to the individuals' histories. Each of these levels of analysis will capture a portion of the richness of the organization. Indeed, the 'hardest' numbers on product performance, company revenues and competitors' market shares are after-the-fact proxy manifestations rather than the actual processes in the firm, including the prioritization of the firm and its related decisions (Johnson and Kaplan, 1987).

QUALITATIVE VERSUS QUANTITATIVE RESEARCH

While it is clear that qualitative research has unique characteristics, this does not mean that qualitative research should be viewed as the opposite of quantitative research. In fact, the quality of research can be increased if scholars can employ a combination of quantitative data (for example, economic data, technology product-market outcomes) and qualitative data (interviews, observations) in their research (Venkatesh, 2009). The benefit of combining these methods is that it increases the validity of the research as scholars are assured that an accurate picture of the situation at hand is developed. Thus, scholars may have a large number of potential variables they could employ, but they will include qualitative methods to help narrow the list of the variables and improve the categorization and definitions of the variables. This has happened to examine and decide the research question to direct the research. Thus, rather than conceptualizing qualitative research as the opposite of qualitative research, we encourage scholars to conceptualize the two methods as complements to each other (Creswell and Clark, 2010). What the scholar is trying to examine should direct which method is chosen as the foundation for the study. Qualitative research can help to clarify data and the variables that could be employed in a study.

Looking deeper into where data for the qualitative study comes from, studies that rely solely on published accounts in the news or other business publications can be problematic (Rosenzweig, 2007). For example, books such as *In Search of Excellence* (Peters and Waterman, 1983) or *Good to Great* (Collins, 2001) are interesting but contribute little to theoretically driven scholarly research. Part of the problem, as highlighted by Carr's (1961) *What Is History?*, is that most historical accounts simply summarize what happened and record the events that they decide were important enough to record. Often, the process of what was recorded (or not) lies hidden, as do potential biases in data collection and post-hoc descriptions of events (Rosenzweig, 2007).

Part of why mixed methods can be effective is that if only quantitative data is employed the issue that must be determined is whether the data are 'objective'. One of the authors of the balanced scorecard, Robert Kaplan, and colleagues showed quite convincingly that the numbers representing revenues, costs and profits that appear in companies' financial statements are typically the result of processes of estimation, allocation, debate and political and public relations processes that can produce grossly inaccurate reflections of true cost and profit (Johnson and Kaplan, 1987). The subjective nature of financial statement data, and the skills and methods used by those who made those judgments, however, are hidden from the view of researchers who use the published numbers only and do not trace the processes behind them or utilize the research of those who have done that work. Qualitative insights combined with the quantitative data help to provide insights to those processes that lie behind the quantitative data or can reassess categorization schemes that may not be robust, particularly in a new research site (Cohen and Basu, 1987; Rosch, 1975).

Researchers of every persuasion ought always to strive to examine phenomena not just through the lenses of different academic or functional disciplines, but through the lenses of multiple forms of data as well. Scholars need not be defensive about the extent to which the data in our or others' research are 'subjective.' Instead, as scholars we are obligated to do our best to be thorough and open to new insight in participating individually within and collectively across the theory-building and improvement stages, particularly in novel research sites.

Thus, rather than conceptualizing qualitative research as an opposite number to quantitative research, we encourage scholars to think of the two research approaches as complimentary to each other (Creswell and

Clark, 2010). Qualitative research can be very helpful in the initial stages of theory-building and creating new variables. It is also important for clarifying what type of data is needed, how it should be categorized and what it is actually saying (Christensen, 2006; Cohen and Basu, 1987). What the scholar is trying to examine should direct which general approach is chosen as the foundation for the study (Creswell, 2006). However, if it is possible to combine the two into a mixed methods approach the study will typically benefit from the methods being combined (Creswell and Clark, 2010). Table 11.1 summarizes the differences in quantitative and qualitative research.

Table 11.1   The differences in quantitative and qualitative research

Qualitative	Quantitative
Answers Why? How?	Answers How many? When? Where?
Conducted in the formative early phases of research to ensure what questions to ask	Tests, hypotheses, later phases
Data are 'rich' and time-consuming to analyze	Data are more efficient, but may miss contextual detail
Design may emerge as study unfolds	Design decided in advance
Reasoning – inductive	Deductive

RICH QUALITATIVE RESEARCH

Qualitative research seeks to provide a deep understanding of the setting being examined (Stake, 2010). Research should continue to seek for new information, whether that is interviews or secondary data, until no new insights are generated; thus, there is saturation of information obtained (Strauss and Corbin, 1990). The methods section needs to detail that information-gathering and saturation process, and the article results subsequently needs to reflect that richness (Ozcan and Eisenhardt, 2009; Stake, 2010). There must be a strong and clear story that illustrates and convinces the reader of the findings in an interesting manner. Such rich stories are particularly important in Asia as many scholars' understanding of Asia is limited and the rich description helps to bring a clarity and depth of understanding to these scholars.

However, in presenting the story in the article it is worth noting that typically that richness no longer takes the form of direct quotes in the paper. Instead, today it is common for scholars to place their supporting quotes in tables at the end of the research. For an illustration of this see Suddaby and Greenwood's (2005) work in *Administrative Science Quarterly* or Khavul et al.'s (2013) work in *Journal of Business Venturing*. Authors often feel that they may not have enough to say if they take the quotes out of the paper. However, it can be liberating to the authors if they remove such quotes as it allows them to concentrate on the theory and the insights rather than working with many direct quotations from their subjects.

Without quotes the authors can focus more clearly on the theory in the development of their qualitative work. For publishing qualitative work it is critical that the authors always recognize that theory-building and improvement is the core of the article. The ability to expand the theoretical understanding of the situation through qualitative research is critical. The goal of qualitative research is not to simply provide a story; such actions are more suited to journalists and diarists. Instead, we use the qualitative research to build an understanding that allows scholars to build the grounded theoretical understanding that will allow them to examine other similar situations (Glauser and Strauss, 1967). There will be no other case in the world exactly like that which the qualitative study examined. The only way to examine in similar settings is to have strong theoretical development that explains the situation and then to utilize that theory to examine other settings.

Finally, it is critical in publishing qualitative research that a detailed methods section be developed. The first part of qualitative papers is commonly shorter, as the issue to be addressed, why it needs to be addressed and some relevant theory are presented. The paper will then present the methods and these methods have to be very detailed. It is not uncommon that a qualitative paper's methods section will be twice as long as an empirical paper's methods section. The reason for this is that the research design must be described and justified, and readers must be shown the steps taken in the study and how their validity and reliability were reasonably assured. The ability of the reader to understand and then replicate the steps to create a similar study is a daunting task, but a task that the qualitative paper's methods section must facilitate. One outcome of the richness needed in the story and in the methods is that it is not uncommon for qualitative research articles to be longer than a typical empirical piece of research.

ASIA EXAMPLES

We will now examine two pieces of Asia-based research that employ qualitative research methods and which have been published in *Financial Times* listed journals. We will then examine a third piece of research that utilizes mixed methods – both qualitative and quantitative – which was also published in a *Financial Times* listed journal. The purpose of these examinations is to focus on the how the scholars formed the article and less so on the findings.

Research on Venture Capitalists

Bruton and Ahlstrom (2003) conducted 36 interviews of 24 venture capitalists to generate a thorough grounding of the venture capital industry in China. The primary theoretical question that the research focused on was how the differing institutional regimes in East Asia affected venture capital there and what those differences were. The venture capitalists in China at the time of this study were all effectively trained in the USA or by US firms. The results were that the scholars found that normative values of the venture capitalists were the same as those that reported in the West. However, how those values were implemented was radically different owing to the cognitive institutions present in their environment (cf. Ahlstrom and Bruton, 2006). To illustrate one aspect of this briefly, venture capitalists in the US will normally spend more time with troubled ventures than with those doing well. They spend time based on where they think they will have the greatest impact. In China, relationships are far more critical than in the USA so the venture capitalists were found to spend roughly equal time with all their ventures no matter how they were doing financially (Bruton and Ahlstrom, 2003). Thus, it was argued that venture capital in China may look outwardly very similar to that in the USA; people in China utilized terms and concepts that are the norm in the USA. However, how venture capital actually operates proved substantively different in China in many dimensions (Ahlstrom et al., 2007; Bruton and Ahlstrom, 2003).

In examining how the article is structured, there is a relatively short beginning to the paper as the authors lay out the growth in venture capital in China but that the assumption that it is similar to the USA may be misplaced. They then provide a relatively long methods section, usually over two full pages of information on the methods. They then provide a relatively rich and long story on how the model of venture capital is the same as or different from that in the USA. The article reflects a relatively older style of qualitative research in that the authors place quotes to support their argument in the paper. Again, today more qualitative research will have relatively limited quotes in the paper but will instead normally place them in the second half of the paper with the results and discussion sections.

COFFEE SHOP PHOTOGRAPHS

Venkatraman and Nelson (2008) employed a qualitative methodology called photo-elicitation in their article in the *Journal of International Business Studies*. In this process consumers record their experiences first, then using photographs of Starbucks in China they elicit, through in-depth interviews, the respondents feelings and experiences at that time. Servicescape refers to the idea of how firms shape their physical setting and how this can impact consumption by consumers. A key theoretical issue is how does a firm that enters a country much different from its home country adapt its physical setting in order to encourage consumer comfort and familiarity. The study was based on seven in-depth inter-actions with consumers through the photo-elicitation process.

Venkatraman and Nelson's (2008) article is structured in a very similar way to the Bruton and Ahlstrom (2003) study. There is a relatively brief beginning to the paper as the problem and its key elements are discussed. There are several pages of carefully described methodology. The photo-elicitation methodology was a rather new methodology in business research and crucial to the thesis of the article. The article then goes on to generate a very rich story of how Starbucks and its environment were perceived and changed by consumers. It again uses the traditional method of including quotes in the text of the article rather than in an appendix or summary table alone. The article opens a new area of investigation on the impact of the physical setting of the store in Asia and how it may differ from the retail outlets in Europe and North America.

The two articles reviewed are similar in that they open new areas of investigation about Asia. Assumptions about how things operate in Asia based on prior research on mature Western economies may appear accurate on the surface, but the qualitative research demonstrates that different research questions need to be asked. The two articles both take particular pains to establish the validity of their research. Thus, Ahlstrom and Bruton (2003) create transcripts of all interviews. It is important that scholars in Asia realize that they must have such transcripts and that they must be in a language which is accessible to other scholars if they wish to check the validity of the interpretation. Thus, scholars in Asia will typically have to have the interviews translated, with English transcripts available so others can view them if they wish.

MIXED METHODS

Tan et al. (2013) provide a valuable illustration of how to use qualitative methods mixed with quantitative methods (Creswell and Clark, 2010). Tan et al. (2013) examine how firms in confined geographical areas deal with the institutional pressures for conformity while also seeking to strategically create differentiation. To ground the study they employ interviews with seven firms, two entrepreneurial founders, two associations, and two governmental officials in order to ensure they are asking the right questions. These interviews occurred over three different time periods with each round of interviews building on the previous one, and some interviewees being interviewed again as greater insight was obtained. They then did a survey of 38 firms.

The mixed methods article again is very similar to the others in that since this research is exploratory there is a relatively short beginning of approximately three pages. There are then over two pages of methods. The results are longer as there are rich insights to provide, with approximately seven pages of results and discussion. The authors provide the insights and grounding of the paper not in quotes in the paper but in a table that summarizes the information and support.

CONCLUSION

Qualitative research can play a crucial role in research on Asia. It should not be assumed that research questions in Asia and mature Western economies are the same. The two research articles with qualitative methods alone opened up new domains to investigation in Asia (venture capital and Servicescape). The findings largely show that while ideas from the mature economies and the West cannot be totally ignored, there are also substantial differences so there should not be an assumption there is commonality either. Future scholars should expand on this insight to examine other questions that we cannot assume are the same in Asia.

NOTE

1. A case study can be contrasted with other, more quantitative research designs such as an experiment or a simulation.

REFERENCES

Aaker, D. (2007), 'Innovation: brand it or lose it', *California Management Review*, **50** (1), 8–24.

Ahlstrom, D. (2012a), 'Continuing the progress at the *Asia Pacific Journal of Management*', *Asia Pacific Journal of Management*, **29** (4), 841–48.

Ahlstrom, D. (2012b), 'On the types of papers the *Asia Pacific Journal of Management* generally publishes', *Asia Pacific of Journal Management*, **29** (1), 1–7.

Ahlstrom, D. and G.D. Bruton (2006), 'Venture capital in emerging economies: networks and institutional change', *Entrepreneurship: Theory and Practice*, **30** (2), 299–320.

Ahlstrom, D. and L.C. Wang (2010), 'Entrepreneurial capitalism in East Asia: how history matters', in H. Landstrom and F. Lohrke (eds), *Historical Foundations of Entrepreneurship Research*, Cheltenham, UK and Northampton, MA, USA: Edward Elgar, pp. 406–27.

Ahlstrom, D., G.D. Bruton and K.S. Yeh (2007), 'Venture capital in China: past, present, and future', *Asia Pacific Journal of Management*, **24** (2), 247–68.

Ahlstrom, D., S.-J. Chen and K.S. Yeh (2010), 'Managing in ethnic Chinese communities: culture, institutions, and context', *Asia Pacific Journal of Management*, **27** (3), 341–54.

Allison, G.T. and P. Zelikow (1999), *Essence of Decision: Explaining the Cuban Missile Crisis*, 2nd edn, New York: Longman.

Bansal, P. and K. Corley (2012), 'Publishing in *AMJ* – part 7: what's different about qualitative research?', *Academy of Management Journal*, **55** (3), 509–13.

Bruton, G.D. and D. Ahlstrom (2003), 'An institutional view of China's venture capital industry: explaining the differences between China and the West', *Journal of Business Venturing*, **18** (2), 233–59.

Bruton, G.D., D. Ahlstrom and H.L. Li (2010), 'Institutional theory and entrepreneurship: where are we now and where do we need to move in the future?', *Entrepreneurship Theory and Practice*, **34** (3), 421–40.

Bruton, G.D, D. Ahlstrom and T. Puky (2009), 'Institutional differences and the development of entrepreneurial ventures: a comparison of the venture capital industries in Latin America and Asia', *Journal of International Business Studies*, **40** (5), 762–78.

Carr, E.H. (1961), *What Is History?* New York: Vintage Books.

Chen, C.C. (1995), 'New trends in reward allocation preferences: a Sino-U.S. comparison', *Academy of Management Journal*, **38** (2), 408–28.

Chen, X.-P. and C.C. Chen (2012), 'Chinese guanxi: the good, the bad, and the controversial', in X. Huang and M.H. Bond (eds), *Handbook of Chinese*

Organizational Behavior: Integrating Theory, Research and Practice, Cheltenham, UK and Northampton, MA, USA: Edward Elgar, pp. 415–35.

Christensen, C.M. (2006), 'The ongoing process of building a theory of disruption', *Journal of Product Innovation Management*, **23** (1), 39–55.

Christensen, C.M. and P. Carlile (2009), 'Course research: using the case method to build and teach management theory', *Academy of Management Learning & Education*, **8** (2), 240–51.

Cohen, J.B. and K. Basu (1987), 'Alternative models of categorization: toward a contingent processing framework', *Journal of Consumer Research*, **13** (4), 455–72.

Collins, J. (2001), *Good to Great*, New York: HarperBusiness.

Creswell, J.W. (2006), *Qualitative Inquiry And Research Design: Choosing among 5 Traditions*, 2nd edn, Thousand Oaks, CA: Sage Publications.

Creswell, J.W. and V.L.P. Clark (2010), *Designing and Conducting Mixed Methods Research*, 2nd edn, Thousand Oaks, CA: Sage Publications.

Fu, P.P. and G. Yukl (2000), 'Perceived effectiveness of influence tactics in the United States and China', *Leadership Quarterly*, **11** (2), 251–66.

Gaddis, J.L. (2002), *The Landscape of History: How Historians Map the Past*, New York: Oxford University Press.

Glauser, B. and A. Strauss (1967), *The Discovery of Grounded Theory*, Chicago, IL: Aldine.

Hargadon, A.B. and Douglas, Y. (2001), 'When innovations meet institutions: Edison and the design of the electric light', *Administrative Science Quarterly*, **46** (3), 476–501.

Harrison, G.W. and J.A. List (2004), 'Field experiments', *Journal of Economic Literature*, **17** (December), 1009–55.

Hofstede, G. and Hofstede, G.J. (2005), *Cultures and Organizations Software of the Mind*, New York: McGraw-Hill.

Huang, X. and M.H. Bond (eds), (2012), *Handbook of Chinese Organizational Behavior: Integrating Theory, Research and Practice*, Cheltenham, UK and Northampton, MA, USA: Edward Elgar, Jia, L., S. You and Y. Du (2012), 'Chinese context and theoretical contributions to management and organization research: a three-decade review', *Management and Organization Review*, **8** (1), 173–209.

Johnson, H.T. and R. Kaplan (1987), *Relevance Lost*, Boston, MA: Harvard Business School Press.

Khavul, S., H. Chavez and G.D. Bruton (2013), 'When institutional change outruns the change agent: the contested terrain of entrepreneurial microfinance for those in poverty', *Journal of Business Venturing*, **28** (1), 30–50.

Kressel, N. and D. Kressel (2004), *Stack and Sway: The New Science of Jury Consulting*, New York: Basic Books.

Lai, J.Y.M., L.W. Lam and Y. Liu (2010), 'Do you really need help? A study of employee supplication and job performance in China', *Asia Pacific Journal of Management*, **27** (3), 541–59.

Lam, L.W., X. Huang and D.C. Lau (2012), 'Leadership research in Asia: taking the road less traveled?', *Asia Pacific Journal of Management*, **29** (2), 195–204.

Larsson, R. (1993), 'Case survey methodology: quantitative analysis of patterns across case studies', *Academy of Management Journal*, **36** (6), 1515–46

Leung, K. (2009), 'Never the twain shall meet? Integrating Chinese and Western management research', *Management and Organization Review*, **5** (1), 121–9.

Lincoln, Y.S. and E.G. Guba (1985), *Naturalistic Inquiry*, Newbury Park, CA: Sage.

Lingo, E.L. and O'Mahony, S. (2010), 'Nexus work: brokerage on creative projects', *Administrative Science Quarterly*, **55** (1), 47–81.

Lohrke, F.T., D. Ahlstrom and G.D. Bruton (2012), 'Extending turnaround process research: important lessons from the U.S. Civil War', *Journal of Management Inquiry*, **21** (2), 217–34.

Luscher, L. and M. Lewis (2008), 'Organizational change and managerial sensemaking: working through paradox', *Academy of Management Journal*, **51** (2), 221–40.

Mao, Y., K.Z. Peng and C.S. Wong (2012), 'Indigenous research on Asia: in search of the emic components of guanxi', *Asia Pacific Journal of Management*, **29**(4), 1143–68.

March, J.G. (2005), 'Parochialism in the evolution of a research community: the case of organization studies', *Management and Organization Review*, **1** (1), 5–22.

Meyer, K.E. (2006), 'Asian management research needs more self-confidence', *Asia Pacific Journal of Management*, **23** (2), 119–37.

Morris, M.W., J.M. Podolny and S. Ariel (2001), 'Culture, norms, and obligations: cross-national differences in patterns of interpersonal norms and felt obligations toward coworkers', in W. Wosinska, R.B. Cialdini, D.W. Barrett and J. Reykowski (eds), *The Practice of Social Influence In Multiple Cultures*, Mahwah, NJ: Lawrence Erlbaum Associates, pp. 84–107.

Moustakas, C. (1994), *Phenomenological Research Methods*, Thousand Oaks, CA: Sage Publications.

Ozcan, P. and K.M. Eisenhardt (2009), 'Origin of alliance portfolios: entrepreneurs, network strategies and firm performance', *Academy of Management Journal*, **52** (2), 246–79.

Peng, M.W. (2005), 'Perspectives – from China strategy to global strategy', *Asia Pacific Journal of Management*, **22** (2), 123–41.

Peters, T. and R.H. Waterman (1983), *In Search of Excellence: Lessons from America's Best Run Companies*, New York: Harper & Row.

Ragin, C.C. (1987), *The Comparative Method: Moving Beyond Qualitative and Quantitative Strategies*, Berkeley, CA: University of California Press.

Ravasi, D., C. Turati, G. Marchisio and C.D. Ruta (2004), 'Learning in entrepreneurial firms: an exploratory study', in G. Corbetta, M. Huse and D. Ravasi (eds), *Crossroads of Entrepreneurship*, Boston, MA: Kluwer Academic.

Rosch, E. (1975), 'Cognitive representations of semantic categories', *Journal of Experimental Psychology*, **104** (3), 192–233.

Rosenzweig, P. (2007), *The Halo Effect:… and the Eight Other Business Delusions that Deceive Managers*, New York: Free Press.

Sarasvathy, S. (2009), *Effectuation: Elements of Entrepreneurial Expertise*, Cheltenham, UK and Northampton, MA, USA: Edward Elgar.

Singh, K. (2007), 'The limited relevance of culture to strategy', *Asia Pacific Journal of Management*, **24** (4), 421–8.

Smith, P.B. (2012), 'Chinese management theories: indigenous insights or lessons for the wider world?', in X. Huang and M.H. Bond (eds), *Handbook of Chinese Organizational Behavior: Integrating Theory, Research and Practice*, Cheltenham, UK and Northampton, MA, USA: Edward Elgar, pp. 502–12.

Stake, R.E. (2010), *Qualitative Research: Studying How Things Work*, New York: Guilford Press.

Strauss, A.L. and J.M. Corbin (1990), *Basics of Qualitative Research: Grounded Theory Procedures and Techniques*, Newbury Park, CA: Sage Publications.

Suddaby, R. and R. Greenwood (2005), 'Rhetorical strategies of legitimacy', *Administrative Science Quarterly*, **50** (1), 35–67.

Tan, J., Y. Shao and W. Li (2013), 'To be different, or to be the same? An exploratory study of isomorphism in the cluster', *Journal of Business Venturing*, **28** (1), 83–97.

Tsang, E.W.K. and K.M. Kwan (1999), 'Replication and theory development in organizational science: a critical realist perspective', *The Academy of Management Review*, **24** (4), 759–80.

Tsoukas, H. (1989), 'The validity of idiographic research explanations', *Academy of Management Review*, **14** (4), 551–61.

Tsui, A.S. (2007), 'From homogenization to pluralism: international research in the academy and beyond', *Academy of Management Journal*, **50** (6), 1353–64.

Tsui, A.S., C.B. Schoonhoven, M. Meyer, C.M. Lau and G. Milkovich (2004), 'Organization and management in the midst of societal transformation: the People's Republic of China', *Organization Science*, **15** (2), 133–44.

Van de Ven, A.H. (2004), 'The context-specific nature of competence and corporate development', *Asia Pacific Journal of Management*, **21** (1–2), 123–47.

Van de Ven, A.H. (2007), *Engaged Scholarship*, Oxford: Oxford University Press.

Venkatesh, S.A. (2008), *Gang Leader for a Day: A Rogue Sociologist Takes to the Streets*, New York: Penguin Books.

Venkatesh, S.A. (2009), *Off the Books: The Underground Economy of the Urban Poor*, Cambridge, MA: Harvard University Press.

Venkatraman, M. and T. Nelson (2008), 'From Servicescape to Consumptionscape: a photo-elicitation study of Starbucks in the New China', *Journal of International Business Studies*, **39** (6), 1010–26.

Whyte, W.F. (1943), *Street Corner Society*, Chicago, IL: University of Chicago Press.

Wosinska, W., R.B. Cialdini, D.W. Barrett J. and Reykowski (eds) (2001), *The Practice of Social Influence in Multiple Cultures*, Mahwah, NJ: Lawrence Erlbaum Associates.

Yin, R.K. (1981), 'The case study crisis: some answers', *Administrative Science Quarterly*, **26** (1), 58–65.

Yin, R.K. (2008), *Case Study Research: Design and Methods*, 4th edn, Thousand Oaks, CA: Sage Publications.

Yin, R.K. (2010), *Qualitative Research from Start to Finish*, New York: Guilford Press.

12. Publishing cases in entrepreneurship journals

Franz Lohrke, Melissa Baucus and Charles Carson

INTRODUCTION

The case method has long played an important role in organizational research as a way to both build and teach theory (Christensen and Carlisle, 2009; Eisenhardt, 1989; Lincoln and Guba, 1985). Classic case studies have provided foundational theory for many research streams, including worker motivations (Roethlisberger and Dickson, 1939), organizational structure (Chandler, 1962) and managerial decision making (Allison, 1971). Like other applied fields (for example, medicine and law), case studies also serve as critical pedagogical tools that immerse students in the richness and complexity of real-world decision making as well as provide them opportunities to learn from historical examples (Summer et al., 1990).

As in others fields, entrepreneurship scholars have employed the case method to generate new theory and to educate aspiring entrepreneurs (Hindle, 2004; Perren and Ram, 2004). Some early entrepreneurship case studies provided key theory in research areas, including entrepreneurial motivation (McClelland, 1961), geographic clusters (Becattini, 1979), corporate entrepreneurship/entrepreneurial orientation (Miller, 1983) and new international ventures (Oviatt and McDougall, 1994). As the field has developed, scholars have continued to generate new theory using the case method. For example, in their review of research conducted in the 1990s, Chandler and Lyon (2001) found that 18 percent of articles in leading entrepreneurship journals employed qualitative techniques, with the majority employing either real-time or retrospective case study methods.

Pedagogical cases provide an important tool that professors can use to lead students through the complex entrepreneurship process of opportunity identification, evaluation and exploitation (Shane and Venkataraman,

2000). Given this important role, some top entrepreneurship journals regularly publish pedagogical cases along with standard journal articles to help disseminate new cases.

In this chapter, we discuss important issues related to publishing theory-development and pedagogical cases in top journals. We first briefly review the case method in organizational research, with a particular focus on its use in entrepreneurship research. Given the large number of excellent sources on this method (for example, Eisenhardt, 1989; Lincoln and Guba, 1985; Yin, 2009), we do not intend this chapter to serve as step-by-step tutorial for conducting case research, per se. Instead, we endeavor to highlight key issues that scholars should consider when trying to publish case-based research in top entrepreneurship journals. To do so, we review case studies published in top journals over the past five years to highlight important issues (see also Tables 12.1 and 12.2). In the final sections, we discuss our findings as well as draw from our collective experience publishing in and reviewing cases for top journals to provide advice we hope will help readers successfully navigate this process.

THE CASE METHOD IN ENTREPRENEURSHIP RESEARCH

The case method requires scholars to examine one or more organizations in depth to discover critical issues impacting the firms' current situation. Scholars can collect data through primary methods such as interviews, surveys or direct observation, and/or they can employ secondary sources such as business press publications. A case study can also examine issues at one or multiple (for example, individual entrepreneur, new venture, and/or industry) levels of analysis (Eisenhardt, 1989).

After collecting the data, the investigator must communicate important issues and findings in sufficient detail to allow the reader to gain insight into the complex situations faced by decision makers in the case. Types of information that must be communicated will depend on whether a scholar is writing a theory-development or a pedagogical case study. In the following sections, we examine important issues related to publishing both types in entrepreneurship journals.

Theory-development Cases

A central goal of scientific research is to develop theories that explain how the world works by parsimonously detailing relationships among important concepts and the circumstances under which these relationships hold (Bacharach, 1989). Scholars can build theory in several ways, including conducting literature reviews, drawing on personal experiences or borrowing theory from other fields (Whetten et al., 2009). To build testable theory grounded in data, however, scholars often employ the case method (Glaser and Strauss, 1967).

In her classic treatise, Eisenhardt (1989) illustrated how the inductive case method both parallels and differs from deductive, quantitative research. Similar to the latter, using the case method involves searching for patterns within the data. In addition, scholars must consider critical research issues such as the external validity of their results, especially because they only employ a small sample of firms.

In terms of differences, goals of the case method and large-sample empirical research often diverge, with the former focusing primarily on generating theoretical propositions and the latter focusing on testing theoretically derived hypotheses (Yin, 2009). Sample sizes are another obvious difference (for example, *n* often equals one for case studies), but some of the prescribed methods for conducting research can also differ. For example, whereas random samples are preferred in large-sample experimental designs to remove possible alternative explanations for findings, scholars conducting case research are often encouraged to employ 'purposeful sampling' to deliberately choose organizations operating on polar opposite ends of a focal construct (for example, environmental turbulence) so as to maximize differences (Glaser and Strauss, 1967). In addition, in contrast to large-sample studies that develop hypotheses based on specific theories, scholars employing the case method may enter the field with a preliminary theory and then further develop or alter the theory as they accumulate additional data (Eisenhardt, 1989).

Employing the case method offers some advantages, including that it provides useful opportunities to generate novel theories, modify existing theory or compare and contrast two or more theories. As an example of the first of these, when Allison (1971) conducted his case study of decision making during the Cuban Missile Crisis, the 'rational decision making' model held sway. Research in this area, however, quickly changed after his results were published to focus on alternative decision-making approaches that deviated from the rational model. Developing theory employing the case method remains important to the entrepreneurship field, given that in academic terms, it is still relatively young compared with other social sciences (Lohrke and Landström, 2010).

The case method can also be a good starting point to modify existing theory as scholars investigate a theory's boundary conditions (cf.

Bachrach, 1989). For example, in examining long-lived family firms, Zellwegger and Sieger (2012) found, contrary to prevailing wisdom in entrepreneurship research, that firms did not have to sustain high levels of entrepreneurial orientation (EO) to succeed over the long term. Their results, therefore, suggest that family firms can successfully adapt their EO levels across time rather than follow the prevailing 'more is better' view of EO within the field.

Cases can also be used to compare and contrast existing theoretical perspectives. For example, Fisher (2012) employed the case method to examine overlap and differences between effectuation (Sarasvathy, 2001) and bricolage (Baker and Nelson, 2005), two prominent theoretical perspectives examining resource scarcity that have generally developed independently of one another.

One major disadvantage to employing the case method is that it can be complex and time-consuming to conduct. Gartner and Birley (2002) introduce the term, 'critical mess' theory, to highlight the overwhelming amount of information that case researchers may encounter when investigating organizations. They argue, however, that such messiness is necessary to examine and develop explanations for entrepreneurial phenomena that are not easily amenable to large-sample, quantitative study.

Pedagogical Cases

Pedagogical cases provide a valuable tool to immerse students in the complexity of entrepreneurial decision making. Cases expose students to issues and situations that can be difficult to reproduce in a classroom setting (for example, managing a start-up) and provide an opportunity for students to learn lessons from entrepreneurs' experiences. Thus, publishing pedagogical cases helps maintain the intellectual capital needed for professors to teach contemporary issues to students (David, 2003; Summer et al., 1990).

Given its value in simulating decision-making situations, professors have long employed the case method of teaching in organizational studies, including entrepreneurship (Dooley and Skinner, 1977). A pedagogical case can be defined as:

> a vehicle by which a chunk of reality is brought into the classroom to be worked over by the class and the instructor. A good case keeps the class discussion grounded upon some the stubborn facts that must be faced in real life situations. It is the anchor on academic flights of speculation. It is the record of complex situations that must be literally pulled apart and put together again before the situations can be understood. (Lawrence, 1953, p. 215)

One long-standing issue in case research has been the source types (that is, primary versus secondary) that authors should use when writing a case. On the one hand, primary sources (for example, interviews or participant observation) provide the opportunity to develop 'thick descriptions' and ask follow-up questions, but also involve time-consuming efforts to gather information. On the other hand, secondary sources allow authors to access and triangulate information about a company's situation from multiple sources as well as facilitate gathering data after an event has occurred without having to rely on a decision maker's fallible memory. Secondary sources, however, may not provide either the depth of information needed or access to managers' thought processes that occurred during an event (Smith et al., 1989). Consequently, as part of our review below, we include whether pedagogical cases employed primary, secondary or both types of sources.

METHODOLOGY

To examine case method use in recent entrepreneurship research, we reviewed leading entrepreneurship and management journals from 2008 through 2012. We examined the 17 journals in Fried's (2003) top two categories (that is, 3 – Significant or 4 – Outstanding) in his review of leading entrepreneurship outlets. In addition, we considered other entrepreneurship journals that have launched since Fried's review, which may have attained high rankings despite being relatively new. Based on this criterion, we added the *Strategic Entrepreneurship Journal* to the journal pool, resulting in a total of 18 journals in our review sample.

Although arguments could be made that other entrepreneurship or case-focused journals could be included, this sampling procedure captured leading management and entrepreneurship journals as well as included both US- and European-based journals. We thought including the latter was particularly important, not only to provide a more global perspective on the field, but also because the European research tradition has generally included wide acceptance of the case method in organizational research (Gartner and Birley, 2002). Thus, we believe this sample provides a useful overview of recent case-based entrepreneurship research published in top outlets.

We conducted database and table of content searches for both theory-development and pedagogical cases, employing terms such as 'case study', 'grounded theory' and 'qualititative methods'.[1] In addition, when examining journals (for example, *Academy of Management Journal*) that did not focus exclusively on entrepreneurship topics, we applied the

Academy of Management Entrepreneurship Division's domain statement to decide whether a given case-based article examined relevant topics.[2] We then classified the resulting studies into one of the major topics in the entrepreneurship process (that is, opportunity recognition, evaluation, or exploitation) or as 'integrative works' if they examined multiple topics.

RESULTS

Our results indicate that the case method remains important in entrepreneurship research with 42 theory-development and 19 teaching cases appearing in major journals the past five years. Although these numbers represent a relatively small percentage relative to the total number of articles published over the same period, our results demonstrate that scholars can publish well-written case-based research in leading entrepreneurship and general management outlets (see Tables 12.1 and 12.2).

The results show that theory-development cases tended to fall into one of two general overlapping areas. First, they examined 'cutting edge' issues where continued theory development remains necessary. For example, despite a strong theoretical underpinning from psychology, research examining cognitive issues in entrepreneurship has needed continued theory development to examine how psychological issues influence the entrepreneurship process (Hindle, 2004).

Second, topics examined also included theoretical areas where large sample-size research remains difficult. For example, studies examining a resource-based view of the firm and effectuation issues remain largely case based, as does research on social entrepreneurship. These findings make sense, given the somewhat nascent state of research on these topics in the entrepreneurship literature. In addition, topics such as entrepreneurial failure, where finding large samples can be difficult, either because of a lack of extant databases or unwillingness of potential subjects to participate, often use the case method (for example, Cope, 2011).

In addition, our results indicate that recent case-based research maintains a healthy diversity of topics, industries and geographic locations. For example, scholars examined issues across the entrepreneurship process and employed cases from developed and developing countries when writing both theory-development and pedagogical cases. In terms of the latter, however, the majority of cases examined opportunity exploitation decisions, suggesting a need exists for more cases examining opportunity recognition and evaluation issues.

Table 12.1 A review of theory-development cases published in top entrepreneurship journals, 2008–12

Study	Sample	Topic					Key findings
		Integrative works	Opportunity recognition	Opportunity evaluation	Opportunity exploitation		
Academy of Management Journal							
Ozcan and Eisenhardt, 2009	Six US firms in the wireless gaming industry				Strategic alliances		Executives are more likely to build high-performing alliance portfolios when they visualize these portfolios in the context of the entire industry rather than as a series of dyadic ties and when they form simultaneous ties with multiple partners
Walsh and Bartunek, 2011	Six large US organizations that had failed				Organizational rebirth following failure		The death and rebirth process proceeds through four stages: disintegration, demise, gestation and rebirth
Almandoz, 2012	271 US banks during the founding process				Impact of different logics on successful founding		Employing a community logic leads to greater firm legitimacy, and, in turn, greater chances of successful founding
Hallen and Eisenhardt, 2012	Nine US Internet security ventures				Network tie formation		Two 'equifinal' paths for how executives efficiently form ties exist

Study	Sample	Topic					Key findings
		Integrative works	Opportunity recognition	Opportunity evaluation	Opportunity exploitation		

Academy of Management Perspectives

Study	Sample	Integrative works	Opportunity recognition	Opportunity evaluation	Opportunity exploitation	Key findings
Pilegaard et al., 2010	One spinoff from a university in Denmark				University spinoffs	Contexts may be structured to better evaluate the entrepreneurial process and the university entrepreneurship process in social sciences and humanities differs from the process in the hard sciences

Administrative Science Quarterly

Weber et al., 2008	41 semi-structured interviews with key US stakeholders	New market emergence				Social movements can bring about cultural change through market creation

California Management Review

Engel and del-Palacio, 2011	Israel and Silicon Valley	Innovation within and among 'clusters of innovation' (COIs)				COIs differ from industrial or Porterian cluster on various characteristics
McCarthy et al., 2010	130 Russian entrepreneurs	Entrepreneurial leadership styles				Most Russian entrepreneurs had an open leadership style similar to US entrepreneurs, providing support for entrepreneurial convergence theory

Entrepreneurship Theory and Practice

West et al., 2008	Local development in Costa Rica and Mexico	Regional economic development	From a resource-based view, entrepreneurial orientation, networks, knowledge and political stability are critical in regional economic development
Lechner and Leyronas, 2009	Entrepreneurs in three French business groups	Realizing, managing and enabling growth	Business group formation helped new ventures overcome liability of newness issues
Terjesen and Elam, 2009	Four transnational entrepreneurs	Internationalization	Economic, social, cultural and symbolic capital are necessary to navigate multiple institutional environments when internationalizing
Khavul et al., 2009	Eight ventures operating in the East African informal economy	Role of network ties in family business	East African entrepreneurs rely on both strong family and strong community ties to establish businesses. These entrepreneurs are more likely to start businesses with the latter, and this effect is greater for female than male entrepreneurs

| | | Topic | | | | |
Study	Sample	Integrative works	Opportunity recognition	Opportunity evaluation	Opportunity exploitation	Key findings
Achtenhagen et al., 2010	30 interviews with Swedish entrepreneurs in young-, high- and continuous-growth firms				Business growth	Entrepreneurs in different types of companies define growth differently from each other and from academics
Ahlstrom and Bruton, 2010	Ten Russian start-ups in a business incubator	Organizational adaptation to changing institutional environments				The general assumption in institutional theory that institutions change slowly does not generally hold in transition economies
Corner and Ho, 2010	One membership-based charity headquartered in New Zealand		Opportunity recognition in social entrepreneurship		Opportunity exploitation in social entrepreneurship	Recognizing and exploiting socially entrepreneurial opportunites require collective action, experience corridors and a 'spark'
Di Domenico et al., 2010	Eight social enterprises in the UK				Bricolage in social entrepreneurship	Social bricolage is conceptually distinct from other forms because it involves social value creation, stakeholder participation, and persuasion

Grimes, 2010	Three case studies based on six organizations across multiple geographic locations	Performance measurement in social entrepreneurship	Performance measurement impacted the sense-making process in socially entrepreneurial firms
Iacobucci and Rosa, 2010	14 entrepreneurs active in Italian business groups	New venture creation by serial entrepreneurs	Business groups grew to enhance the specialization of and access additional management talent for a firm
Kistruk and Beamish, 2010	Ten cases of social intrapreneurship in Africa and Latin America	Role of cognitive, network, and cultural embeddness on organizational form	Social intrapreneurship in nonprofit firms experienced greater difficulty in shifting goals compared with efforts in for-profit forms
Autio et al., 2011	Ten Finnish firms operating globally (eight of which were start-ups)	New capability development and firm adaptation	Environmental uncertainty relates positively to new capability development. Resource fungibility and shared prior experiences positively and negatively moderate this relationship, respectively

| | | Topic | | | | |
Study	Sample	Integrative works	Opportunity recognition	Opportunity evaluation	Opportunity exploitation	Key findings
Knockaert et al., 2011	Nine high technology Belgian start-ups			Role of tacit knowledge and top management team (TMT) composition on commercialization of technology transfer		TMT commercialization experience needs to be complemented by technical experience to enhance commercialization success
Biniari, 2012	Two large, multinational corporations				Corporate venturing	Emergence of envy within a company can jeapordize corporate venturing initiatives
Datta and Gailey, 2012	Six Indian female entrepreneurs				Social entrepreneurship and economic empowerment	For-profit socially entrepreneurial ventures promote empowerment for groups underrepresented in entrepreneurship
Fisher, 2012	Six US Internet-based new ventures	Entrepreneurial behaviors based on different theories				Effectuation and bricolage share four dimensions related to the entrepreneurship process

Gemmel et al., 2012	32 entrepreneurs in US high-technology industries	Social behaviors and cognitive processes	Entrepreneurs frequently employ complex but well-defined social interactions as part of a cycle of learning and experimentation in innovation
Katre and Salipante, 2012	31 founders of 23 North American socially entrepreneurial (SE) firms	Social entrepreneurship	Three sets of entrepreneurial behaviors differentiated successful and unsuccessful SE ventures
Marlow and McAdam, 2012	Life history of a female tenant in a high-technology incubator	Gender influences on entrepreneurship	Interaction of masculinized culture of high-technology venturing and self-imposed role expectations create tensions that female entrepreneurs must reconcile

Journal of Business Venturing

| Dutta and Thornhill, 2008 | 30 Canadian entrepreneurs | Cognitive issues in growth intentions | Entrepreneurs' cognitive styles moderate the relationship between environmental perceptions and growth intentions |

Study	Sample	Topic					Key findings
		Integrative works	Opportunity recognition	Opportunity evaluation	Opportunity exploitation		
Mair and Marti, 2009	40 semi-structured interviews in a Bangladeshi non-governmental organization (NGO)				Institutional voids and bricolage in developing economies		Bricolage requires sense-making by the bricoleur, involves political processes and, in some cases, can have negative outcomes in alleviating poverty
Mujamdar, 2010	Interviews with ten Indian entrepreneurs				Organizational growth		Entrepreneurs define and hold different attitudes toward venture growth
Vaghely and Julien, 2010	Interviews with CEOS and staff members in ten small and medium-sized businesses		Information processing issues				Opportunities can be both recognized and constructed
Cope, 2011	Eight UK and US entrepreneurs	Recovery and learning from organizational failure					Through failure, entrepreneurs learn about themselves and are increasingly prepared for future entrepreneurship

Journal of Management Studies

Kiel et al., 2008	Five large, global information and communication technology firms	Corporate venture capital (CVC) in high uncertainty environments	CVC investments allow incumbent firms to identify voids in their existing capabilities and influence investment decisions in building future capabilities
McInerney, 2008	Ethnographic study of non-profit technology assistance providers and conferences	Field formation process	Institutional entrepreneurs use political processes to shape new fields and influence the institutions that govern them

Organization Science

Tracey et al., 2011	One UK social enterprise	Emergence of new organizational forms	Individual-, organizational- and societal-level processes affect the emergence of new organizational forms

Research Policy

Doganova and Eyquem-Renault, 2009	One French spinoff firm	Innovation	A firm's business model can be examined as a market device
DiVito, 2012	Interviews in five UK and six Dutch biotechnology firms	Innovation strategy	Firms adopted alternative high-risk innovation strategies when facing institutional constraints

Study	Sample	Topic				Key findings
		Integrative works	Opportunity recognition	Opportunity evaluation	Opportunity exploitation	
He et al., 2011	Interviews with CEOs and employees in 41 Chinese firms	Geographic clusters				Clusters can self-organize based on a process including landscape design, positive feedback, boundary constraints and novel outcomes
Small Business Economics						
Zellweger and Sieger, 2012	Three case studies of Swiss firms in three different industries	Importance of entrepreneurial orientation in family firms				The entrepreneurial orientation – firm performance relationship may differ between family and non-family firms
Strategic Entrepreneurship Journal						
Dyer et al., 2008	Case studies of innovative entrepreneurs		Information acquisition			Entrepreneurs differ from executives on four dimensions of information accumulation: questioning, observing, experimenting and idea networking
Clarysse et al., 2011	Six case studies of young technology-based, high-growth firms				Resource accumulation	Specific high-growth paths result from structuring resource portfolios based on environmental demands
Sieger et al., 2011	Four case studies of European and Latin American family firms				Portfolio entrepreneurship based on the resource-based perspective	Six different resource categories are relevant to the portfolio entrepreneurship process

Table 12.2 A review of pedagogical cases published in top entrepreneurship journals, 2008–12

Study	Industry	Topic				Sources
		Integrative works	Opportunity recognition	Opportunity evaluation	Opportunity exploitation	
California Management Review						
Alexander et al., 2012	Thermoelectric technology				Market entry	Primary and secondary
Chesbrough, 2012	Green/renewable energy	Corporate entrepreneurship				Primary and secondary
Zafar and Chang, 2012	Computer software				Building a new venture to permit exit via acquisition	Primary and secondary
Entrepreneurship Theory and Practice						
Plant et al., 2008	Business procurement software in Chile				New venture growth	Primary and secondary
Sharma and Smith, 2008	Road construction materials in the USA				Succession planning	Primary and secondary
Stetz et al., 2008	Bowling supplies in East Asia			Re-evaluation of risks following international expansion		Primary and secondary

Study	Industry	Topic				Sources
		Integrative works	Opportunity recognition	Opportunity evaluation	Opportunity exploitation	
Ivanova, 2009	Small chemical trading company in Belarus	Ethical dilemmas in a venture operating in a transition economy				Primary and secondary
Kammermeyer and Naumes, 2009	Natural foods in the USA				Strategic positioning and entrepreneurial lifestyle	Primary and secondary
Croonen and Brand, 2010	Franchised pharmacy in the Netherlands				Franchisor–franchisee relationships	Primary and secondary
Hudnut and DeTienne, 2010	Motorcycle engines				Product launch in bottom of the pyramid markets	Primary and secondary
Huser and Swartz, 2010	Medical testing kits in the USA				New venture valuation and growth	Primary and secondary
Baucus et al., 2011	Laundry detergent in the USA				Proposed purchase of a corporate spinoff	Primary and secondary
Grove and Cook, 2011	Snow shoes in the USA				Valuing a firm during management exit decisions	Primary and secondary

Reference	Context	Topic	Topic	Data
McCrea and Torres-Baumgarten, 2011	Mailing and mail box services in the USA		Converting an existing to a new franchise	Primary and secondary
Reed and Brunson, 2011	Health care facilities in the USA	Risk assessment in acquiring a business		Primary and secondary
Fernandes et al., 2012	Self-propelled scooters from Brazil in the USA		Product positioning in international markets	Primary and secondary
Finkle, 2012	Internet search engines	Corporate entrepreneurship		Mostly secondary
Schenkel et al., 2012a	Online auctions	Opportunity recognition based on changing technology		Primary and secondary
Schenkel et al., 2012b	Agricultural equipment in the USA		New venture growth	Primary and secondary

Interestingly, some studies employed the case method even though they had sample sizes sufficient to use parametric research methods. For example, Gemmel et al. (2012) interviewed 32 entrepreneurs in high-technology industries, which could have allowed the authors to employ parametric statistical methods. Their goal in the study, however, was to develop rather than to test theory, thereby requiring the case approach. In addition, Katre and Salipante (2012) interviewed 31 social entrepreneurs, but noted that qualitative research provided the fine-grained analysis necessary to study behaviors that differentiated successful from unsuccessful socially entrepreneurial ventures. Other authors (for example, Cope, 2011; Dyer et al., 2008) have incorporated both qualitative and quantitative research methods into 'mixed method' studies.

Finally, the results also show that pedagogical cases frequently employed both primary and secondary sources to provide readers with sufficient information to make strategic decisions. We will elaborate on this point further in the following section.

SUGGESTIONS FOR PUBLISHING CASES

Results from our review of recent literature show that the case method continues to play an important role for both developing theory in entrepreneurship literature and providing cases to teach critical entrepreneurship concepts to aspiring entrepreneurs. In this section, we draw from our experience of publishing cases in and reviewing cases for top entrepreneurship journals to provide suggestions to those interested in employing the case method.

The process of publishing cases has similarities to and differences from other submission types. In terms of similarities, much of the advice in this volume about publishing in general holds for case-based research. For example, cases must conform with the mission and editorial guidelines of the targeted journal, be free of grammatical and typographical errors, and provide sufficient methodological detail for the reviewers to determine the quality of the research conducted (Chrisman, 1990).[3]

Based on our results and experience, we note that those that successfully navigated the publication process had some similar characteristics. First, authors successfully overcame some unique challenges to writing cases. Those publishing theory-development cases must follow prescribed methods for building grounded theory including incorporating an overwhelming amount of information into a scholar's working theory during the research process (Eisenhardt, 1989; Yin, 2009). Those publishing pedagogical cases face challenges including collecting primary and secondary data, choosing a decision point and developing a teaching note. For both types of cases, scholars must also provide sufficient relevant data for readers to follow a study's theoretical development or to perform the requisite analysis of a focal company. In addition, scholars must assume the role of 'storyteller' by leading the reader through a complex narrative. Cases submitted to journals for review often have problems in one or more of these areas, often leading reviewers and editors to reject them for publication. We discuss each, in turn.

Collecting Data

Case research requires scholars to collect and scrutinize an immense amount of information. Those developing new theory must continuously incorporate this information into their preliminary theory by searching for patterns within the data. This process suggests the need to collect data using methods (for example, recording interviews) that will allow scholars to revisit the data over time as this search unfolds.

Those writing pedagogical cases must consider the debate about the relative merits of using primary versus secondary data in these cases (see, for example, Chrisman, 1990; David, 2003). In fact, some case-specific research outlets (for example, *Case Research Journal*) will only accept submissions based on primary data. In our experience, it is often difficult for a case to provide the necessary insight into important issues without both types. The results above show that although most cases contain some secondary data, all include at least some primary data gathered through surveys or interviews.

For example, Baucus et al. (2011) included primary data based on interviews with two aspiring entrepreneurs and secondary data providing critical information about a venture's competitors to examine issues related to buying a corporate spinoff. In terms of secondary data, they also relied on newspaper and magazine articles written about the entrepreneurs and their start-up without providing any references that might lead students to discovering the actual outcome of the case. This practice can be problematic for case researchers as the need to provide accurate references and citations may conflict with the need to withhold source documents to facilitate students' working through the issues presented in the case rather than performing a web search to find out what 'really happened' to the firm in question.

Primary data typically involves interviewing the entrepreneur(s) and possibly other individuals that can provide valuable information related to a case's key decision. For example, a case one of the present authors reviewed discussed a family business where the founder was struggling with the succession decision; interviews with the founder and several other family members provided a clearer picture of the family dynamics as well as the different management styles between the founder and his son, who was being considered as a possible successor. The case also presented primary data gathered by surveying the founding entrepreneur and several family members in key management positions on communication patterns, such as who communicated with whom on particular types of issues as well as frequency and type of communication (for example, email or in person). Such information can add value if it is presented in a way that relates to the central decision in the case. When possible, primary data should usually include financial information about the company, given that it provides critical insights into a firm's current strengths and weaknesses.

Scholars using primary sources should be prepared to seek a release from the subject and/or the firm under study. This can be problematic if there are sensitive or unflattering issues discussed in the case. Entrepreneurs may wish to protect their image and avoid public dissemination of a new venture's 'dirty laundry'. It is, therefore, advisable for case authors to secure written releases from all relevant parties very early in the development stages of the research project.

Secondary data, in contrast, generally do not require any release to publish the associated data. For example, the founder(s) of the company may have developed a business plan for the venture that contains relevant information related to the founder(s) and history of the company. The company's website sometimes has links to magazine and newspaper articles written on the firm or these may be found through online searches. Again, these sources are useful, but the risk exists of 'giving away' the story to a resourceful student who does even a cursory web search based on any references and citations within the case.

These same sources may help in locating industry and competitor information. Government agencies can also provide important data. For example, the Food and Drug Administration in the USA provides details of the process companies must go through to get new products or medical devices approved, and this sort of secondary information is essential for readers when analyzing a case about a firm that has to go through this process. As these examples illustrate, secondary information can add robust and essential data for analyzing a case.

It is also worth noting, based on our experience, that the data gathered from both primary and secondary sources must be high-quality, reliable information. For example, pedagogical cases published in top outlets in the past five years relied heavily on high-quality primary information resulting from engaging a firm's key stakeholders. Cases that do not

engage stakeholders, in contrast, often have to rely on scholarly speculation about what decision makers were thinking during the events covered
in the case. Although this has become common practice, it may be more
advisable to allow students to speculate during class discussion rather
than having case authors 'fictionalize' aspects of a case that lacks
primary sources.

When using secondary sources, these case studies generally relied on
high-quality business press articles or data services (for example, financial press articles or industry surveys) rather than sources that summarize
information from other sources (for example, textbooks or online ency-
clopedias). Because the latter are not subject to scholarly peer review or
the discipline of the market in terms of their accuracy about business
information, they do not constitute high-quality sources for pedagogical
(or theory-development) cases.

Choosing a Decision Point

One of the biggest challenges for pedagogical case authors, especially
after gathering copious information from interviews and other primary or
secondary data sources, involves selecting a single decision point for the
case. Good pedagogical cases reach a decision point (Chrisman, 1990).
Lacking this, cases remain stories about 'a day in the life' of an
entrepreneur or a new venture and, thus, do not fulfill the role of a
pedagogical case. They are analogous to a murder mystery that describes
the characters and setting but lacks the chilling event and the 'who done
it?' question.

Many entrepreneurship cases we have reviewed for journals present
multiple decisions points in their initial form, an outcome that seems to
occur because cases offer so many possible decisions and contain
numerous potential directions for discussion that authors seem to believe
the added complexity enhances the case. Returning to the analogy of the
murder mystery, a case with multiple decision points resembles a 'who
done it?' with so many murders and murderers that readers often cannot
sort clues to make sense out of the story. An initial manuscript of a case
recently reviewed by one of the present authors was presented as a
hodgepodge of decisions related to what exit strategy an entrepreneur
should use, including when to exit, how to deal with conflicting
preferences (and equity holdings) of different investors, how to contend
with challenges in continuing to try to grow the company, and so forth.
This initial draft may have depicted the messy reality faced by the
entrepreneur, but students would have had great difficulty fully understanding any of the decisions presented, analyzing the various decisions,

and recommending and supporting a course of action. The reviewer's recommendation was to focus the case on only one decision point, which allowed the authors of the manuscript to revise their case into a well-presented situation of an entrepreneur facing an exit decision: is it time to sell the firm? Some of the other issues remain in the case but as important side issues, such as how to convince the various groups of investors that the exit decision, once made, is the right one.

A specific decision point makes it easier for scholars to focus on a core decision or issue because cases are often chosen to illustrate particular theories or concepts. Scholars writing pedagogical cases can often become mesmerized by all the interesting facets of a situation and forget that a good teaching case focuses the analysis and discussion on a central issue. In our opinion, most great teaching cases do not require students to make decisions about four or five different issues. This is not to say that professors cannot revisit a case throughout a semester as they cover new material, students develop new understandings, and a more developed analysis of a situation unfolds. Well-written, well-focused cases, however, generally grab students' attention, put them in the decision makers' shoes, require them to carefully analyze the situation, and support a course of action without overwhelming them with too many issues to consider simultaneously.

One option for scholars faced with writing up cases that address multiple decisions over time involves writing a series of cases. For instance, Branzei and Valente (2007a; 2007b; 2007c) wrote their case in three parts, with each case focusing on a different decision point and building on the information presented in the prior case. This allows students to see how prior decisions can affect the options available at a later point in time. Yet, even within a series of cases such as this, each individual case should be written so it focuses on a primary issue and could be used as a stand-alone case without the other parts.

Developing the Teaching Note

Pedagogical cases include a teaching note, although its form may vary by the journal's or publication's requirements. Generally, the teaching note provides a synopsis of the case with the decision point clearly laid out, as well as a description of the topics or issues in a particular course that the case could be used to illustrate. For example, case authors could recommend if a case involving whether or not to start a venture would likely work best at the very beginning of the course to get students thinking about what they need to learn or later in the course after they have studied critical start-up issues.

The teaching note usually provides key questions for discussion, laying them out in logical order so a professor could read and follow the teaching note as a road map for the class. Usually the note also includes a few supplemental questions or readings that allow a professor to expand the discussion into a side issue or two. In all situations, the teaching note provides guidance as to key points that should be addressed and brought out during class discussion of each question listed in the teaching note.

A good teaching note often includes the author's explanation of how he or she has used the case in class and options that may have worked well. For instance, an author writing a teaching note for a case on a succession decision might report that he or she assigns roles to various class members, with one student playing the firm's founder who must choose a successor, three or four students playing family members who work in the firm and would like to have family run the firm, another group of students representing a firm wanting to purchase and run the firm, and perhaps the remaining students acting as observers and consultants to the founder. The case author might then explain how he or she instructs the students prior to the role play, what typically happens during the role play, how he or she transitions from the role play to discussion of the case, and how he or she summarizes the case at the end of class to ensure students grasp the main points. The case might even include other options the author has experimented with that other professors can consider when using the case.

Providing Sufficient Information

Well-written theory-development cases contain sufficient information for the reader to follow a theory's development through the messy process of data collection and analysis. Well-written pedagogical cases provide readers with copious information both about a firm's internal and external environment, its history and founders. Lacking this information in a pedagogical case, the reader is forced to rely on speculation or must conduct additional research to provide data needed for a decision. For example, we have read cases where the teaching note directed professors to have students conduct outside research. Although encouraging students to gather important outside information to make strategic decisions is a valuable skill, it should not be a requirement to supplement information missing from a case.

Pedagogical cases should also include numerical data, such as financial statements, industry data or any other numbers related to the central decision point. For instance, a case involving entrepreneurs trying to decide whether to leave their current jobs to start a new venture should provide several years of pro forma financial statements for start-up, industry data showing major competitors and their relative market shares, industry growth rates and so forth, so students can determine if the venture represents a good opportunity for the entrepreneurs (see Baucus et al., 2011, as one example).

A case one of the present authors reviewed that involved a succession decision lacked financial data, so it was difficult to determine if the founder was correct in thinking his son did not have a realistic strategy for the firm's future growth or survival (or if a possible buyer for the firm had a better strategy and was offering a reasonable price for the venture). Students analyzing the succession case cannot make a decision based solely on hearsay or descriptive information about the relationship between the founder and his son; instead, they need to be able to look at the founder's and son's financial projections relative to past financial performance and competitors' performance.

Entrepreneurs may be reluctant to share their financial data because competitors might gain access to it. Scholars might be able to convince them that by the time the case is published, the data will be several years old, and the entrepreneurial venture will be in a very different position. Another approach that one of the present authors has used is to agree to multiplying all financial numbers by some odd multiple (for example, 2.3847). By doing this, the financial ratios will remain the same for students' analysis but an entrepreneur's competitors will typically not be able to determine the precise numbers for sales, expenses and so on. It can also help to agree to change the firm's and entrepreneur's names to disguise their identity.

The data presented in the case should relate directly to making the key decision in the case. For instance, if an entrepreneur with a pharmaceutical firm faces a decision of whether to acquire another firm or expand current operations to increase capacity, the case does not need to provide information on the cost of each phase of the US Food and Drug Adminstration's (FDA's) drug approval process. If instead the entrepreneur must determine whether to invest in developing new promising drugs versus investing in ones currently in the pipeline that might have lower profitability, the case should include the costs associated with the FDA's phases of drug testing and approval.

Performing the Role of Storyteller

Case writers must tell compelling stories that interest their readers whether they write theory-development or pedagogical cases. For the former, scholars must lead the reader through the complex research process used in theory development. In studies having more than one organization as a case study, sufficient background information needs to be provided to give readers a flavor for the key issues that scholars considered when developing their theory. For example, in their study of economic development based on the resource-based view of the firm, West et al. (2008) included copious information about the Costa Rican and Mexican regions they employed as case studies.

Pedagogical cases should also be 'good stories'. Academics tend to rely heavily on jargon or terminology specific to their field, such as entrepreneurship scholars discussing effectuation, cognition, entre-preneurial orientation and so forth. They learn the basic formula of writing a manuscript for a journal (for example, introduction, literature review, hypothesis development, methods, results and conclusion), and they write in a scholarly fashion that often appears to be a foreign language to the uninitiated.

Pedagogical case writing has little in common with other forms of academic writing and more closely resembles storytelling. Case writers need to master the art of crafting each sentence to concisely convey key information while avoiding jargon or getting bogged down in unnecessary details. For example, when writing pedagogical cases, most authors attempt to 'set the hook' in an opening paragraph with a compelling story, anecdote or scenario that compels the reader to invest in the remainder of the case.

One of the present authors remembers writing a pedagogical case for the first time and realizing that each sentence had to be interesting: it needed to make students and other readers want to keep reading. This often means telling the story through the eyes of one person in the case (often the entrepreneur) and presenting the information in an engaging manner.

Avoiding jargon in pedagogical cases can be difficult because many of the terms commonly used appear obvious to entrepreneurship scholars. We forget that even a term as simple as 'family business' needs to be briefly explained or placed in context in a way that clarifies the meaning; otherwise, students might accidently misinterpret it to mean a business that focuses on families such as planning family reunions or researching a family's genealogy. Similarly, students will not understand terms such as 'dot.com era', 'rounds of funding', 'angel investors', 'venture capital-ists' or, even, 'succession'. If these terms must be used, then a brief explanation (often in footnote form) should be included that makes the meaning clear for the reader. Sometimes diagrams also can help illustrate complex processes involved in entrepreneurship.

Many aspiring case writers can master many key challenges in the process but have difficulty moving from a dry rendition of the central decision point to a vibrant story that brings the entrepreneur and a new venture's dilemma to life. Suggestions for casewriters, who struggle to craft the story, include studying well-written published cases to see how the authors told their stories, such as cases in our review, analyzing an excellent work of fiction (for example, Helprin's 1983 book, *Winter's Tale*) that demonstrate extraordinary use of language to create scenes and characters, reading 'how to' case writing books,[4] or even hiring a copyeditor to transform the case from a straightforward description of events leading to the decision point to a story where readers identify with the entrepreneur and care about the decision he or she faces.

Pedagogical cases present factual information but may have some minor fictional elements. For instance, Baucus et al. (2011) provided some information from the viewpoint of one of the entrepreneurs in the case. Direct quotes used in the case were used exactly from interviews with the entrepreneurs but a minor word or two might be altered to help the quote better fit in the context of the case (that is, poetic license). Other factual data might be presented as if one of the entrepreneurs was thinking or in terms of how the entrepreneur felt about a particular option. For example, in Baucus et al.'s case, the entrepreneurs were said to feel they would be giving up their dream of being entrepreneurs if they had to agree to allow a venture capitalist to put his own proven entrepreneur in as chief executive officer (CEO) and work under that person in order to get funding for the venture. Often interviews provide case authors with insights into an entrepreneur's perspective, thoughts and feelings, and these can be woven into the case to add interest and help in developing the context surrounding the decision. The basic facts of the decision point remain the same but minor elements may be presented in a way that enhances the story.

CAREER ISSUES AND CASE WRITING

We should also note some important career issues that can arise from publishing cases. Summer et al. (1990) advised PhD students in strategic management both to publish a case, as a way to hone their organizational study abilities, and to teach using the case method because it was one of the only ways to simulate the complex decision making situations in strategic situations. We suggest the same holds true for nascent entrepreneurship scholars. Although writing and publishing cases can be a time-consuming process, the insights gained and the questions generated can make the experience valuable.

At the same time, scholars need to balance the time commitment needed to conduct and write a case with the potential career issues that arise. For example, employing the case method to conduct research can lengthen the time needed to finish a PhD program or can consume valuable time while a junior faculty member faces tenure clock pressure (Gartner and Birley, 2002). That said, at least one theory-development case in our sample (Croonen and Brand, 2010) resulted from a dissertation, showing that this type of research can be published in top outlets by new scholars.

Based on our experiences, publishing theory-development cases are probably more valuable (that is, they will 'count' for more) than pedagogical cases when moving through the promotion and tenure (P and T) process at PhD-granting institutions in the USA, where scholars may still face P and T committee members with biases favoring large-sample, empirical research. As shown in the results, top journals do accept both kinds of cases. Our experience is that Asian, Canadian, European and South American institutions have a much more favorable perspective on all types of case research than their US counterparts, although this may be changing in some countries as schools adapt their publishing requirements of faculty in order to score well in national research assessment exercises.

In terms of other career advice, scholars should be alert to the possibility of conducting case-based research from opportunitistic situations in addition to any deliberate efforts to seek out possible research sites. For example, case-based research can develop out of consulting projects, student ventures, or occur as part of a 'natural experiment'. Hudnut and DeTienne (2010) detail the development of a student enterprise where one of them served on the new venture board that started in one of their entrepreneurship classes. In addition, Meyer (1982) was investigating hospital administration issues in three hospitals when a 'natural experiment' (that is, an unexpected doctors' strike) in the San Franscisco area provided an opportunity to write a theory-development case about managerial reactions to environmental shocks. Additionally, student written instructor faciliated (SWIF) case writing provides an appealing mix of student engagement and faculty involvement and oversight, particularly for students at the Master's and undergraduate levels (Bailey et al., 2005).

We should also note that along with leading journals, some top entrepreneurship conferences also accept research employing the case method. For example, the Babson College Research Conference accepts a large amount of case-based research annually. In addition, some conferences (for example, the North American Case Research Association – NACRA) focus on developing pedagogical cases. These conferences can provide important feedback to scholars that are hoping to publish their cases in top journals.

The scope of this chapter has been to address case research in top entrepreneurship journals. We believe that it is also important, however, to note continued growth in case-focused journal outlets (for example, *Case Research Journal*). The increase in viable peer-reviewed journal outlets should have trickle-down effects on the numbers of submisisons to and interest in publishing high-quality cases in top tier entrepreneurship journals. NACRA has also supported the development of theory-based and theory-development cases with prestigious, generous (for example, $10 000) research grants that reinforce the importance of using case research as a valuable tool in the theory building process.

CONCLUSION

In this chapter, we have discussed important issues related to publishing theory-development and pedagogical cases in top journals. Based on our literature review, we can confidently conclude that case-based research remains important in entrepreneurship research. In the past five years, scholars have found top journals receptive to publishing well-written, methodologically sound cases.

We have also endeavored to provide guidance to the reader on how to navigate the publication process for case-based research. This research can be time-consuming and messy, with myriad details that scholars must consider simultaneously. Scholars who follow generally prescribed methods for conducting case research and consider the advice we have provided, however, may see their efforts rewarded by publishing research that generates novel theory for the entrepreneurship field. Those who employ their organizational investigations to develop pedagogical cases that tell good stories can provide intellectual capital that professors can use to train the next generation of aspiring entrepreneurs. Both of these outcomes represent important contributions to the entrepreneurship field.

NOTES

1. We included 'qualitative methods' in the search, even though this term is not necessarily synonymous with the case method. The latter, for example, can also employ quantitative methods. The two terms, however, are frequently used interchangeably in organizational research (Eisenhardt, 1989).
2. The Division's current domain statement is '(a) the actors, actions, resources, environmental influences and outcomes associated with the emergence of entrepreneurial opportunities and/or new economic activities in multiple organizational contexts, and (b) the characteristics, actions, and challenges of owner-managers and their businesses' ('Academy of Management … statements', 2013).
3. See, for example, 'Information for contributors of cases', http://www.baylor.edu/business/ETP/ index.php?id=24903.
4. Two excellent sources are Vega's (2013) *The Case Writing Workbook: A Self-Guided Workshop* and Naumes and Naumes (2011) *The Art and Craft of Case Writing*.

REFERENCES

'Academy of Management division and interest group domain statements' (2013), accessed 24 January 2013 at http://aom.org/Divisions-and-Interest-Groups/Academy-of-Management-Division – Interest-Group-Domain-Statements.aspx#ent.

Achtenhagen, L., L. Naldi and L. Melin (2010), 'Business growth – do practitioners and scholars really talk about the same thing?', *Entrepreneurship Theory and Practice*, **34** (2), 289–316.

Ahlstrom, D. and G. Bruton (2010), 'Rapid institutional shifts and the co-evolution of entrepreneurial firms in transition economies', *Entrepreneurship Theory and Practice*, **34** (3), 531–54.

Alexander, B., A. Boscoe, M. Cabot, P. Dawsey, L. Emmanuel Barreau and R. Griffith (2012), 'Alphabet energy: thermoelectrics and market entry', *California Management Review*, **55** (1), 149–60.

Allison, G. (1971), *Essence of Decision: Explaining the Cuban Missile Crisis*, Boston, MA: Little Brown.

Almandoz, J. (2012), 'Arriving at the starting line: The impact of community and financial logics in new banking ventures', *Academy of Management Journal*, **55** (6), 1381–406.

Autio, E., G. George and O. Alexy (2011), 'International entrepreneurship and capability development: qualitative evidence and future research directions', *Entrepreneurship Theory and Practice*, **35** (1), 11–37.

Bacharach, S. (1989), 'Organizational theories: some criteria for evaluation', *Academy of Management Review*, **14** (4), 496–515.

Bailey, J., M. Sass, P.M. Swiercz, C. Seal and D.C. Kayes (2005), 'Teaching with and through teams: student-written, instructor facilitated case writing and the signatory code', *Journal of Management Education*, **9** (1), 39–59.

Baker, T. and R. Nelson (2005), 'Creating something from nothing: resource construction through entrepreneurial bricolage', *Administrative Science Quarterly*, **50** (3), 329–66.

Baucus, M., S. Human, T. Clark and D. Rosenthal (2011), 'P&G is selling Oxydol!', *Entrepreneurship Theory and Practice*, **35** (2), 395–407.

Becattini, G. (1979), 'Sectors and/or districts: some remarks on the conceptual foundations of industrial economics', in E. Goodman, J. Bamford and P. Saynor (eds), *Small Firms and Industrial Districts in Italy*, London: Routledge, pp. 133–45.

Biniari, M. (2012), 'The emotional embeddedness of corporate entrepreneurship: the case of envy', *Entrepreneurship Theory and Practice*, **36** (1), 141–70.

Branzei, O. and M. Valente (2007), 'Honey Care Africa (A): a different business model', Richard Ivey School of Business Foundation, London, Ontario.

Branzei, O. and M. Valente (2007), 'Honey Care Africa (B): opportunity knocks', Richard Ivey School of Business Foundation, London, Ontario.

Branzei, O. and M. Valente (2007), 'Honey Care Africa (C): growth alternatives', Richard Ivey School of Business Foundation, London, Ontario.

Chandler A. (1962), *Strategy and Structure: Chapters in the History of American Industrial Enterprise*, Cambridge, MA: MIT Press.

Chandler, G. and D. Lyon (2001), 'Issues of research design and construct measurement in entrepreneurship research', *Entrepreneurship Theory and Practice*, **25** (4), 101–13.

Chesbrough, H. (2012), 'GE's ecomagination challenge', *California Management Review*, **54** (3), 140–54.

Chrisman, J. (1990), 'Writing a publishable case: some guidelines', *Case Research Journal*, **10** (Spring), 4–9.

Christensen, C. and P. Carlile (2009), 'Course research: using the case method to build and teach management theory', *Academy of Management Learning and Education*, **8** (2), 240–51.

Clarysse, B., J. Bruneel and M. Wright (2011), 'Explaining growth paths of young technology-based firms: structuring resource portfolios in different competitive environments', *Strategic Entrepreneurship Journal*, **5** (2), 137–57.

Cope, J. (2011), 'Entrepreneurial learning from failure: an interpretative phenomenological analysis', *Journal of Business Venturing*, **26** (6), 604–23.

Corner, P. and M. Ho (2010), 'How opportunities develop in social entrepreneurship', *Entrepreneurship Theory and Practice*, **34** (4), 635–59.

Croonen, E. and M. Brand (2010), '"Dutch druggists in distress." Franchisees facing the complex decision of how to react to their franchisor's strategic plans', *Entrepreneurship Theory and Practice*, **34** (5), 1021–38.

Datta, P. and R. Gailey (2012), 'Empowering women through social entrepreneurship: case study of a women's cooperative in India', *Entrepreneurship Theory and Practice*, **36** (3), 569–87.

David, F. (2003), 'Strategic management case writing', *SAM Advanced Management Journal*, **68** (3), 36–43.

Di Domenico, M., H. Haugh and P. Tracey (2010), 'Social bricolage: Theorizing social value creation in social enterprises', *Entrepreneurship Theory and Practice*, **34** (4), 681–703.

DiVito, L. (2012), 'Institutional entrepreneurship in constructing alternative paths: a comparison of biotech hybrids', *Research Policy*, **41** (4), 884–96.

Doganova, L. and M. Eyquem-Renault (2009), 'What do business models do? Innovation devices in technology entrepreneurship', *Research Policy*, **38** (10), 1559–70.

Dooley, A. and W. Skinner (1977), 'Casing case method methods', *Academy of Management Review*, **2** (2), 277–88.

Dutta, D. and S. Thornhill (2008), 'The evolution of growth intentions: toward a cognition-based model', *Journal of Business Venturing*, **23** (2), 307–32.

Dyer, J.H., H.B. Gregersen and C. Christensen (2008), 'Entrepreneur behaviors, opportunity recognition, and the origins of innovative ventures', *Strategic Entrepreneurship Journal*, **2** (4), 317–38.

Eisenhardt, K. (1989), 'Building theories from case study research', *Academy of Management Review*, **14** (4), 532–50.

Engel, J. and I. del-Palacio (2011), 'Global clusters of innovation: the case of Israel and Silicon Valley', *California Management Review*, **53** (2), 27–49.

Fernandes, B., A. da Rocha and R. Junior (2012), 'Trikke Tech Inc', *Entrepreneurship Theory and Practice*, **36** (5), 1075–99.

Finkle, T. (2012), 'Corporate entrepreneurship and innovation in Silicon Valley: the case of Google, Inc. *Entrepreneurship Theory and Practice*, **36** (4), 863–84.

Fisher, G. (2012), 'Effectuation, causation, and bricolage: a behavioral comparison of emerging theories in entrepreneurship research', *Entrepreneurship Theory and Practice*, **36** (5), 1019–51.

Fried, V. (2003), 'Defining a forum for entrepreneurship scholars', *Journal of Business Venturing*, **18** (1), 1–11.

Gartner, W. and S. Birley (2002), 'Introduction to the special issue on qualitative methods in entrepreneurship research', *Journal of Business Venturing*, **17** (5), 387–95.

Gemmell, R., R. Boland and D. Kolb (2012), 'The socio-cognitive dynamics of entrepreneurial ideation', *Entrepreneurship Theory and Practice*, **36** (5), 1053–73.

Glaser, B. and A. Strauss (1967), *The Discovery of Grounded Theory: Strategies of Qualitative Research*, London: Wiedenfeld and Nicholson.

Grimes, M. (2010), 'Strategic sensemaking within funding relationships: the effects of performance measurement on organizational identity in the social sector', *Entrepreneurship Theory and Practice*, **34** (4), 763–83.

Grove, H. and T. Cook (2011), 'Whitetracks Design, Inc', *Entrepreneurship Theory and Practice*, **35** (4), 831–48.

Hallen, B. and K. Eisenhardt (2012), 'Catalyzing strategies and efficient formation', *Academy of Management Journal*, **55** (1), 35–70.

He, Z., L. Bacchus and Y. Wu (2011), 'Self-organization of industrial clustering in a transition economy: a proposed framework and case study evidence from China', *Research Policy*, **40** (9), 1280–94.

Helprin, M. (1983), *Winter's Tale*, Boston, MA: Houghton Mifflin Harcourt.

Hindle, K. (2004), 'Choosing qualitative methods for entrepreneurial cognition research: a canonical development approach', *Entrepreneurship Theory and Practice*, **28** (6), 575–607.

Hudnut, P. and D. DeTienne (2010), 'Envirofit International: a venture adventure', *Entrepreneurship Theory and Practice*, **34** (4), 785–97.

Huser, E.A. and E. Swartz (2010), 'Opt-e-scrip, Inc.', *Entrepreneurship Theory and Practice*, **34** (2), 399–416.

Iacobucci, D. and P. Rosa (2010), 'The growth of business groups by habitual entrepreneurs: the role of entrepreneurial teams', *Entrepreneurship Theory and Practice*, **34** (2), 351–77.

Ivanova, Y. (2009), 'Can this business be rescued?', *Entrepreneurship Theory and Practice*, **33** (4), 989–95.

Kammermeyer, J. and M. Naumes (2009), 'Blue Moon Natural Foods', *Entrepreneurship Theory and Practice*, **33** (3), 789–803.

Katre, A. and P. Salipante. (2012), 'Start-up social ventures: blending fine-grained behaviors from two institutions for entrepreneurial success', *Entrepreneurship Theory and Practice*, **36** (5), 967–94.

Khavul, S., G. Bruton and E. Wood (2009), 'Informal family business in Africa, *Entrepreneurship Theory and Practice*, **33** (6), 1219–38.

Kiel, T., E. Autio and G. George (2008), 'Corporate venture capital, disembodied experimentation and capability development', *Journal of Management Studies*, **45** (8), 1475–505.

Kistruck, G. and P. Beamish (2010), 'The interplay of form, structure, and embeddedness in social intrapreneurship', *Entrepreneurship Theory and Practice*, **34** (4), 735–61.

Knockaert, M., D. Ucbasaran, M. Wright and B. Clarysse (2011), 'The relationship between knowledge transfer, top management team composition, and performance: the case of science-based entrepreneurial firms', *Entrepreneurship Theory and Practice*, **35** (4), 777–803.

Lawrence, P. (1953), 'The preparation of case materials', in K. Andrews (ed.), *The Case Method of Teaching Human Relations*, Cambridge, MA: Harvard University Press, pp. 215–24.

Lechner, C. and C. Leyronas (2009), 'Small-business group formation as an entrepreneurial development model', *Entrepreneurship Theory and Practice*, **33** (3), 645–67.

Lincoln, Y. and E. Guba (1985), *Naturalistic Inquiry*, Newberry Park, CA: Sage.

Lohrke, F. and H. Landström (2010), 'History matters in entrepreneurship research', in H. Landström and F. Lohrke (eds), *The Historical Foundations of Entrepreneurship Research*, Cheltenham, UK and Northampton, MA, USA: Edward Elgar, pp. 1–11.

Mair, J. and I. Marti (2009), 'Entrepreneurship in and around institutional voids: a case study from Bangladesh', *Journal of Business Venturing*, **24** (5), 419–35.

Majumdar, S. (2010), 'How do they plan for growth in auto component business? A study on small foundries of western India', *Journal of Business Venturing*, **25** (3), 274–89.

Marlow, S. and M. McAdam (2012), 'Analyzing the influence of gender upon high-technology venturing within the context of business incubation', *Entrepreneurship Theory and Practice*, **36** (4), 655–76.

McCarthy, D., S. Puffer and S. Darda (2010), 'Convergence in entrepreneurial leadership style: evidence from Russia', *California Management Review*, **52** (4), 48–72.

McClelland, D.C. (1961), *The Achieving Society*, Princeton, NJ: Van Nostrand.

McCrea, E. and G. Torres-Baumgarten (2011), 'Mail Boxes Etc. or the UPS Store? A decision from a franchisee's perspective', *Entrepreneurship Theory and Practice*, **35** (3), 595–610.

McInerney, P. (2008), 'Showdown at Kykuit: field-configuring events as loci for conventionalizing accounts', *Journal of Management Studies*, **45** (6), 1089–116.

Meyer, A. (1982), 'Adapting to environmental jolts', *Administrative Science Quarterly*, **27** (4), 515–37.

Miller, D. (1983), 'The correlates of entrepreneurship in three types of firms', *Management Science*, **29** (7), 770–91.

Naumes, W. and M.J. Naumes (2011), *The Art and Craft of Case Writing*, 3rd edn, Armonk, NY: M.E. Sharpe.

Oviatt, B. and P. McDougall (1994), 'Toward a theory of international new ventures', *Journal of International Business Studies*, **25** (1), 45–64.

Ozcan, P. and K. Eisenhardt (2009), 'Origin of alliance portfolios: entrepreneurs, network strategies, and firm performance', *Academy of Management Journal*, **52** (2), 246–79.

Perren, L. and M. Ram (2004), 'Case-study method in small business and entrepreneurial research', *International Small Business Journal*, **22** (1), 83–101.

Pilegaard, M., W. Moroz and H. Neergaard (2010), 'An auto-ethnographic perspective on academic entrepreneurship', *Academy of Management Perspectives*, **24** (1), 46–61.

Plant, R., S. Wills and C. Valle (2008), 'Creative entrepreneurship at iconstruye: a pan Andean e-Procurement market maker', *Entrepreneurship Theory and Practice*, **32** (3), 575–88.

Reed, M. and R. Brunson (2011), 'Proton Cancer Therapy Center: An entrepreneur's dilemma', *Entrepreneurship Theory and Practice*, **35** (5), 1091–100.

Roethlisberger, F.J. and W.J. Dickson (1939), *Management and the Worker: An Account of a Research Program Conducted by the Western Electric Company, Hawthorne Works, Chicago*, Cambridge, MA: Harvard University Press.

Sarasvathy, S. (2001), 'Causation and effectuation: toward a theoretical shift from economic inevitability to entrepreneurial contingency', *Academy of Management Review*, **26** (2), 243–63.

Schenkel, M., J. Cornwall and J. Finley (2012a), 'Snappy auctions', *Entrepreneurship Theory and Practice*, **36** (3), 589–606.

Schenkel, M.T., J. Finley and W. Chumney (2012b), 'RHS, Inc.: innovation "guiding" agriculture', *Entrepreneurship Theory and Practice*, **36** (2), 415–25.

Shane, S. and S. Venkataraman (2000), 'The promise of entrepreneurship as a field of research', *Academy of Management Review*, **25** (1), 217–26.

Sharma, P. and B. Smith (2008), 'Ed's dilemma: succession planning at Niagara Paving', *Entrepreneurship Theory and Practice*, **32** (4), 763–74.

Sieger, P., T. Zellweger, R.S. Nason and E. Clinton (2011), 'Portfolio entrepreneurship in family firms: a resource-based perspective', *Strategic Entrepreneurship Journal*, **5** (4), 327–51.

Smith, K., M. Gannon and H. Sapienza (1989), 'Selecting methodologies for entrepreneurship research: trade-offs and guidelines', *Entrepreneurship Theory and Practice*, **14** (1), 39–49.

Stetz, P., T. Finkle and L. O'Neal (2008), 'A-1 lanes and the currency crisis of the East Asian Tigers', *Entrepreneurship Theory and Practice*, **32** (2), 369–84.

Summer, C., R. Bettis, I. Duhaime, H. Grant, D. Hambrick, C. Snow and C. Zeithaml (1990), 'Doctoral education in the field of business policy and strategy', *Journal of Management*, **16** (2), 361–98.

Terjesen, S. and A. Elam (2009), 'Transnational entrepreneurs' venture internationalization strategies: a practice theory approach', *Entrepreneurship Theory and Practice*, **33** (5), 1093–120.

Tracey, P., N. Phillips and O. Jarvis (2011), 'Bridging institutional entrepreneurship and the creation of new organizational forms: a multilevel model', *Organization Science*, **22** (1), 60–80.

Vaghely, I. and P.-A. Julien (2010), 'Are opportunities recognized or constructed? An information perspective on entrepreneurial opportunity identification', *Journal of Business Venturing*, **25** (1), 73–86.

Vega, G. (2013), *The Case Writing Workbook: A Self-Guided Workshop*, Armonk, NY: M.E. Sharpe.

Walsh, I. and J. Bartunek (2011), 'Cheating the fates: organizational foundings in the wake of demise', *Academy of Management Journal*, **54** (5), 1017–44.

Weber, K., K. Heinze and M. DeSoucey (2008), 'Forage for thought: mobilizing codes in the movement for grass-fed meat and dairy products', *Administrative Science Quarterly*, **53** (3), 529–67.

West, G., C. Bamford and J. Marsden (2008), 'Contrasting entrepreneurial economic development in emerging Latin American economies: applications and extensions of resource-based theory', *Entrepreneurship Theory and Practice*, **32** (1), 15–36.

Whetten, D., T. Felin and B. King (2009), 'The practice of theory borrowing in organizational studies: current issues and future directions', *Journal of Management*, **35** (3), 537–63.

Yin, R. (2009), *Case Study Research: Design and Methods*, Thousand Oaks, CA: Sage.

Zafar, N. and V. Chang (2012), 'SpeedSim: made to exit!', *California Management Review*, **54** (4), 143–55.

Zellweger, T. and P. Sieger (2012), 'Entrepreneurial orientation in long-lived family firms', *Small Business Economics*, **38** (1), 67–84.

13. Getting published in entrepreneurship policy

David B. Audretsch

INTRODUCTION

The relationship between entrepreneurship scholarship and policy is complicated and nuanced. On the one hand, scholarship in entrepreneurship might seem to be a field that is distant from any policy considerations. After all, entrepreneurship typically involves the smallest of analytical units of analysis, such as a small business, new startup or venture, or even tinier, an idea that leads to action in someone's mind.

On the other hand, entrepreneurship has become a focal point for policy. In 'A strategy for American innovation: securing our economic growth and prosperity', the President of the USA, Barack Obama, emphasizes that entrepreneurship policy takes on a key role in generating economic growth, employment creation and global competitiveness:

> Entrepreneurship plays an essential role in generating innovation and stimulating U.S. economic growth. New firms account for most net job growth, and small businesses employ 30% of high-tech workers. Yet market obstacles limit entrepreneurship, as would-be entrepreneurs struggle to raise funding without an established reputation or without giving ideas away. The Obama Administration is committed to helping entrepreneurs build vibrant businesses that lead to new jobs and economic growth.[1]

Similarly, entrepreneurship policy is a key priority within the European Union (Commission of the European Union, 2003).

Despite this keen policy interest, the emerging scholarly field of entrepreneurship has not had an explicit policy focus. Rather, much policy focus has been on small business. Still, it would be erroneous to conclude that there are no possibilities for publishing policy research relevant to entrepreneurship. The purpose of this chapter is to explain the role of policy research in the scholarly field of entrepreneurship and how to publish policy-relevant research.

In the second section of this chapter, the inherent link between policy and the field of entrepreneurship, or what is characterized as the policy shadow in entrepreneurship research, is explained. In clarifying between what actually does and does not constitute entrepreneurship policy research, the third section identifies five distinct types or levels of entrepreneurship policy research.

In the fourth section of this chapter, a link between each of these five types of entrepreneurship policy research and actual publication modes or outlets is analyzed and explained. Some of the entrepreneurship policy research types or levels are more conducive to publishing in a particular outlet or publication mode, such as entrepreneurship scholarly journals, than are others.

In the final section, a summary and conclusions are provided. In particular, this chapter finds that, despite what might superficially appear as little priority being placed on entrepreneurship policy research, in fact the scholarly field of entrepreneurship is rife with publication opportunities for policy-relevant research. However, care must be taken to match up the type or level of policy research with the actual mode of publication or publication outlet.

THE POLICY SHADOW INHERENT IN ENTREPRENEURSHIP SCHOLARSHIP

Alexander Humboldt transformed the university in the early 1800s away from its role as a vassal for the church and the state to a new and uncharted role where knowledge in both research and teaching could be concerned for its own sake. The Humboldt model of the university reshaped the role of the university, bringing a new emphasis on intellectual independence and autonomy, freedom of thought and freedom of expression as the cornerstones of the university.

A very different tradition of research and teaching was initiated by the advent of the land grant university in the USA. Rather than being driving solely by a quest for knowledge for its own sake, the mandate for the land grant universities was to also prioritize the actual contribution to the economic development of the community or state. Thus, there was an expansion from not just knowledge for its own sake but to knowledge that would fuel economic growth and create jobs and economic competitiveness.

The modern, contemporary university, certainly in the North American context, but increasingly throughout the world, can be understood as consisting of a broad range of disciplines, fields, programs and subjects that draw on various degrees of knowledge for its own sake and knowledge because it could potentially be economically or socially valuable to the greater community and society. At the typical university both types of research and teaching can be found. For example, theoretical physics is a traditional academic discipline, where its inherent value is derived from addressing the most compelling questions and issues as defined by the discipline itself, that is, knowledge for its own sake. By contrast, interdisciplinary fields, such as biochemistry or informatics, derive their value by addressing questions and issues coming from outside of the traditional disciplines and have their roots in society and the economy. The driving mandate for these fields is not just knowledge for its own sake but rather because it can create value in society and the economy.

Entrepreneurship as a field of scholarly research did not emerge simply because of a mandate to understand the phenomenon 'for its own sake'. Rather, the sharp and dramatic explosion in entrepreneurship research was a response to the increased importance in and role played by entrepreneurship in society (Audretsch, 2007). As long as entrepreneurship seemed to play a marginal and peripheral role in the economy, it remained a marginal and peripheral topic for scholarship and teaching at the university. However, with the emergence of entrepreneurship as a driving force spurring economic growth, performance, jobs and competitiveness, there also emerged a corresponding demand for understanding in and learning about the topic (Audretsch, 2007). Thus, in many, if not most academic contexts, the prima facie mandate for entrepreneurship scholarship is essentially policy driven. As long as entrepreneurship remains as a driving engine of economic performance, the academic field of entrepreneurship is likely to remain strong, dynamic and robust. However, if the primacy of entrepreneurship as a force of economic and social dynamism yields to other forces, I would anticipate that the academic interest and value for the field would also correspondingly diminish.

WHAT ENTREPRENEURSHIP POLICY RESEARCH IS AND WHAT IT IS NOT

Considerable confusion shrouds the common view about what actually does and does not constitute entrepreneurship policy research. The myth is that what could be classified as, or constitutes, bona fide entrepreneurship policy research are papers that provide explicit instructions to a specific government agency about a very exact policy intervention along with the instruments that should be utilized to implement such a policy intervention (Henrekson and Stenkula, 2010). While such research certainly falls within the domain of entrepreneurship policy research, it is not the only type of research that actually constitutes entrepreneurship policy research.

The dimension of what actually constitutes entrepreneurship policy is considerably broader and more inclusive. The domain of entrepreneurship policy research can include any one of the following five levels or types. The first, which can be referred to as the underlying force level, involves identifying the link between the underlying force – entrepreneurship, in this case – and economic performance. If the mandate for the field is ultimately driven by such a policy concern, research probing whether and in what ways entrepreneurship is linked to economic performance is ultimately of interest to policy. For example, a paper linking an underlying force such as start-up activity, either at the regional or national level, to economic performance, perhaps measured by growth or employment creation, can be considered to be a policy-relevant paper in that it focuses the attention of a key goal for policy – growth and employment creation – on a key force underlying that policy goal. Thus, the contribution of an underlying-force level paper can be to identify those forces that are conducive to a particular goal of policy.

A second type of entrepreneurship policy paper, which could be called an underlying-force influence level paper, identifies what actually influences the entrepreneurial force(s) that are linked or found to be conducive to the policy goal. For the above example, this could be trying to identify what exactly generates start-ups and what deters them. Such a paper is important to policy because it clarifies what tends to facilitate more of the desired phenomenon and what tends to impede it.

A third type of entrepreneurship policy paper, which could be called a policy impact paper, examines the impact of a particular policy on an element of the underlying forces, and perhaps even on the ultimate policy goal. For the above example, this would involve analyzing which policies are most conducive to increasing startup activity. A slightly different variant would link the policies to changes in the relevant performance variable, such as employment creation or economic growth.

The fourth type of entrepreneurship policy paper, which could be referred to as an instrument recommendation paper, provides a focus on and analysis of an actual particular instrument, or group of instruments, that have been or could be used to implement the policy target. For the above example, a particular type of instrument that could be considered to enhance the policy target, start-up activity might be a specific scheme providing funds for starting a new firm. Other particular types of policy instruments used to implement this policy target could be an incubator or science and technology park.

The fifth type of entrepreneurship policy paper, which could be named as a policy evaluation paper, provides an assessment or evaluation of the impact of a particular policy on a specific policy target. Such an evaluation may consider not just the impact of the policy on the targeted goal, but also the costs incurred to obtain that goal. Such papers tend to be written within the context of an explicit or implicit benefit-cost framework, although many notable exceptions exist.

A specific example of a first-level entrepreneurship policy paper, or underlying force paper, might involve examining the impact of start-up activity on economic growth at some spatial level of analysis. Specific examples of such a study include, but are certainly not limited to, Fritsch and Mueller (2004), Henrekson and Johansson (2010), Ács and Mueller (2008), Audretsch and Keilbach (2004; 2007), Audretsch et al. (2006) and van Praag and Versloot (2007).

For example, in 'What is the value of entrepreneurship? A review of recent research', van Praag and Versloot (2007) provide a comprehensive and compelling review of recent empirical studies providing evidence between what we are calling here the underlying force of entrepreneurship and various measures of economic and social performance. In particular, van Praag and Versloot (2007) focus on 57 separate studies that link various measures of entrepreneurial activity to four main performance indicators. These performance measures are, first, job creation and related measures of employment dynamics and performance. The second type of economic performance measure is innovative activity. The third economic performance criterion or measure involves productivity and economic growth. Finally, the fourth type of economic performance measure is based on increasing the utility levels of individuals. The underlying force level is relevant for policy because it contributes to identifying which phenomena are linked to a particular desired policy target.

Another example of the second-level underlying forces entrepreneurship policy paper is 'The more business owners, the merrier? The role of tertiary education' (Van Praag and van Stel, 2012). This paper challenges the findings and assumption that a higher entrepreneurship rate, measured in terms of the business owner rate, leads to a higher level of economic output. Rather, the authors find that not only does an optimal business ownership rate exist, but that the optimal business ownership rate tends to decrease with greater levels of tertiary education.

A specific example of the second-level entrepreneurship policy paper, or underlying force influence paper, might involve examining which types of factors and characteristics are most conducive to start-up activity. Specific examples of such a study include, but are not limited to, Audretsch and Keilbach (2004), who link the knowledge conditions of regions in Germany to startup activity. Similarly, Davidsson and Honig (2003) examine the impact of human capital on entrepreneurial activity. Almeida and Kogut (1999), in 'Localization of knowledge and the mobility of engineers in regional networks', examine the impact of localized knowledge on measures of entrepreneurial activity. Other examples include Bates (1995), Eisenhardt and Schoonhoven (1990), Gilbert et al. (2006; 2008), Minniti and Nardone (2007) and Mosey and Wright (2007).

The underlying-force influence paper is relevant for policy because it identifies phenomena that tend to promote, or alternatively deter, the policy target, which would involve start-up activity in this particular example.

A specific example of the third-level entrepreneurship policy paper, or policy impact paper, might involve examining the impact of a particular policy such as the US Small Business Innovation Research (SBIR) program on the underlying force, in this case, start-up activity (Link and Scott, 2009). Specific examples of such a study include, but are not limited to, Link and Scott (2009) and Aldridge and Audretsch (2010). The policy impact paper is relevant for policy because it draws a clear link between policy and an underlying force, in this case, entrepreneurship.

A specific example of a fourth-level entrepreneurship policy paper, or instrument recommendation, is a recommendation for science parks or specific strategies, practices and policies undertaken by the technology transfer offices of universities. Link (1995; 2002) provides an analysis of the Research Triangle Park in North Carolina. Similarly, Chapple et al. (2005), Clarysse et al. (2005), Link et al. (2007) and Lockett et al. (2003) provide analyses of technology transfer policies of universities.

A specific example of the fifth-level entrepreneurship policy paper, or policy evaluation paper, is 'Effectiveness and efficiency of SME innovation policy', which provides an assessment of innovation policy in the UK (Foreman-Peck, 2012). The impact is measured in terms of a policy goal, the innovative activity of small and medium-sized enterprises (SMEs). In particular, the impact of specific policy instruments, such as tax credits for SMEs, is analyzed, and the return on this type of policy investment is estimated.

While the five types or categories of papers identified in this section in no way exhaust the universe of entrepreneurship policy papers, much if not most research which could be either directly or indirectly considered to constitute, or at least be relevant to, entrepreneurship policy can be classified in one of these five categories. What does not constitute an entrepreneurship policy paper? The most compelling examples of types of papers that do not constitute an entrepreneurship policy paper or research involve pure theory that may be of interest to scholars of entrepreneurship but sheds little or no light on issues of policy. Examples of non-policy papers that make key theoretical contributions include, 'Entrepreneurship as social construction: a multilevel evolutionary approach' (Aldrich and Martinez, 2010), 'The psychological basis of opportunity identification: entrepreneurial alertness,' (Gaglio and Katz, 2001), and 'What are we talking about when we talk about entrepreneurship?' (Gartner, 1990).

THE LINK TO THE SCHOLARLY LITERATURE

The five different types or levels of entrepreneurship policy papers are not homogeneous with respect to the types of publication outlets. Scholarly journals in entrepreneurship are most focused on, and give priority to, advancing the theoretical understanding of entrepreneurship, which generally involves the formulation of new theoretical approaches and subjecting such theories to empirical scrutiny. For example, the aims and scope of the *Journal of Business Venturing* have an explicit mandate, 'to deepen our understanding of the entrepreneurial phenomenon in its myriad of forms'.[2] The mission of understanding the entrepreneurial phenomenon is not unique to the *Journal of Business Venturing*, but rather typical of entrepreneurship journals.

Even with such an explicit aims and scope, what exactly is meant by 'understanding of the entrepreneurial phenomenon' needs to be interpreted and explained. In fact, such an interpretation and explanation is gleaned by examining actual papers and articles published in the entrepreneurship scholarly journals. There are three main categories of research dealing with 'understanding of the entrepreneurial phenomenon'. The first category of research examines what actually constitutes the entrepreneurial phenomenon. This type of research tends to be not only theoretical in nature, but also epistemological. Such research has a central focus on what exactly constitutes the entrepreneurial phenomenon in its 'myriad of forms' and what distinguishes entrepreneurial activity from non-entrepreneurial activity (Aldrich and Martinez, 2010; Gaglio and Katz, 2010; Gartner, 1990). While such research provides a cornerstone for scholarly inquiry about entrepreneurship, it is not particularly relevant for public policy.

The second category of entrepreneurship research devoted to understanding the entrepreneurial phenomenon has a focus on conditions, factors and characteristics that alternatively generate or impede that phenomenon. It is important to note that this type of entrepreneurship research corresponds to the underlying-force type or level of entrepreneurship policy research. A central concern of the scholarly literature in understanding the entrepreneurial phenomenon in its myriad of forms is the impact of entrepreneurial activity on performance. Even though such papers may never explicitly mention the word 'policy', they are relevant for policy in that they shed light on the links between the underlying phenomenon, entrepreneurship and its impact on performance, broadly considered.

The third category of entrepreneurship research devoted to understanding the entrepreneurial phenomenon has a focus on the impact of entrepreneurship or the outcomes emanating from entrepreneurial activity. This type of entrepreneurship research corresponds to the second level of entrepreneurship policy research, or the underlying-force influence paper, and is conducive for consideration by the entrepreneurship journals. The central focus of the underlying-force influence paper is on identifying conditions, characteristics or factors that are conducive to entrepreneurship. Addressing the question of what facilitates, or alternatively inhibits, entrepreneurship is a central concern in understanding the entrepreneurial phenomenon in its myriad forms.

This third category of entrepreneurship research also corresponds to the policy impact type of research, which examines the impact of a particular policy on an element of the underlying forces. For example, Markman et al. (2005) and Lockett et al. (2003) analyze the impact of university technology transfer on entrepreneurship, Lockett et al. (2005) examine the entrepreneurial activity emanating from public research institutions, and Link and Scott (2009) analyze the impact of the US SBIR on entrepreneurial activity.

The fourth type of entrepreneurship policy research, the instrument recommendation paper, provides a focus on and analysis of an actual particular instrument, or group of instruments. Research focusing on which particular policy instruments can best be utilized to attain policy targets are of great interest to policy makers but of less concern and relevance to 'understanding entrepreneurial phenomena', which is the major focus of entrepreneurship scholarly journals. The same holds true for the fifth type of entrepreneurship policy research, policy evaluation, which provides an assessment or evaluation of the impact of a particular policy on a specific policy target. Such papers fall outside of the three types of research typifying the published entrepreneurship literature.

Thus, such research may be less suited to scholarly journals in entrepreneurship and more conducive to being published as a book or policy report. Such research addresses key policy concerns that do not fall within the primary focus of the entrepreneurship scholarly journals. For example, Link (1995; 2002) evaluates a specific research park, Research Triangle Park in North Carolina, using the publication outlet of a book.

CONCLUSIONS

It would be erroneous to suggest that the interest and focus of the entrepreneurship journals coincides perfectly with that of policy. In fact, the *raison d'être* of policy is considerably different from that of the entrepreneurship scholarly community. The mandate for entrepreneurship research is focused on understanding the phenomenon of entrepreneurship. By contrast, the primary motivation for policy is to undertake action with the goal of improving some situation or solve some problem(s). Entrepreneurship becomes relevant only as a means to an end. To the extent that entrepreneurship can facilitate a policy goal, it becomes interesting and relevant for policy. However, it is imperative for scholars of entrepreneurship to keep in mind that entrepreneurship is generally never a policy goal or concern in and of itself. The policy goal is typically a value that has inherent economic or social value to society, while entrepreneurship provides, at best, a vehicle for perhaps attaining that goal.

Still, it would also be a mistake to conclude that the opportunities for publishing research that is relevant for policy are few or severely limited in the field of entrepreneurship. Rather, as this chapter has shown, opportunities abound for publishing entrepreneurship research that is relevant for policy.

In particular, this chapter has classified policy research into five distinct categories. The first type links the underlying phenomenon, in this case entrepreneurship, to a desired or targeted policy goal. Since analyzing the outcomes or impact of entrepreneurship is a bona fide concern of the entrepreneurship literature and focus of scholarly journals in entrepreneurship, such research not only falls within the domain of the scholarly journals but is also of considerable interest to and relevance for policy.

The second type of policy research focuses on conditions, factors and characteristics that either facilitate or impede that underlying force. While this is of interest to policy because it sheds light on where to look to generate more of the desired activity that will ultimately lead to improving a policy goal or target, it is also of interest to the scholarly community since understanding what generates or impedes entrepreneurship is a central concern of the academic field.

The third type of policy research links a particular policy to an element of the underlying forces. While such research guides policy by identifying which instruments will enhance the underlying force, or entrepreneurial activity, in this case, it also may fall within the domain of the entrepreneurship journals to the extent that it influences the underlying phenomenon – entrepreneurship.

The fourth and fifth types of policy research involve a focus on particular policy instruments along with their evaluation. This is the domain of policy research that is of more interest and concern to the policy community than it is to entrepreneurship scholars. Therefore, there are few examples of such research to be found in the entrepreneurship journals. Rather, a more appropriate outlet for publication will be in books or reports.

It is important to note that, while we conclude that there are considerable opportunities for policy-relevant research available within the domain of the entrepreneurship journals, this does not necessarily suggest that such articles will be read directly by or communicated to the policy community. Rather, the orientation and targeted audience of the entrepreneurship journals is scholars. Even if the policy-making community had the requisite background, training and competence, the orientation and focus of such articles do not provide a context and level of communication that facilitates understanding by a broader audience.

Thus, if a research goal is to have some influence in the policy community, other publication outlets may help facilitate the diffusion and impact of research ideas. Such other publication outlets typically include reports and papers for policy agencies, as well as books written for a broader, policy-oriented audience. Examples abound, including Ács et al. (2008), Allen et al. (2007), Anyadike-Danes et al. (2009) and Audretsch and Thurik (2001).

Entrepreneurship has emerged as a vibrant and dynamic academic field not because of a compelling theoretical and empirical coherence, but because of the policy relevance of the topic. The demand for insights and knowledge about entrepreneurship, along with the response by the scholarly community, has been the catalyst for a dynamic and robust field. Therefore, that opportunities abound for publishing policy relevant research in entrepreneurship is both a welcome and nurturing dimension of the scholarly field of entrepreneurship.

NOTES

1. 'A strategy for American innovation: securing our economic growth and prosperity', National Economic Council, Council of Economic Advisers, and Office of Science and Technology Policy, Washington, DC: The White House, February 2011, http://www.whitehouse.gov/sites/default/files/uploads/InnovationStrategy.pdf.
2. http://www.journals.elsevier.com/journal-of-business-venturing/.

REFERENCES

Ács, Z.J. and Mueller, P. (2008), 'Employment effects of business dynamics: mice, gazelles and elephants,' *Small Business Economics*, **30** (1), 85–100.

Ács, Z.J., W. Parsons and S. Tracy (2008), 'High-impact firms: gazelles revisited', unpublished manuscript prepared for the United States Small Business Administration.

Aldrich, H.E. and M.A. Martinez (2010), 'Entrepreneurship as social construction: a multilevel evolutionary approach', in Z.J. Ács and D.B. Audretsch (eds), *Handbook of Entrepreneurship Research: An Interdisciplinary Survey and Introduction*, New York: Springer, pp. 387–430.

Aldridge, T.T. and D. Audretsch (2010). 'Does policy influence the commercialization route? Evidence from national institutes of health funded scientists', *Research Policy*, **39** (5), 583–88.

Allen, I.E., N. Langowitz and M. Minitti (2007), '2006 report on women and entrepreneurship', *Global Entrepreneurship Monitor*, Wellesley, MA: Babson College.

Almeida, P. and B. Kogut (1999), 'Localization of knowledge and the mobility of engineers in regional networks', *Management Science*, **45** (7), 905–17.

Anyadike-Danes, M., K. Bonner, M. Hart and C. Mason (2009), 'Measuring business growth – high growth firms and their contribution to employment in the UK', NESTA, October.

Audretsch, D.B. (2007), *The Entrepreneurial Society*, Oxford: Oxford University Press.

Audretsch, D.B. and M. Keilbach (2004), 'Does entrepreneurship capital matter?', *Entrepreneurship Theory and Practice*, **28** (5), 419–30.

Audretsch, D.B. and M. Keilbach (2007), 'The theory of knowledge spillover entrepreneurship', *Journal of Management Studies*, **44** (7), 1242–54.

Audretsch, D.B. and R. Thurik (2001), 'Linking entrepreneurship to growth', OECD Science, Technology and Industry Working Papers, 2001/02, OECD Publishing, http://dx.doi.org/10.1787/736170038056.

Audretsch, D.B., M. Keilbach and E. Lehmann (2006), *Entrepreneurship and Economic Growth*, New York: Oxford University Press.

Bates, T. (1995), 'Self-employment entry across industry groups', *Journal of Business Venturing*, **10** (2), 143–56.

Blanchflower, D. and A.J. Oswald (1998), 'What makes an entrepreneur?' *Journal of Labor Economics*, **16** (1), 26–60.

Chapple, W., A. Lockett, D. Siegel, D. and M. Wright (2005), 'Assessing the relative efficiency effects of UK University Technology Transfer offices: a comparison of parametric and non-parametric approaches', *Research Policy*, **34** (3): 369–84.

Clarysse., B., M. Wright, A. Lockett, A. Van de Velde and A. Vohora (2005), 'Spinning out new ventures: a typology of incubation strategies from European research institutions', *Journal of Business Venturing*, **20** (2), 183–216.

Commission of the European Union (2003), *Entrepreneurship Green Paper*, COM 2003, Brussels: Commission of the European Union, accessed 1 July 2013 at http://eur-lex.europa.eu/LexUriServ/site/en/com/2003/com2003_0027 en01.pdf.

Davidsson, P. and B. Honig (2003), 'The role of social and human capital among nascent entrepreneurs', *Journal of Business Venturing*, **18** (3), 301–31.

Eisenhardt, K.M. and C.B. Schoonhoven (1990), 'Organizational growth: linking founding team, strategy, environment, and growth among U.S. semiconductor ventures, 1978–1988', *Administrative Science Quarterly*, **35** (3), 504–29.

Foreman-Peck, J. (2012), 'Effectiveness and efficiency of SME innovation policy', *Small Business Economics*, March, forthcoming, DOI 10.1007/s11187-012-9426-z.

Fritsch, M. and P. Mueller (2004), 'The effects of new business formation on regional development over time', *Regional Studies*, **38** (8), 961–75.

Gaglio, C.M. and J.A. Katz (2001), 'The psychological basis of opportunity identification: entrepreneurial alertness', *Small Business Economics*, **16** (2), 95–111.

Gartner, W. (1990), 'What are we talking about when we talk about entrepreneurship?', *Journal of Business Venturing*, **5** (1), 15–28.

Gilbert, B.A., P.P. McDougall and D.B. Audretsch (2006), 'New venture growth: a review and extension', *Journal of Management*, **32** (6), 926–50.

Gilbert, B.A., P.P. McDougall and D.B. Audretsch (2008), 'Clusters, knowledge spillovers and new venture performance: an empirical examination', *Journal of Business Venturing*, **23** (4), 405–22.

Henrekson, M. and D. Johansson (2010), 'Gazelles as job creators – a survey and interpretation of the evidence', *Small Business Economics*, **35** (2), 227–44.

Henrekson, M. and M. Stenkula (2010), 'Entrepreneurship and public policy', in Z.J. Ács and D.B. Audretsch (eds), *Handbook of Entrepreneurship Research: An Interdisciplinary Survey and Introduction*, New York: Springer, pp. 595–638.

Link, A. and J.T. Scott (2009), 'Private investor participation and commercialization rates for government-sponsored research and development: would a prediction market improve the performance of the SBIR programme?', *Economica*, **76** (302), 264–81.

Link, A., D. Siegel and B. Bozeman (2007), 'An empirical analysis of the propensity of academics to engage in informal university technology transfer', *Industrial and Corporate Change*, **16** (4), 641–55.

Link, A.N. (1995), *A Generosity of Spirit: The Early History of the Research Triangle Park*, Research Triangle Park, NC: The Research Triangle Park Foundation of North Carolina.

Link, A.N. (2002), *From Seed to Harvest: The Growth of the Research Triangle Park*, Research Triangle Park, NC: Research Triangle Park Foundation of North Carolina.

Lockett, A., M. Wright and S. Franklin (2003), 'Technology transfer and universities' spin-out strategies,' *Small Business Economics*, **20** (2), 185–201.

Lockett, D.S., M. Wright and M. Ensley (2005), 'The creation of spin-off firms at public research institutions: managerial and policy implications', *Research Policy*, **34** (7), 981–93.

Markman, G., P. Phan, D. Balkin and P. Gianiodis (2005), 'Entrepreneurship and university-based technology transfer', *Journal of Business Venturing*, **20** (2), 241–63.

Minniti, M. and C. Nardone (2007), 'Being in someone else's shoes: the role of gender in nascent entrepreneurship', *Small Business Economics*, **28** (2–3), 223–38.

Mosey, S. and M. Wright (2007), 'From human capital to social capital: a longitudinal study of technology based academic entrepreneurs', *Entrepreneurship Theory and Practice*, **31** (6), 909–35.

Van Praag, M. and A. van Stel (2012), 'The more business owneres, the merrier? The role of tertiary education', *Small Business Economics*, June, DOI 10.1007/s11187-012-9436-x.

Van Praag, M.C. and P.H. Versloot (2007), 'What is the value of entrepreneurship? A review of recent research', *Small Business Economics*, **329** (4), 351–82.

14. Positioning entrepreneurship research for general management journals

Andrew Corbett

INTRODUCTION

Why do seemingly well-crafted entrepreneurship manuscripts have a difficult time getting published in broader management journals? Part of the answer lies in the fact that publishing in scholarly outlets continues to become more difficult every day (Ashansky, 2010). Additionally, 'competition' from management scholars in emerging scholarly markets around the globe suggests this trend is only going to continue (Delios et al., 2014) as researchers from Asia, South America and other parts of the world ramp up their focus on management scholarship.

More directly, however, entrepreneurship researchers attempting to publish in broad management journals need to take care to construct their manuscripts quite differently than when they are submitting to an entrepreneurship journal. Both the broader audience and the convergence of disciplines and communities of scholars who address entrepreneurial issues impact how you craft your research findings.

Manuscripts are all vying for limited publication space. In this chapter we examine how entrepreneurship scholars need to build their manuscripts to fit well within general management journals. This chapter contributes to the growth of each entrepreneurship scholar's toolkit by expanding their view and providing insights into how to shape and develop their research for a broader management audience. The chapter examines differences in the review process and how to prepare for them. It also focuses on the importance of clarity, impact and a differentiated contribution that needs to take into account related research from scholars outside of the entrepreneurship research community. I begin with some definitions and boundary conditions, and explain some benefits for why entrepreneurship scholars would want to publish in broader management journals.

WHO AND WHY?

As we begin to investigate the process of positioning entrepreneurship research for a broader management audience, allow me first to clarify what I mean by 'entrepreneurship researchers' and why these scholars would want to publish in journals that go beyond the scope of entrepreneurship.

When I use the term 'entrepreneurship researchers' or 'entrepreneurship scholars' I have in mind someone who has been primarily trained in entrepreneurship and/or someone who considers entrepreneurship to be their home field. As someone who has been intimately involved with the leadership of the Entrepreneurship Division of the Academy of Management for the past decade, when I use these terms within this chapter I am generally referring to the scholars who inhabit this division and those across the globe who may act, think and research in a similar way. These researchers have a commonality in that their first purpose is to investigate entrepreneurial phenomena. To be sure, there are many researchers investigating entrepreneurship issues that are not housed within the Entrepreneurship Division of the Academy of Management (or other similar entrepreneurship groups across the globe) who are doing excellent research in entrepreneurship. These scholars come from other management traditions (organizational behavior, strategy, finance, operations, and so on) and generally use that foundation to investigate entrepreneurship phenomena. Why do I make this distinction? As you will see unfold on the following pages, entrepreneurship scholars who are attempting to break out of entrepreneurship niche journals and break into broader management journals need to recognize the differing perspectives of these two groups of entrepreneurship researchers.

So, why would entrepreneurship researchers want to publish their entrepreneurship work in a broad management journal? Both the changing landscape of global business and the evolution and demands of higher education have come together over the past few decades to motivate entrepreneurship scholars to broaden their reach. The impact and importance of entrepreneurship across the globe is at a heightened level as policy makers, government officials, corporate leaders and entrepreneurs of all types recognize entrepreneurship as the vital engine to generate economic, social and personal wealth (Kelley et al., 2012;

Xavier et al., 2013). This has created a 'pull' from these constituents for a greater understanding of the phenomenon of entrepreneurship and how it manifests in every conceivable environment. This, in turn, has created a demand for scholars from various traditions and backgrounds to provide new insights into the phenomenon. Therefore, broad management journals are publishing more entrepreneurship research.

For entrepreneurship scholars there is an opportunity to expand your reach and the potential to make a larger impact; to demonstrate the implications of entrepreneurship research to other disciplines. Based upon their more diverse audiences, the top broad management journals reach a much larger audience. The academy journals (*Academy of Management Journal*, *Academy of Management Review*, and so on) are in the hands of nearly 20 000 members. As editor of the *Journal of Management Studies*, I know that our journal is read broadly in over 3000 institutions across the globe. While a few entrepreneurship journals may have comparable numbers, the issue is reach. You will not get the broad reach or the opportunity to cross-fertilize your work into other disciplines, nor create an impact, by publishing only in entrepreneurship specific journals. The latest impact factors – from the 2011 Social Sciences Citation Index (SSCI) – show that on average the top-five management journals have twice the impact that the top-five entrepreneurship journals have. Table 14.1 shows that the leading entrepreneurship journal has an impact that is more than a full point less than the number five general management journal.

Broad management journals allow entrepreneurship scholars to directly reach researchers who work in entrepreneurship, innovation, invention and related management topics. They also allow you to reach back further to scholars of the mother disciplines of economics, sociology, psychology, and so on, who publish some of their applied research in general management journals. Let me be clear, I am not trying to state that you should only publish in broad management journals – that is not the point. It is not an issue of 'either or', but a question of broadening your portfolio of research. When you have something that should be in a conversation beyond the borders of entrepreneurship journals, you should strive to publish in a general management journal. What follows in this chapter is a guide to how to manage and regulate this change of outlet, beginning with the differences you can expect in the review process.

Table 14.1   Impact factors of leading journals

Top Five General Management Journals	
Academy of Management Review	6.169
Academy of Management Journal	5.608
Journal of Management	4.595
Journal of Management Studies	4.255
Administrative Science Quarterly	4.212
Top Five Entrepreneurship Journals	
Journal of Business Venturing	3.062
Family Business Review	2.600
Entrepreneurship Theory and Practice	2.542
Journal of Product Innovation Management	2.109
Strategic Entrepreneurship Journal	2.053

Source: Social Sciences Citation Index 2011.

DIFFERING PERSPECTIVES IN THE REVIEW PROCESS

Is the review process for broad management journals all that different from the process of getting published in top entrepreneurship journals as outlined by Wright in Chapter 2 in this volume? In general, no. The process for most any general management journal follows a similar path. So if the process is the same, what is the issue at hand here? The difference entrepreneurship scholars have to prepare for is one of perspective and expectation. The perspective and intellectual grounding of those who will examine your work during the submission process – general editors, action editors and reviewers – can vary greatly when you are submitting your entrepreneurship work to a broad management journal. Box 14.1 examines the reach of some of the top entrepreneurship journals by exploring the scope of each journal. While there certainly is a difference in focus between each of these outlets, the scope of the journals as a group is relatively tight when compared to general management journals.

BOX 14.1   AIMS AND SCOPE OF LEADING
                      ENTREPRENEURSHIP JOURNALS

The *Journal of Business Venturing: A Journal Dedicated to Entrepreneurship* provides a scholarly forum for sharing useful and interesting theories, narratives and interpretations of the antecedents, mechanisms and/or consequences of entrepreneurship. This multidisciplinary, multifunctional, and multi-contextual journal aspires to deepen our understanding of the entrepreneurial phenomenon in its myriad of forms. The journal publishes entrepreneurship research from: (1) the disciplines of economics, psychology and sociology, and welcomes research from other disciplines such as anthropology, geography, history, and so on; (2) the functions of finance/accounting, management, marketing and strategy, and welcomes research from other functions such as operations, information technology, public policy, medicine, law, music, and so on; and (3) the contexts of international and sustainability (environmental and social), and welcomes research from other contexts such as high uncertainty, dynamism, time pressured, emotional, and so on.

Entrepreneurship Theory and Practice is a leading scholarly journal in the field of entrepreneurship studies. The journal's mission is to publish original papers which contribute to the advancement of the field of entrepreneurship. *Entrepreneurship Theory and Practice* publishes conceptual and empirical articles of interest to scholars, consultants and public policy makers. Most issues also feature a teaching case. Article topics include, but are not limited to: national and international studies of enterprise creation; small business management; family-owned businesses; minority issues in small business and entrepreneurship; new venture creation; research methods; venture financing; and corporate and non-profit entrepreneurship.

The *Strategic Entrepreneurship Journal* (SEJ) is a research journal that publishes original work recommended by a developmental, double-blind review process conducted by peer scholars. Strategic entrepreneurship involves innovation and subsequent changes which add value to society and which change societal life in ways which have significant, sustainable, and durable consequences. The SEJ is international in scope and acknowledges theory- and evidence-based research conducted and/or applied in all regions of the world. It is devoted to content and quality standards based on scientific method, relevant theory, tested or testable propositions, and appropriate data and evidence, all replicable by others and all representing original contributions. The SEJ values contributions which lead to improved practice of managing organizations as they deal with the entrepreneurial process involving imagination, insight, invention, and innovation and the inevitable changes and transformations that result and benefit society.

The *Journal of Product Innovation Management* is an interdisciplinary, international journal that seeks to advance our theoretical and managerial knowledge of product and service development. The journal publishes original articles on organizations of all sizes (start-ups, small and medium-sized, large) and from the consumer, business-to-business and institutional domains. The journal is receptive to all types of quantitative and qualitative methodologies. Authors across the world from diverse disciplines and functional perspectives are welcome to submit to the journal.

The *Family Business Review* (FBR) combines scholarly research and practical experience in the only scientific journal in the world devoted exclusively to exploration of the dynamics of the family firm. Its interdisciplinary forum captures the insights of professions from such diverse fields as management, family therapy, organizational behavior, finance, consulting, law and government as well as managers and owners of family businesses. The FBR covers such vital topics as succession planning, impact of family dynamics on managerial behaviors, estate and tax planning, liquidity issues, financial management, generation and gender issues, international family-owned business, organizational structures, and strategic planning and organizational changes in family firms.

While the perspective and intellectual grounding of editors and reviewers of entrepreneurship journals may be relatively wide, it will be strongly focused upon entrepreneurship. I recognize that this is only a representative list of the five entrepreneurship journals with the highest impact factors, but even if I include other entrepreneurship journals that focus on other divergent entrepreneurship topics (*Venture Capital, Journal of Small Business Management, Entrepreneurship & Regional Development, Journal of Technology Transfer, Small Business Economics*, and so on) the story is still the same. These scholars tend to focus first on entrepreneurship issues and may look to other areas for input and insight into entrepreneurship questions.

When you send your entrepreneurship work to a broad management journal there is a distinct shift or perhaps difference in priority and perspective that you will see from the editors and reviewers. Is there a likelihood that your paper might be in the hands of some of the same people? Sure, there is some overlap with respect to who is on the editorial boards of the top entrepreneurship journals and the leading general management journals. This overlap is relatively small, however. The review team at an entrepreneurship journal is going to be focused on entrepreneurship first. However, the scholars working at the general management journals will come from different and perhaps broader management traditions (for example, organizational behavior, strategy, finance, operations) and will generally use that foundation to investigate entrepreneurship phenomenon. So they may view your work first through the lens of broader management research looking to see how you work informs this larger corpus of research. So a contribution to entrepreneurship is not enough; your work has to have implications for a broad management audience.

As noted above, interest in entrepreneurship research and the need for it has likely never been greater than it is today. As such we are seeing a confluence of scholars researching entrepreneurship questions from the micro issues of the individual and opportunity to the macro issues of economic development, industry diversification and national competitiveness. Many of these researchers and their work converge in the communities of general management journals. So the work of entrepreneurship scholars – work that you might regularly submit to niche entrepreneurship journals – needs to be built and developed to match the interests and expectations of editors, reviewers and readers who come from a related but different perspective.

Again with apologies for my North American bias, allow me to use the Academy of Management and its subgroups of divisions and interest groups to illustrate the point. Today scholars from strategy, technology management, organizational behavior, finance and myriad other foundations are likely to be reviewing and editing your entrepreneurship work when you submit it to a general management journal.

You are unlikely to get three reviewers and an action editor who come from a pure entrepreneurship background. Your article is likely to be reviewed by scholars who have their intellectual home in technology and innovation management, business policy and strategy, or perhaps organizational behavior. Depending upon the intended contribution of your work, you may also find scholars from the following divisions of the Academy reviewing your work: Organizational Development and Change; Organizations and the Natural Environment; Managerial and Organizational Cognition, Human Resources, and Social Issues in Management. Outside the Academy you have interested parties from finance or marketing or perhaps mother disciplines of economics, sociology or psychology. Scholars from across the globe in all of these areas are converging on and researching in entrepreneurship issues. The benefit here is that your review team is not going to be the relatively homogenous set of scholars that comes from the Academy of Management's Entrepreneurship Division and thinks first and exclusively about entrepreneurship.

A quick comparison of the domain statements of the divisions listed in Box 14.2 will give you an appreciation for the differences between these sets of scholars and those who see entrepreneurship as their home discipline. Even though we are all converging to research entrepreneurship issues, our perspectives and base of research differs widely. Entrepreneurship scholars are primarily focused upon the emergence of opportunities and all of the actors, actions, resources, and different contexts of entrepreneurship. Strategy scholars come from a tradition of examining performance. Organizational behavior scholars focus on individuals and groups within organizations whereas technology and innovation management researchers look at the management of innovation and technological change.

BOX 14.2   DOMAIN STATEMENTS OF SELECTED ACADEMY OF MANAGEMENT DIVISIONS

Business Policy and Strategy Specific domain: the roles and problems of general managers and those who manage multi-business firms or multi-functional business units. Major topics include: strategy formulation and implementation; strategic planning and decision processes; strategic control and reward systems; resource allocation; diversification and portfolio strategies; competitive strategy; cooperative strategies; selection and behavior of general managers; and the composition and processes of top management teams.

Entrepreneurship Specific domain: (a) the actors, actions, resources, environmental influences and outcomes associated with the emergence of entrepreneurial opportunities and/or new economic activities in multiple organizational contexts, and (b) the characteristics, actions, and challenges of owner-managers and their businesses. (Revised 8/2011)

Organizational Behavior Specific domain: organizational behavior is devoted to understanding individuals and groups within an organizational context. The field focuses on attributes, processes, behaviors, and outcomes within and between individual, interpersonal, group, and organizational levels of analysis. Major topics include:

- individual characteristics such as beliefs, values, personality, and demographic attributes, and individual processes such as learning, perception, motivation, emotions, and decision making
- interpersonal processes such as trust, justice, power/politics, social exchange, and networks
- group/team characteristics such as size, diversity, and cohesion, and group/team processes such as development, leadership, decision making, and cooperation and conflict
- organizational processes and practices such as leadership, goal setting, work design, feedback, rewards, communication, and socialization
- contextual influences on individuals and groups such as organizational and national culture, and organizational identity and climate
- and the influence of all of the above on individual, interpersonal, group, and organizational outcomes such as performance, creativity, attachment, citizenship behaviors, stress, absenteeism, turnover, deviance, and ethical behavior.

Technology and Innovation Management Specific domain: encourages interdisciplinary scholarship and dialogue on the management of innovation and technological change from a variety of perspectives, including strategic, managerial, behavioral, and operational issues. The problem domain includes the management of innovation processes, research and development, information technologies, e-commerce, and process technologies. Participants in this broad academic endeavor come from a wide range of disciplines and draw on an extensive array of theoretical and research paradigms. We enter this complex problem domain in the spirit of dialogue, debate, and deepened understanding. Major topics include: studies of the strategic management of technology; innovation processes; innovation diffusion and the development, implementation and use of technologies; technology development trajectories; intellectual capital; organizational processes by which technically-oriented activities are integrated into organizations; product development strategies; technical project management; behaviors and characteristics of technical professionals; technological forecasting and policies; information technology; impacts of new technologies on organizational forms and electronic commerce. (Revised 11/99)

While it is easy to see the potential commonality between these groups of researchers when they are addressing questions of entrepreneurship, their foundational differences matter for how they are going to read and review your manuscript. Each reviewer's years of study and intellectual home strongly impact their schema, that is, the manner in which they organize their prior knowledge in order to understand new information (Fiske and Taylor, 1991). Simply stated, a scholar from another tradition is going to look at your manuscript very differently than someone that comes from a singular entrepreneurship tradition. This is because their schema influences how they encode new information, make connections between new and old information, and make inferences about what is important or what is missing.

As an example, take a manuscript that is being developed about the knowledge, capabilities, and roles necessary for developing entrepreneurial ventures in existing organizations. At a general management journal, a topic such as this has the potential to be put in front of editors and reviewers whose primary research focus may not be entrepreneurship but is instead knowledge management, dynamic capabilities, strategy, human resources, organizational change, innovation management or, perhaps, a handful of other intellectual bases.

Now think about a current entrepreneurship project you are working. Think about how you view this research and its importance. Then attempt to mentally run it through the schema of a reviewer or editor that comes from a related intellectual home, using Box 14.1 as a guide if necessary. You need to do this if you want to publish your entrepreneurship work in a general management journal. You should conduct this brief exercise at varying points through your manuscript development to make sure you are positioning it and its potential contribution to fit in the outlet you are submitting it to.

In sum, you need to recognize who is reading your manuscript when you submit it to a general management journal. It is unlikely to be just your colleagues from the Entrepreneurship Division of the Academy of Management. It is very likely that the reviewers and action editor come from a different entrepreneurial tradition than you. Think about it this way: you are trying to reach a broader audience with your work and the first micro version of a broad audience are going to be the general editor of the journal you submitted to, the action editor and the three reviewers. Given this you need to be very clear at the beginning of your manuscript.

CLARITY AND IMPACT UP FRONT

Publishing in general management journals is more competitive than ever (Ashansky, 2010; Delios et al., in press) and space is extremely limited. For instance, in past years the *Academy of Management Journal* has received approximately 1500 manuscripts yearly, but the journal only publishes on average ten papers a year in each of its six volumes. Similarly, my journal, the *Journal of Management Studies*, received slightly over 900 manuscripts in 2011 for about 48 open slots (after special issues and other special topic sections). The numbers at other top general management journals are similar and show that acceptance rates range from about only 4–6 percent.

So, the necessity for clarity and impact at the start of your manuscript is paramount. The diversity and breadth of primary interest of your review team requires precise definitions and clarity of constructs. The tightness of your abstract and introduction are crucial. You may say, 'OK, that's true but it is no different from when I am writing for an entrepreneurship journal'. Perhaps, but as noted above, your review team will likely not share your worldview of entrepreneurship concepts and constructs.

So you need to be extremely clear about what you are studying and what you are not. As an editor I often see researchers from two different camps converging on a similar idea or research question but they often define the same phenomenon or construct completely differently. So it is incumbent upon the author to break through this morass of potentially competing definitions and constructs.

Remember, the review team is made up of individuals with certain schemas about what entrepreneurship is and how it works – and the likelihood is they do not share your exact outlook. So you need to break free of your world of entrepreneurship and be sure to more thoroughly understand the potential perspectives of anyone who may end up on your review team. As an editor I have reviewed hundreds of manuscripts, read thousands of reviews, and I can tell you that reviewers do rely heavily upon their schemas. I see this from the reviews I read and from the comments to editors that you, as an author, never see.

Here is a shorthand and stylized version of what schemas do to reviewers. Your title cues for the reviewer particular thoughts about what your manuscript is about. As they read the abstract he or she gets a clear sense of what the paper is about and as they continue through to the introduction their schema about (1) what is important in this line of inquiry, (2) what is currently missing, and (3) what you have to say comes together for them. Generally at this point their schema and your work come together for them to make a decision as to whether your work has potential or not. That early. Really.

This is why the abstract and introduction of your entrepreneurship paper that is submitted to a general management journal needs such extra care. If they like what they see and it does not completely oppose their worldview of entrepreneurship, they will look for confirmation for why your paper is good as they continue to read. However, if their schema suggest to them that what you are doing has already been done (perhaps you were not aware of what was going on in one of the other research camps) or isn't that important they will look for reasons to verify why they do not think the paper is worthy of a revise and resubmit.

To help increase the odds and make sure your manuscript is one of the 4–6 percent that makes it through, you have to start by taking care as you would with any manuscript. However, you also need to take extra care to properly position your entrepreneurship work to align its contribution for a general management journal.

ENTREPRENEURSHIP RESEARCH IN GENERAL MANAGEMENT JOURNALS: POSITIONING A DIFFERENTIATE CONTRIBUTION

Positioning one's contribution effectively is built upon the connections and relationships between your introduction and theoretical development at the front end of your manuscript and the discussion and conclusions on the back end (see Figure 14.1).

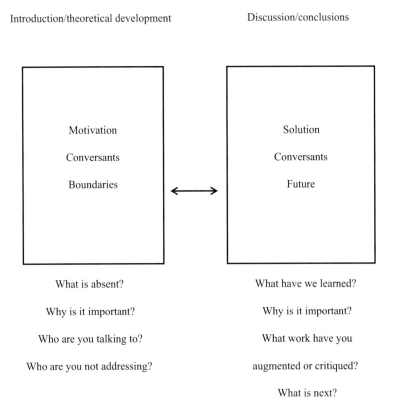

Figure 14.1   An explicit link between the introduction and discussion/ conclusions

Well-written papers are motivated by a true need: they demonstrate that the research is needed because it is filling an important and specifically defined gap. You must go beyond what I term 'motivation by neglect'. Motivation by neglect is when someone simply states that no one has yet to research in a certain area or that no one has simultaneously looked at a couple of constructs. Neglect is not good enough; it could be very likely that work examining the constructs you proposed has not been published because it is not that important. More than likely it is because the relationship is obvious and does not need to be investigated. 'Motivation by need' demonstrates not just that the research is currently absent but that it also fills an important need.

This is where scholars porting their work from entrepreneurship-specific journals into general management journals need to take care. You need to be sure that you have thoroughly explored the literature in all of the areas tangential to your primary area of contribution. Again, using the example noted above you may craft an entrepreneurship manuscript about the roles and responsibilities necessary for corporate entrepreneurship. Even though you are focused upon the concept of entrepreneurship and trying to make a contribution to further it, your work is likely to end up in the hands of reviewers who specialize in human resources, knowledge management and perhaps even strategy (from a 'managerial dynamic capabilities' perspective).

Given this, you need to scour the literature for scholarship in each of these primary areas to understand what work has been done there with respect to entrepreneurship or innovation within organizations. Only by doing this can you find the right conversants (the other scholars upon whose work you will build and/or whose work you will augment, extend or critique) to allow you to set the proper boundaries and motivation for your own work. If not, members of your review team may see the arguments you build for your motivation as lacking in importance, interest or potential for contribution. They may believe some of the assumptions or boundaries you take for granted are not so.

SUMMARY

This chapter began by bemoaning the fact that many good entrepreneurship manuscripts with potentially strong contributions to management never see the light of day in general management journals. Using the differing mindsets of entrepreneurship researchers 'born and raised' within the field as opposed to those who come to entrepreneurship from a different but related tradition, I show how entrepreneurship research can become mired and trapped within this gap of schemas. I then explore how entrepreneurship scholars can bridge this gap to move their work into general management journals.

What should you do? You need to build from the ground up and recognize that your motivation, positioning, conversants and contribution need to be reworked out of an entrepreneurship centric mindset to include the broader areas of management that you hope to contribute to. Your goal is to publish your entrepreneurship work in a general management journal so it has to have a contribution for both entrepreneurship researchers and researchers in at least one other management discipline. You need to set a motivation that shows clearly why the paper extends outside of the entrepreneurship domain but also contributes to the broader general management audience.

If you take the extra time to think clearly about the perspective, interests and schemas of your potential readers, editors and reviewers of the broad management journal you submit to, your success rate in publishing entrepreneurship research in general management journals will increase.

REFERENCES

Ashansky, N.M. (2010), 'Publishing today is more difficult than ever', *Journal of Organizational Behavior*, **31** (1), 1–3.

Delios, A., A. Corbett, J. Cornelissen and B. Harley (in press), 'Variety, novelty and perceptions of scholarship in research on management and organizations: an appeal for ambidextrous scholarship', *Journal of Management Studies*, **51** (1).

Fiske, S.T. and S.E. Taylor (1991), *Social Cognition*, New York: McGraw Hill.

Kelley, D., A. Ali, E. Rogoff, C. Brush, A. Corbett, M. Majbouri and D. Hechavarria (2012), *Global Entrepreneurship Monitor United States Report 2011*, Babson Park, MA: Babson College.

Xavier, S., D. Kelley, J. Kew, M. Herrington and A. Vorderwulbecke (2013), *Global Entrepreneurship Monitor 2012 Global Report*, London: Global Entrepreneurship Research Association.

Index